Endeavour
on
Location

J. P. Sperati
&
Antony J. Richards

Edited by Louise Cissel

All correspondence for
Endeavour on Location
should be addressed to:

Irregular Special Press
Endeavour House
170 Woodland Road
Sawston
Cambridge
CB22 3DX

ISBN: 1-901091-73-2 (10 digit)
ISBN: 978-1-901091-73-1 (13 digit)

Proof reading & editing: Louise Cissel
Front cover picture: Courtesy of ITV Press centre, Patrick Smith.

This publication is not part of the official Endeavour series. It has not been
endorsed or authorised by Mammoth Screen, Masterpiece or ITV Studios. It
does not claim or imply any rights to the Colin Dexter characters or creations
and is a review of those locations already in the public domain used in filming
the Endeavour television series. Episode titles, character names and other
information that might be copyright protected are used for reference only.

Every effort has been made to ensure accuracy, but the publishers do not hold
themselves responsible for any consequences that may arise from errors or
omissions. Whilst the contents are believed to be correct at the time of going to
press, changes may have occurred since that time or will occur during the
currency of this publication.

Contents

Part I - Episode Synopses, Scene by Scene & Locations*

---

* Unique to the episode in question. For locations used more than once see
Part II - The Usual Suspects.

3

Contents

PART II - THE USUAL SUSPECTS*

*Locations used more than once in the series.

Contents

PART I
EPISODE SYNOPSES, SCENE BY SCENE & LOCATIONS*

PLEASE NOTE THAT THERE ARE SOME SPOILERS IN THE EPISODE SYNOPSES

*Unique to the episode in question. For locations used more than once see
PART II - THE USUAL SUSPECTS.

THIS PUBLICATION COVERS THE *ENDEAVOUR* PILOT ALONG WITH EVERY EPISODE FROM SERIES 1-4 INCLUSIVE

ALL BOLD NUMBERS IN BRACKETS WITHIN THE TEXT E.G. **(54)** ARE PAGE NUMBER REFERENCES TO FILMING LOCATIONS. THESE ARE ONLY USED AT THE FIRST OCCURRENCE OF A PARTICULAR LOCATION WITHIN A GIVEN EPISODE.

THE ABBREVIATIONS USED FOR THE POLICE RANKS ARE OUTLINED BELOW. THESE ARE ONLY USED FOR THE FIRST OCCURRENCE OF A PERSON WITHIN A GIVEN EPISODE.

CC - CHIEF CONSTABLE
ACC - ASSISTANT CHIEF CONSTABLE
CS - CHIEF SUPERINTENDENT
DCI - DETECTIVE CHIEF INSPECTOR
DI - DETECTIVE INSPECTOR
DS - DETECTIVE SERGEANT
DC - DETECTIVE CONSTABLE
PS - POLICE SERGEANT
PC - POLICE CONSTABLE
WPC - WOMAN POLICE CONSTABLE

First Bus to Woodstock
Pilot Episode

Premier: 2nd January 2012

Length: 98 minutes

Audience: 8.2 million

Director: Colm McCarthy

Guest Stars: Richard Lintern, Patrick Malahide, Flora Montgomery.

Synopsis

The disappearance of 15 year-old schoolgirl, Mary Tremlett, and the apparent suicide of her boyfriend, Miles Percival, leads to an investigation by Oxford City Police. The subsequent discovery of Mary's body sends them on a search that will lead to the uncovering of a cabal of local politicians, businessmen, Oxford dons, and policemen who are attending sex parties where under-aged girls are made available to them. The gathering and sifting of evidence is thus made very difficult, but fortunately for the Oxford City Police, a young constable, Endeavour Morse, has been temporarily seconded to them, under the supervision of DI Fred Thursday. Thursday, recognising in Morse someone he can trust, takes him under his wing, determined, with Morse's help, to bring the case to a successful conclusion.

This episode, perhaps more than any other, sets the scene for what is to come. It fills in background details alluded to in the earlier *Inspector Morse* films, and has subtle nods to other aspects of the series. For a start Colin Dexter was very proud of the title, *First Bus to Woodstock*, which reminds the viewer of Colin's first Inspector Morse novel, *Last Bus to Woodstock*, published in 1975. As Colin put it Biblically at the time of filming, 'the first shall be last and the last shall be first'.

Scene by Scene

As the film begins the viewer sees somebody, looking not unlike Michael Caine's Harry Palmer persona in *The Ipcress File*, in a car with a camera keeping surveillance outside a large residence. Inside, Patrick Malahide's character is playing backgammon. Patrick Malahide is no stranger to Morse, having been the chief suspect in the episode *Driven to Distraction*. Soon we see a single decker No. 7A bus passing along a country lane past a bus stop – this is the first bus to Woodstock of the episode title – and it is followed by an excerpt from Madame Butterfly as the camera pans in on Carshall Newtown police station (a fictitious location) which has a variety of period cars outside.

The action now moves to the Cowley School for Girls, which is actually the Royal Masonic School for Girls in Rickmansworth **(17)**. The school can also be seen in the Inspector Morse episode *Cherubim and Seraphim*. Soon Morse is seen arriving by coach along with other officers who have been drafted to Oxford on the missing schoolgirl case. The coach passes familiar Oxford landmarks and is seen going under the Bridge of Sighs **(182)** and into New College Lane **(217)**. This is a little inappropriate, for if the coach continues much further down New College Lane (which today is a cul-de-sac) it would have to negotiate a couple of very sharp turns, and a bridge, which would be impossible for such a vehicle to do safely.

However, the coach does make it to Cowley Road police station (which in reality is some miles from the centre of Oxford) where the officers are seen being assigned their new duties. The building used was actually on the site of the old School of Languages in Beaconsfield **(13)**. On closer inspection it can be seen that the building is in need of repair with out of control ivy climbing up the outside walls.

It is here that Morse now sees Thursday for the first time, albeit at a distance. The subsequent scene introduces Richard Lintern, as Dr. Rowan Stromming, who is lecturing at college (and although the college name is never mentioned, from what transpires later it is meant to be Lonsdale College). For this, and subsequent college scenes, an amalgam of Merton College **(187)** and St. John's College **(192)** was used. Meanwhile the priority for Morse is lodgings, and these are provided in Park Town **(218)**. It is at this juncture that there is a reference to Philip Larkin's poem, Mr. Bleaney, when Morse's landlady informs him that, "This was Mr. Bleaney's room. He stayed here the whole time he was at the Bodleian".

The action now moves to the Tremlett household, somewhere near St. John Street **(224)** if the establishing shot is to be believed, then back to the police station, and finally to the river, supposedly Thrupp but really a location nearer to Binsey **(249)**. Here an artist finds the body of Mary Tremlett's boyfriend, Miles Percival. It is now that Morse meets another major character in the form of James Bradshaw, who plays Dr. Max DeBryn the pathologist. He soon discovers two things about Morse. First that he is "not entirely a fool", and second that he squeamish around dead bodies. Morse next visits Percival's flat in Jericho, though it is actually on the corner of King Edward Street **(213)** and Oriel Square **(19)** – a favourite Morse location – in the very centre of the city.

The trail also takes Morse to his *alma mater*, Lonsdale College (which does not exist, although there is a Lonsdale Road – named after the Earl of Lonsdale – in North Oxford). In *Inspector Morse*, it was invariably Brasenose College **(177)** that stood in for Lonsdale, but here, it is once again the exterior of Merton College that is seen. There is a difference between the television adaptations and the Inspector Morse novels, for in the latter Morse was an undergraduate at St. John's

College. Morse meets a contemporary of his student days, Alexander Reece, but does not find the person he seeks, Dr. Stromming. For this he has to travel to Stromming's magnificent home where he meets Stromming's wife, the opera singer Rosalind Stromming, née Calloway, someone Morse has admired for years and is rather star struck to meet.

Some rooftop shots of Oxford follow, accompanied by more opera music as Morse finds a clue in a crossword puzzle. This leads him to the *Oxford Mail*, which, as unlikely as it may seem for a major newspaper, has offices not in New Inn Hall Street where it was actually located until 1972, but in a small room at the top of a spiral staircase, adjacent to The Turf Tavern in St. Helen's Passage **(224)**. It is here that Morse meets the editor, Dorothea Frazil, played by Abigail Thaw (John Thaw's eldest daughter) and so there remains a Thaw association with the newest Inspector Morse franchise. There follows a lovely verbal exchange as Frazil asks Morse if they have met before. Morse answers in the negative to which Frazil rejoins poignantly, "Another life then".

Back at the police station, Morse is informed that he has to go and fetch Thursday for which he is allowed the use of a car – but not just any car for Morse is next seen in a Mk I Jaguar looking very content as he drives from the police station, with the security fencing of the disused military base clearly visible in the background.

Soon the body of Mary Tremlett is discovered in Bagley Wood (an actual place) and subsequently Morse faints during the post mortem examination, again proving that he is squeamish around dead bodies. To recover Thursday takes him to the Victoria Arms **(18)** in Old Marston for a drink, and it is here beside the river that Colin Dexter can be spotted making his cameo appearance as a customer. The pub has featured several times in both *Inspector Morse* and *Lewis* – its most notable appearance to date being in *The Remorseful Day* as the place where Morse recites the last verse of the Housman poem that lends its name to the title of that final *Inspector Morse* episode. It is also here that Morse professes not to drink alcohol. Despite this he has a pint of beer, forced upon him by Thursday, which he seems to enjoy. Hence the Victoria Arms is the location for Morse's first and last on-screen alcoholic drink.

After further enquiries back at the girl's school, the investigation takes Morse to the establishment of seedy used car dealer Teddy Samuels. On his forecourt Morse admires a MkII Burgundy Jaguar with registration plate 248 RPA – the vehicle which has become inextricably linked to Morse since it was first seen in *The Dead of Jericho*. It was originally intended that, at the conclusion of *First Bus to Woodstock*, Morse would return and purchase the car and thus explain how he came by it in the first place. There are problems here since Samuels states that the car is only nine months old, implying that the car was manufactured in 1965, given that the car's tax disc displays an expiry date of December 1965. However, the car was actually manufactured in 1960. Maybe Morse saw through the shady salesman and decided not to purchase, or more likely the asking price of £1,227 (with just 9,000 miles on the clock) was too high given that brand new the car would only have cost £1,534. The location of the garage was not in Oxford, but was the Wargrave Auto Centre near Henley-on-Thames. Unfortunately, it has since been demolished and is now a housing development.

It is then back to college to interview Dr. Stromming and another chance encounter with Alexander Reece, who reminds the viewer that Morse dropped out of university as he "was never Oxford material" being "too decent by half". In the next scene the viewer finally gets another chance to see Patrick Malahide, as Sir Richard Lovell, at his home. Morse makes a further visit to college to see Dr. Stromming, then to the Stromming home to see Mrs. Stromming, before returning to the police station to give his current theory to CS Crisp. He initially supports Morse, until it is revealed that a member of the public saw Mary Tremlett waiting for the first bus to Woodstock, at a time when according to Morse she would have been dead some twelve hours. It further transpires that Morse may have withheld important information about the case, a fact that does not please Thursday.

All this investigating is thirsty work so it is time for a drink at the Lamb and Flag **(202)** – nowhere near Cowley Road police station – which Morse is seen entering via Lamb and Flag Passage. Here, by chance, he meets Rosalind Stromming to whom he apologies, and over a drink fills in more background detail by revealing that his father was a taxi driver and his mother a Quaker. It is now time for contemplation with Morse seen sitting on a bench in Christ Church Meadow **(200)** with the cathedral in the background.

The following morning, as he is about to hand in his resignation at the police station, he discovers a clue which leads him back to the girl's school, the used car dealership, the police station again, and finally, in the company of Thursday, to what is described as a Crown Estate property where the sex parties have taken place. The location is actually Syon House **(15)** on the outskirts of London. Not before time the viewer meets that Harry Palmer character from the opening shots. It transpires that he is known just a Dempsey, and does, indeed, work for the secret service. He invites Thursday to verify his credentials by phoning his superior, Colonel Doleman, at the Home Office. The connection with the *Ipcress File* is complete since Michael Caine's boss in the that film was Colonel Ross who was played by Guy Doleman.

The trail now takes Thursday and Morse back to the used car garage, followed by another drink. This time it is the Royal Standard of England **(229)** at Forty Green in Buckinghamshire. Back at the police station Morse resigns and subsequently needs a further drink at the Royal Standard of England. Later Morse feels the need to say goodbye to Mrs. Stromming (and to get his favourite record signed by the opera singer). Here he reveals some more personal details about his past – this time the fact that he had once been engaged (this being most likely a reference to Wendy Spencer a fellow student with whom Morse was in love as mentioned in the Colin Dexter novel *The Riddle of the Third Mile*). Meanwhile Thursday is still on the case and tells Crisp how useful Morse has been in the investigation, and while so doing surreptitiously manages to retrieve Morse's resignation letter.

Back on the case once again, there are more interviews for Morse to conduct. He makes a breakthrough at the hospital that in turn leads to Sir Richard Lovell's house, which is said to be in Woodstock. There is a visit to a dress shop to complete the evidence after which Morse is able to identify the murderer to Thursday. This involves some more college shots with the climax taking place at the New Theatre in Oxford where Rosalind Calloway has been persuaded to come out of retirement for one last performance. The actual location is the Richmond Theatre **(16)**.

There remain only a few loose ends to tie up before Morse is seen leaving his lodgings for his journey back to Carshall Newtown, and an uncertain future. Thursday is there to pick him up, and Morse asks if he can drive the Jaguar to the railway station. On the way they discuss Morse's career. Thursday says that he could be his 'bag man' and that he would look after him and get him through his DS's exam. They stop at traffic lights at which point Thursday says, "You've got to ask yourself where you see yourself in 20 years." Morse is preoccupied in thought, and as he adjusts the rear view mirror he sees in it the reflection of the face, mainly just the eyes, of John Thaw as DCI Morse twenty years in the future. And so ends the pilot episode to the strains of the haunting *Inspector Morse* theme, with Thursday bringing Morse back from his distraction with the single word "Endeavour". This final touching scene is actually more subtle than it first appears, for the location chosen was the corner of Pusey Street **(220)** and St. John Street. In fact, it was filmed outside No. 22 St. John Street, the address given in *The Riddle of Third Mile* for Wendy Spencer, that ex-girlfriend of Morse, who was largely responsible for him dropping out of college and joining the police force in the first instance.

WILTON PARK

Wilton Park, on the outskirts of Beaconsfield, has a long and distinguished military history. The estate once belonged to the monks of Burnham Abbey, who leased it from the de Wheltons. It subsequently passed through various hands until 1702, when it was acquired by the Basill family and, by which time it had become

Whilton Park. In turn it was sold it to Josias Du Pre, who had served in the East India Company and become the Governor of Madras. It was he who had a mansion, known as the White House, built on the estate in 1779. It wasn't well received, being described by Lipscombe, in his book on Buckinghamshire published in 1847, as 'an inferior manor'.

During World War II Wilton Park was leased to the War Office and used as an interrogation centre for high ranking German officers. Among those who passed through the establishment were Marshall Messe, Field Marshalls von Rundstedt and Busch as well as Rudolph Hess. Later it came under the Foreign and Commonwealth Office and was used to re-educate prisoners of war into the British way of life.

[The White House just prior to demolition in 1968]

The White House became home to the Army School of Administration, and also the Army College of Military Education. From 1954 to 1972 it was also the headquarters of Eastern Command. In the 1960s a School of Languages was established, with one Colonel Gaddafi of Libya being one of the students of note. Its main objective was to provide foreign language training for the British Army, and English language training for military personnel from overseas.

Subsequently the estate was purchased in its entirety by the Government, and in 1968 The White House was demolishe to make way for the construction of army buildings, which included a 15-storey accommodation block. A bunker to accommodate the London District War Headquarters Communications Centre was added. The bunker also served, until the opening of the Thames Barrier in 1982, as the Thames Valley Flood Coordination Headquarters.

At the time of filming *First Bus to Woodstock* in 2011, much of the area was already disused awaiting redevelopment of up to 350 new homes which commenced in 2014. Several standing sets have been built for *Endeavour* since then, with Wilton Park also being the home of the *Endeavour* production office.

SYON HOUSE

The area takes its name from the monastery of the Bridgettine Order founded in 1415 by King Henry V, which stood until the 16th century on the north bank of the River Thames, close to Isleworth in west London. The monastery took its name from the Biblical 'Holy City of David', so Syon is a corruption of Zion.

[**The Great Conservatory, designed by Charles Fowler**]

After the Dissolution of the Monasteries it was used as a place of confinement for Catherine Howard prior to her execution in 1542. Later in 1547 King Henry VIII's coffin rested here on its way from Westminster to Windsor. During the night it burst open and the following morning dogs were discovered licking up certain remains.

The house seen today dates from the time of King Edward VI when Edward Seymour, Duke of Somerset, Protector of the Realm, acquired the estate from the Crown. However, he was executed in 1552 for felony with the estate passing to John Dudley, Duke of Northumberland, and it was here that his daughter-in-law Lady Jane Grey was offered the Crown. Dudley was also executed so the estate once again reverted to the monarch. In 1594 Queen Elizabeth I granted a lease to

15

Henry Percy, 9th Earl of Northumberland – the house remains in the family to this day, and has since 1995, during the time of the 12th Duke, been open to the public. The main house is a stone-built turreted quadrangle with various additions having been made over the centuries. The 10th Earl had Inigo Jones make repairs and improvements, while the 1st Duke had Robert Adam improve the house during which time Lancelot 'Capability' Brown landscaped the grounds. It was Adam that was responsible for creating a magnificent suite of rooms which includes the great hall, the ante-room which is lavishly gilded and adorned in the Roam style, the dining room with its richly ornamented half-domes screened by columns at each end, the red drawing room with its crimson silk walls, and the long gallery which has unusual proportions of 41.5 metres long and only 4.3 metres wide and high.

Of particular note is the Great Conservatory, which was designed by Charles Fowler and constructed from gunmetal and Bath stone. It is said that it was the inspiration for Joseph Paxton who studied it before designing Crystal Palace.

RICHMOND THEATRE

[The red brick and terracotta exterior of Richmond Theatre]

Originally just a few cottages and a simple manor house beside the River Thames, the area of Shene did not become important until King Henry VII rebuilt the manor house after a fire in 1497. The new structure, now a palace, he called Rychemonde after his earldom in Yorkshire. Queen Elizabeth I spent her last days here. The 18th century saw the construction of Richmond Bridge and many fine terraces around Richmond Green and Richmond Hill. The latter is adjacent to Richmond Park, the largest of London's Royal Parks and a site of Special Scientific Interest, as well as a Special Area of Conservation. The park, which may be driven through between the hours of dawn and dusk, supports over 600 red and fallow deer.

However, for the *Endeavour* enthusiast it is Little Green that must be visited, for here is to be found one of the most beautiful of all the Frank Matcham theatres. It was built in 1899 as the Theatre Royal and Opera House in red brick and terracotta. The auditorium is a mixture of gilt detailing and red plush fabrics. There was a major refurbishment along with the addition of a side extension in 1991, since when it has been operated by the Ambassador Theatre Group. The theatre was the location for the poignant scene in *First Bus to Woodstock* in which Rosalind Calloway is arrested by Morse who walks on stage at the end of her performance and gently leads her away from her admiring fans, not least of whom her husband Rowan Stromming who is looking on from a box in the circle.

THE ROYAL MASONIC SCHOOL FOR GIRLS

[The Royal Masonic School for Girls main tower]

17

In 1788 a group of Freemasons met to discuss plans to establish a charitable institute for the daughters of brethren who had fallen upon hard times, or whose death had meant hardship for their families. The first location was in the slum area of Somers Place, but after several moves and expansions, a more suitable and permanent home was found in June 1926 – the 204 acres of land in Rickmansworth, complete with a mansion (albeit in a state of disrepair) named Rickmansworth Park. Considerable alterations and building work had to take place such that it could accommodate up to 400 pupils, with boarding houses for the girls and classrooms to hold 30 children. The executed plan included an acoustically magnificent chapel with an organ and delicate frescoes, an impressive Great Hall, and a large Dining Hall with its exquisite cameos of deer, rabbits and plants. It opened in 1934 and today has 315 acres of stunning grounds along with additional sporting facilities.

Since 1978, the school has been a fee paying establishment accepting girls from every background and faith. It accepts both day pupils and boarders, with there being no prerequisite to have any Freemasonry connections.

Away from *Endeavour*, the school also featured prominently in the 1981 Indiana Jones film *The Raiders of the Lost Ark*, and again in 1991 in *Indiana Jones and the Last Crusade*.

THE VICTORIA ARMS

[The Victoria Arms where Oliver Cromwell is said to have waited
for news of the end of the Civil War]

Marston, or more correctly Old Marston, is situated to the north-east of Oxford on the River Cherwell, and is probably a corruption of 'marsh town'. The first mention of a church at Marston is in a charter of 1122 in which the chapel of Marston was granted to the Augustinian canons of St. Frideswide. The present church of St. Nicholas dates from the 12th century, with substantial additions from the 15th century.

The village played an important part in the Civil War, during the siege of Oxford. While the Royalist forces were besieged in the city, which had been used by King Charles I as his capital, the parliamentary forces under Sir Thomas Fairfax had their headquarters in Marston, and used the church tower as a lookout post for viewing the enemy's artillery positions in what is now the University Parks **(121)**.

The Victoria Arms is a riverside public house sitting on the banks of the River Cherwell. Indeed, the pub was the site of the old Marston rope ferry, which was the only way of getting from Marston and Headington to North Oxford and Summertown, until the construction of the Marston Ferry Link Road. The land and surrounding area is owned by the Oxford Preservation Trust, and is carefully managed to keep a unique rural feeling despite being almost in Oxford city centre. Inside the public house there is a brass plaque commemorating the filming of *Inspector Morse* – it was sponsored by The Inspector Morse Society, and unveiled by Colin Dexter in 2003.

ORIEL SQUARE

[In *First Bus to Woodstock* Morse walks across Oriel Square on his way to interview Lomax, who lives in the house at the very left of the picture]

Oriel Square was formerly known as Canterbury Square because of the Canterbury Gate of Christ Church College in the south-west corner. The name was changed after World War II at the request of Oriel College which maintained that it had originally be called Oriel Square. The name change was logical since Oriel College dominates the east side of the square. There are various 18th century town houses along the north side, which are also owned by the College, and are distinctive for their vivid individual colours that brighten the otherwise unremarkable features of the square. Oriel Square is a no through road during the day, and therefore relatively quiet, which maybe why it is so popular with film makers.

GIRL
SERIES 1 EPISODE 1

PREMIER: 14th April 2013   **AUDIENCE:** 7.4 million

LENGTH: 94 minutes   **DIRECTOR:** Edward Bazalgette

GUEST STARS: Olivia Grant, Jonathan Hyde, Jonathan Guy Lewis, Sophie Stuckey.

SYNOPSIS

It was no great surprise that following the successful pilot episode of *Endeavour*, which not only garnered critical acclaim but also had the highest audience figures of any ITV drama for the entire year, that a series would be commissioned. Hence just over a year later, with the same principle actors and many of the same people in the production team (one notable exception being that each episode had a different Director), the first of four new cases was screened on consecutive Sunday evenings, commencing April 2013.

The first of these episodes, *Girl* (and henceforth all *Endeavour* episodes to date have been given single word titles), has DC Morse under the wing of, and bag man to, the experienced DI Thursday. The apparent death by heart attack of 22 year-old Margaret Bell, arouses Morse's suspicions concerning the nature of her demise. The subsequent fatal shooting of Dr. Frank Cartwright, the practice partner of Margaret's general practitioner, Dr. Bill Prentice, further confirms Morse's hypothesis of foul play.

Add to this that Cartwright's widow, Helen, and her father, Sir Edmund Sloan, an eminent nuclear scientist at Beaufort College, are at odds with her younger sister, the epileptic and seemingly unstable Pamela Walters whose child they mind, and the plot deepens.

Morse soon finds a connection between Margaret and Sir Edmund. Sloan, who has been receiving anonymous letters accusing him of murder, is the tutor of Margaret's boyfriend Denis Bradley. The puzzle is complete when it transpires that the latest victim of a spate of post office robberies seems to have been involved with Dr. Cartwright in the supply of illegal drugs to among others, Margaret Bell.

In this case Morse must tread carefully, for although he has the support of Thursday, their superior, CS Bright, very much disapproves of Morse's maverick ways and wants him removed from the case. Morse, however, is able to use his love of puzzles and former experience in code breaking at the Royal Signal Corps (obtained during his National Service) to draw all the threads together and to solve the murders.

SCENE BY SCENE

By the time the opening titles have finished, the viewer has had glimpses of most of the important elements of the episode. First, as always, are the establishing shots of Oxford – this time focussing on Broad Street **(210)** and the Bridge of Sighs **(182)**, where a double-decker bus **(176)**, on which Pamela Walters and Morse exchange glances. Next are a room in which Sir Edmund is lecturing students, Morse at choir practice, Margaret Bell at secretarial college, Denis Bradley getting a hair cut, a parade of shops **(25)** – which includes the post office that will later play a central role in the investigation. Following her day at college, Margaret Bell is at home getting ready to go out. She fails, however, to answer the telephone call from Denis Bradley, who is calling from a telephone box in Catte Street **(211)** – just opposite the Bridge of Sighs and adjacent to where a ban the bomb demonstration is taking place. Here the audience is introduced to the Reverend Monkford, who will also become a key character in the plot. The action then moves to Morse in his new flat, now located in Rewley House **(203)** at the corner of St. John Street **(224)** and Wellington Square **(226)**. Sir Edmund's luxury home **(25)** follows, where Helen Cartwright is putting baby Walters to bed. Ending the title sequence is Radcliffe Square **(222)** and Brasenose Lane **(209)** where Margaret Bell walks alone.

The following day Morse is on the trail of a bogus gas metre reader who has been emptying the gas metres of unsuspecting residents, one of whom mentions the current spate of post office robberies in the area. Back at Cowley Road police station Bright is introducing himself to his new staff and puts everyone on notice as to what he terms 'Spanish practices' (which is defined as 'irregular or restrictive practices in the interests of the workers'). Morse is soon sent to Margaret Bell's house where he meets PC Jim Strange for the first time (the two of them not getting off to the best of starts). Upstairs Dr. DeBryn has examined Margaret's body and concluded that she probably died from a heart attack.

The scene now passes to Sir Edmund's house and then quickly back to the police station where Bright is impressing upon Thursday the need to clear up the bogus gasman case. He also expresses his doubts about having the inexperienced Morse as Thursday's bag man. Meanwhile Morse is at Bell's surgery, where he discovers that since Margaret was on the heart drug Digoxin, she would be unlikely to suffer a heart attack. Morse interviews Denis Bradley at college – supposedly Beaufort but actually St. Edmund Hall **(26)** – where he learns that he had been stood up on the night of his girlfriend's death.

22

Next it is time for the usual liquid lunch at a public house. This time it is the White Horse **(28)** where Morse discusses his findings with Thursday, who advises him to keep his head down in light of Bright's earlier comments. The investigation takes Morse to Margaret's secretarial college, and from there to another possible boyfriend, Derek Clark. Clark works with his father at the post office seen in the opening titles. It is also the post office used by Pamela Walters, who is cashing a 10/- postal order, and also doing a bit of shoplifting. Morse observes this and follows her to the adjacent launderette **(25)** but takes no further action.

The next morning, in a public convenience beside the river, the body of Dr. Frank Cartwright is found shot dead. Bright is on the scene and wants Morse replaced by somebody more senior. It does not help Morse's case when he rather arrogantly announces his Sherlock Holmes-like deductions, which contradict the senior officer's own remarks about a bicycle found abandoned at the scene of crime. Morse will later be proved correct as the bicycle owner will turn out to be a clergyman, the Reverend Monkford.

Scenes at the doctors' surgery, the post office, and Sir Edmund's house follow in quick succession. During an interview Morse inevitably feels sympathy for Pamela Walters who is kept by her father and sister from spending time with her baby, Bobby, due to her epilepsy.

There now follows an aside to the main plot when, on his way home, Morse comes across a gas metre reader in St. John Street. Unfortunately for him, he does not have any identification with him, and so, despite protestations, he is arrested by Morse. After a night in the cells it is found that the man was indeed a genuine employee of the gas board, something that does not improve Bright's humour or impression of Morse.

Luckily Morse can make himself scarce, as he has traced the discarded bicycle to Reverend Monkford. He visits Monkford at his church, located in Hambledon **(231)**, and is surprised that (a) he has a knowledge of science (having a framed periodic table of the elements hanging on the wall) (b) that he shares Morse's passion for puzzles and crosswords and (c) that the church has an association with the Sloan family, with one member being buried there while another was married in the church.

The action soon moves to Beaufort College (where Sir Edmund invites Morse to dinner in the Old Dining Hall), to the police station, to the mortuary, to the post office, to the river (which is being dragged for a murder weapon) and finally back to Beaufort College where Morse has tracked down the writer of the hate mail to Sir Edmund. Here Morse is rather lenient with the culprit, and learns that Sir Edmund is about to leave Oxford for a lucrative position in America.

Morse visits the flat of Pamela Walters at No. 17 Holywell Street **(212)** where another clue is forthcoming. Then it is off down the pub for drinks with Strange, where the latter helps Morse revise for his sergeant's exam, remarking that Morse is "alright, actually, aren't you?". It is at this point that Morse realises the significance of the toilet where Dr. Cartwright's body was found – it was the drop off location for drugs (hiding them in the toilet cistern). He immediately heads for the public convenience only to discover that Thursday has also come to the same conclusion. Morse thinks that Derek Clark might also be involved, so he and Thursday head for the post office, only to find that it has been robbed. Father and son have been tied up in the back room, with the former having had two fingers cut off to encourage him to open the safe.

From here it is back to Hambleden, for in the interim Reverend Monkford has been murdered in the aisle of his church, but not before managing to leave a clue. This clue, which only Morse will recognise – but not until the end of the episode – is in the form of hymn numbers. It is also revealed that recently the Reverend Monkford had taken pity a man he had found sleeping in the church doorway, but that the following morning had discovered that he had robbed him of valuables, including his prized coin collection.

Despite Morse's good work, Bright insists that he is returned to general duties. Morse, though, does not give up, and revisit's Pamela Walters' flat where he discovers that she is in possession of Sir Edmund's revolver. Unhappily for Morse, Thursday is soon on the scene to arrest her for murder, and also to reprimand Morse most severely.

Back on general duties, Morse makes a breakthrough and telephones Somerset House to confirm his theory of the crimes, while Strange manages to apprehend and arrest the bogus gasman, along with his haul of coins. On counting them, Morse realises that amongst the money are some of the Reverend Monkford's stolen coin collection. This immediately leads him to identify the rough sleeper who stole them in the first place. The ensuing interview leads Morse back to Monkford's church where he discovers that Monkford was a member of the Government Code and Cipher School. At last everything becomes clear to him. With this information, Morse is able to solve the clue left by Monkford, and reveal the murderer in front of an astonished Bright who can only proclaim, "Good grief!".

An arrest is made, and for good measure, the episode ends with Morse doing yet another good deed as he ensures that Bobby is returned to Pamela Walters as Sir Edmund heads off for America. Morse is only able to achieve this by citing police regulations, thus illustrating that he has the capacity to be both a good policeman and detective. The final scene sees Pamela Walters and Bobby boarding a coach in Market Street **(214)** for an unknown destination and uncertain future, but, one hopes, a happier life away from the control of Sir Edmund.

MUNDEN HOUSE

[Munden House, a favourite television filming location]

From the remains of a villa excavated in the 1950s it is known that a Roman settlement existed where the Munden Estate now stands. The first formal mention of a manor was in 1097 when the owner was Robert de Meriden (of which Munden is most likely a corruption). The descendants of the present family at Munden can be traced to 1607 when Thomas Ewer of the Lea acquired the property. In 1828 the property passed to the Hibbert family having come through the female line, and it remained a Hibbert home until 1874 when the estate was left to a grandson, Arthur Holland, who later became the 3rd Viscount Knutsford. Today the 6th Viscount Knutsford lives on the estate and his son, Henry Holland-Hibbert is the present incumbent of Munden.

The present house dates from at least 1795, with additions having been made in 1829 with more extensive building works in the late 19th century. It was in the early part of the 19th century that the gardens and woods were laid out.

Among productions filmed here are series such as *Poirot, Rosemary & Thyme, Midsomer Murders, Jonathan Creek* and *Silent Witness.*

GLEBE AVENUE

Originally called Ticheham in the Domesday book the area around Ickenham was mainly agricultural until the 1930s. In 1909 it was described as being 'a small quiet village scattered around a tiny patch of green, on which is a picturesque pump'. In 1921 the population was just 443, but by 1961 this had risen to over 10,000. Part of the rise in popularity of the area was due to the expansion of the railways which in 1904 came to a station in Glebe Avenue. In the early days it was just a small halt with a hut run by the Metropolitan Railway, who were reluctant to have any station at all given the lack of revenue it generated. At that time Ickenham was seen as a day out from London in rural surroundings. Villagers in the vicinity of Glebe Avenue sold flowers from their gardens and served teas to the visitors. In 1910 the District line also stopped at Ickenham. Today in excess of 1 million passengers, mainly commuters to London, use the station every year. At the junction of Glebe Avenue and Long Lane is the parade of shops featured in *Girl*.

[The parade of shops in Glebe Avenue which became (from left to right) a launderette (unchanged), greengrocers, funeral directors (unchanged), newsagents and post office]

St. Edmund Hall

The history of St. Edmund Hall goes back to the 13th century, although it has only been a college in the strict sense since 1957. It is the sole survivor of the medieval academic halls that provided student accommodation and tuition. The saint in question is St. Edmund of Abingdon, who was also archbishop of Canterbury

(1234-40). It is not certain when the hall was founded, but early in the 13th century it is known that what is now the front quadrangle was owned by John de Bermingham, who is likely to have kept a student hall. At that time part of the land belonged to Magdalen College, and there was also a close relationship with Queen's College. In 1546 the Crown sold the hall to a property speculator, William Burnell, who in turn sold it in 1553 to William Denysson, who was the Provost of Queen's College. However, although part of Queen's College under a statute of 1564, St. Edmund Hall was to be a 'separate identity... under the aegis of The Queen's College'.

[The medieval well and sundial in the front quadrangle]

Undergraduate numbers fluctuated and were always small, ranging from just 6 in 1552 to 65 in 1660. Throughout its history there was conflict between the hall and both the Church and State. It was a stronghold of John Wycliffe's supporters (Lollards), with the College principal, William Taylor, being burnt at the stake for his beliefs. During the late 17th century it was home to non-jurors, those men who remained loyal to the House of Stuart and would not recognise the House of Hanover.

It was not until 1934 that Queen's College agreed to relax its control, and in due time allowed the freehold of the site to be vested in an Official Trustee of Charity

Lands. The hall also received statutes of its own, and in 1957 Queen Elizabeth II approved the grant to the hall of its charter of incorporation as a college in its own right.

Notable features of St. Edmund Hall are the entrance in Queen's Lane, over which there is the college coat of arms, a quadrangle with a medieval well inscribed *haurietis aquas in gaudio de fontibus salvatoris* (with joy, draw water from the wells of salvation) in its centre, the chapel whose stained glass window is one of the earliest works by Sir Edward Burne-Jones and William Morris, and library which is housed in the deconsecrated 12th century church of St. Peter-in-the-East **(35)**.

THE WHITE HORSE

The White Horse at No. 52 Broad Street is sandwiched between two branches of Blackwell's bookshop. It is a small 2-roomed 18th century timber-framed tavern, although the frontage was completely rebuilt in 1951. It has been a favourite watering hole in both the *Inspector Morse* and *Lewis* series.

FUGUE
SERIES 1 EPISODE 2

PREMIER: 21st April 2013   **AUDIENCE:** 7.0 million

LENGTH: 93 minutes   **DIRECTOR:** Tom Vaughan

GUEST STARS: Will Featherstone, Laura Rees, Geoffrey Streatfeild.

SYNOPSIS

Episode 2 is perhaps the darkest of the first series, and certainly the most personal for DC Morse himself. It starts with a body found in a railway freight van, and several murders later ends on the roof of Trinity College (37) with Morse and DI Thursday fighting for their respective lives. At first the killings seem random, the work of a deranged individual, but it soon becomes apparent that everything has been meticulously planned and staged with Morse in mind. Indeed, it is Morse who unravels the elaborate staging of the crimes, and recognises the operatic connections. It is also Morse who is sent cryptic clues from the murderer. These goad both Morse, and Oxford City Police, who must solve the clues in order to prevent further murders. The plot has elements of Agatha Christie's *And Then There Were None* mixed in with the *ABC Murders*. The photography and direction by Tom Vaughan is superb, especially in the final climatic scenes at Trinity College which have all the suspense of Alfred Hitchcock's *Vertigo* with a little of *The Man Who New Too Much* thrown in for good measure.

SCENE BY SCENE

As with other episodes, there is a busy opening title sequence in which the viewer is introduced to Trinity College where Morse has been singing in The Oxford Scholars' Choral Association. Afterwards at a reception, he meets Dorothea Frazil (last seen in *First Bus to Woodstock*) from the *Oxford Mail*, and has his photograph snapped for the newspaper. This image is cut out of the newspaper by our murderer who is an admirer of Morse's intellect. There is then the usual rooftop establishing shot of Oxford – this time it is of Exeter College chapel (179) – and then to the Madison family home, followed by an introduction to a frustrated Phillip Madison at a piano practicing for a recital, to psychiatrist Dr. Daniel Cronyn's home in Park Town (218), to a plumber's yard (237), to Morse doing some more studying for his Sergeant's exam, and finally to a solemn looking Lionel Balfour sitting alone in his dining room in front of a plate of food that he is shortly to throw onto the floor in a fit of rage. Only two minutes into the episode the viewer has already been provided with at least one vital clue. Without delay it is onto the first murder victim, Evelyn Balfour, who is found in a freight van in a railway siding, actually filmed at the Buckinghamshire Railway Centre (237). She has been strangled, but as a clue in her mouth is a handkerchief embroidered with the letter 'D'.

Evelyn Balfour appears to have been having an affair. At this point Morse is still on general duties, but he questions why the freight van door had been left open, and sensing that something is wrong, returns to the railway sidings that night. He discovers a vital clue, for written in chalk on the inside of the door, and hidden from view when the door is open, are the words '*un bacio ancora*' from the opera *Otello*. The significance being that these are the last words by Otello, sung just after he has strangled his wife, Desdemona, in a fit of jealousy. In the opera he believes that she has given her handkerchief to another man as a sign of love, and so Morse deduces that Evelyn Balfour, unlike the innocent Desdemona, was having an affair.

With no pausing for breath, it is onto the next victim, Grace Madison, who is found at home by her niece, Faye Madison. Grace, a botanist of some note, had been expecting to have tea and discuss her garden with journalist, Benjamin Nimmo. It is Grace's tea, laced with *detura menstromium*, that is found to have poisoned her.

Next, a connection is found between Lionel Balfour and one Roy Adamson, an employee at the plumber's yard seen in the opening titles. Adamson's fingerprints have been lifted from Evelyn Balfour's handbag. He was her lover, and Thursday promptly has him arrested for her murder. Meanwhile, Morse is on the track of Benjamin Nimmo and so goes to Nimmo's Oxford flat, only to be told that even his neighbour hasn't seen him for three years. She does, however, confirm that he likes classical music, and plays it loudly at all hours.

Unusually, lunch and discussion of the case thus far between Morse and Thursday, is not taken at a public house, but while driving back to the Madison home. Here Morse is soon to find a link to the opera *Lackmé* in Grace's greenhouse. The theory until now has been that the Balfour case is all but solved, and that it is one of the surviving Madisons who is responsible for poisoning Grace for her money.

Some quick scenes follow as Morse does some research back at his flat to verify his findings, birds fly over Exeter College, and CS Bright is in his office listening to Morse's theory that the killings are all linked by operatic last words, and committed in the same manner as that in the opera. It is now that Bright allows Thursday to transfer Morse to the detective squad for the duration of the investigation, owing to his specialist operatic knowledge.

Following the usual drink with Strange down the pub, Morse revisits the home of Faye Madison, listens to some more opera at home, and is seen next morning picking up Thursday from his home, the interior of which is actually located not in Oxford, but in a street in Finchley, North London **(245)**. No wonder he needs a car to get to work! Here we are introduced to Thursday's daughter Joan, who works in a bank, and son Sam, who expresses an ambition to join the army – this provides background information to future episode plots.

At the police station Bright has called upon the services of Dr. Daniel Cronyn, who gives his expert opinion on the psyche of the murderer. The trail takes Morse, Thursday and Dr. Cronyn to the rural location of Drover's Rest, a slaughter yard belonging to Benjamin Nimmo. It is here that another operatic clue, this time from *Aida*, is discovered along with the body of the unfortunate Nimmo, who has been bricked up behind a wall.

It is now obvious to all that someone evil is toying with the police, particularly since the musical score of the *Little List Song*, from the *Mikado*, is found in the dead man's pocket. Add to this the photograph of Morse from the newspaper found pinned to the wall, and it is clear that the killer has Morse in his sights. This prompts Dr. Cronyn to tell Morse the tail of a previous case involving an insane patient called Keith Miller, who spoke of having a 'Little List' of persons who had rubbed him up the wrong way, whom he wanted to kill in revenge. Cronyn believes that Miller has been released from a psychiatric hospital recently, allegedly having been cured. Could Miller be the killer? At this point the plot is looking not too dissimilar from that of the *Inspector Morse* episode *Masonic Mysteries*.

Another clue arrives at the *Oxford Mail*, and a girl, Debbie Snow, is abducted outside her house. Morse finally realises that the deaths are not random, but in the order of the pneumonic 'Every Good Boy Deserves Favour' used to remember the notes on a treble clef. A red shoe is left behind at the scene of Miss Snow's abduction, and inside is a piece of paper with the words 'No Alibi Err Badly' and 'Near By Libra Idol'. This time the opera is *The Snow Maiden* in which the subject melts in the morning sun. Morse is tasked with solving the clue before the girl is surely killed at sunrise the next day. The clue takes him to the Bodleian Library **(197)** where he finds that a Mr. Keith Miller is a frequent reader. He has also recently requested the score for *The Snow Maiden*, and, moreover, he is currently in the building. Morse has the library closed and a chase ensues through the underground stacks culminating in Morse emerging from the Sheldonian Theatre **(204)** having been stabbed. He collapses on the steps at the side of the Museum of the History of Science **(33)**.

Having had stitches applied by Dr. DeBryn, and then been lent a new shirt, Morse finds another clue in Catte Street **(211)** in the form of a double proposition or *bocardo* (a mnemonic for a traditional syllogism) – 'Some Coppers Have No Brains' and 'All Coppers Are Bastards' with the mathematical sign for 'therefore' underneath. Morse needs to consult Dr. Cronyn at Park Town, but the doctor seems more interested in Morse's own background than he is in answering the detective's questions.

Time is now short for Debbie Snow, so Morse decides to drive around the empty streets of the city to clear his head, where he comes to a stop beside the Martyrs' Memorial **(34)**. He suddenly realises the meaning of the syllogism, as it was at the Bocardo prison that the Oxford Martyrs' were held prior to their execution. That is the clue, not the syllogism itself. The prison was located near the Church of St. Michael at the North Gate in Cornmarket Street. Today visitors can see the original cell door which remains on display in that church. However, although the episode clearly states that Debbie Snow is rescued alive from a coffin in the Church of St. Michael at the North Gate, the location used for filming was St. Peters-in-the-East **(36)** in Queen's Lane **(221)** adjacent to St. Edmund Hall **(26)**. Following the rescue Morse talks with Strange in Queen's Lane as he is suspicious that, although the ordeal was horrific for a small girl to endure, she was never really in any danger of being killed.

To seek more expert advice a return is made to Park Town where the body of Dr. Cronyn is found, at least what remains of a body after it has been exposed to *aqua regia* (a mixture of nitric and hydrochloric acids). Morse realises why it was so 'easy' to locate Debbie Snow – she was not the intended victim, just a diversion for the actual murder in which the body was melted away by acid.

There are some short scenes as Morse visits Faye Madison at home again, Lionel Balfour at home, Roy Adamson now back at work after his release, the mortuary, and finally Merton Street **(216)** where he nearly falls asleep at the wheel of the car while driving Thursday. Taking pity on him Thursday takes Morse to his home where he is allowed to sleep, and have a home-cooked meal.

Morse, now rested and back at work, is provided with a valuable clue by Dorothea Frazil at the *Oxford Mail*. Later in the police station, with the help of the murderer phoning him and playing some *Tosca*, 'the penny drops' and Morse finally knows the identity of the killer. On explaining everything to his superiors he hears the usual exclamation of "good grief" from Bright. A search of the murderer's house, or more accurately their bolt hole, is made, but it is found to be empty. However, the reason why the four victims thus far were chosen now becomes clear after Thursday finds some papers, which reveal that all those killed were connected in some way, and form part of the killer's revenge plan.

From this evidence Morse deduces that the fifth and final victim will be Faye Madison, whom he knows will be at Trinity College watching Phillip Madison giving his piano recital that afternoon. However, he is wrong, and the intended victim is not Faye at all, but Thursday. Morse and Thursday confront the murderer, who would have succeeded in their plan, if it were not for Morse's ability to overcome his vertigo (from which he suffers in the *Inspector Morse* episode *Service of All the Dead*), and clamber about the roofs of the College. After the arrest is made Bright arrives at the scene. All he has to say to Morse, who under any other circumstances would be awarded a Queen's Police Medal, is, "I imagine that getting back to general duties after all this will seem like a holiday".

MUSEUM OF THE HISTORY OF SCIENCE

[Side entrance, where Morse recovers on the steps in
***Fugue*, of the Museum of the History of Science]**

In 1924 the upper floor of the Old Ashmolean building in Broad Street **(210)**, which had been built in 1683 to house the collection of Elias Ashmole, was given over to the Lewis Evans collection of scientific instruments. To this ensemble was added that of James Billmeir in 1957, and Cyril Beeson in 1966. As the collections grew it was clear that more space was going to be needed, so in 1935 The Museum of the History of Science was established, occupying the whole building. The original Ashmole exhibits were moved to the current Ashmolean Museum in Beaumont Street. Today the museum holds an unrivalled collection of early astronomical and mathematical instruments from Europe and the Middle East, and an exceptionally rich set of microscopes. Complementing the wide range of objects are manuscripts and early printed works, early photographs, portraits of scientists and scientific prints.

MARTYRS' MEMORIAL

[A 19th century print of the Martyrs' Memorial]

The history of this memorial really begins in 1553 when Queen Mary came to the throne. She was a Roman Catholic and ordered Thomas Cranmer (Archbishop of Canterbury), Nicholas Ridley (Bishop of London) and Hugh Latimer (Bishop of Worcester) to appear before a commission in Oxford on a charge of Protestant heresies.

Thomas Cranmer had already been found guilty of treason on two counts. First, that on the 10th July 1553 when he entered the Tower of London, along with other traitors, that he there did proclaim Lady Jane Dudley to be Queen, and second that he and others had send men in arms to help the Duke of Northumberland against Queen Mary. He was sentenced to be hanged, drawn and quartered for these crimes, but Mary also wanted him tried for the greater offence of heresy.

The trial started on 16th April 1554 in the Divinity School and took the form of a disputation conducted in Latin. Each of the accused were to defend their beliefs on the subjects of the 'Real Presence at the Mass', 'Transsubstantiation' and the 'Mass as a Sacrifice'. On 20th April all three were told that they had failed to prevail and that they should recant their statements. They refused, and thereby became heretics. Fortunately, the burning of heretics had been repealed in 1547 and a new bill before Parliament to reverse this law was defeated by the House of Lords. It was then decided that they should be tried by the courts of the Papal Legate. Meanwhile a new Parliament re-enacted the heresy statutes. Cranmer was tried before the Pope's commissioners in September 1555 and the proceedings sent to Rome, during which time Cranmer was able to appeal. Ridley and Latimer were also tried, found guilty, excommunicated, and burned at the stake on 16th October 1555 after refusing to recant. The burning took place in a ditch just outside the northern city wall. Cranmer, however, being an Archbishop had to be 'degraded' by being ceremoniously stripped of his vestments first before he could be burned. He was made to watch the burning of Ridley and Latimer from a parapet in the City wall.

'Be of good comfort, Master Ridley; we shall this day light such a candle, by God's grace, in England as I trust shall never be put out' are the reported last heroic words of Latimer at the stake.

The 80 days given to Cranmer to appeal ran out in November 1555, but in January 1556 he did write a recantation. However, his accusers were not satisfied and demanded 2 more recantations to be written and sent to the Pope.

In fact, he was to write 6 recantations in all but to no avail. On 21st March 1556 he appeared at the church of St. Mary the Virgin **(206)**, where he was to speak to the congregation and proclaim that he believed in the Catholic faith. He actually read out a speech repudiating his recantations. He was burnt shortly afterwards.

It was not until the 19th century that an appeal was launched to build a memorial for these martyrs. The memorial was situated in St. Giles' on the site of the Robin Hood Inn and other houses on the north side of the church of St. Mary Magdalen. The monument was designed by Sir George Gilbert Scott and took two years to construct (1841 to 1843). The design was based on the 13th century Eleanor Cross at Waltham in Essex, which was one of the crosses erected by King Edward I in memory of Queen Eleanor. The statues were carved by Henry Weekes and have

Cranmer facing north holding his Bible marked May 1541. The significance of the date is that this was when the Bible was allowed to be circulated by royal authority, something for which Cranmer had long pleaded. Ridley faces east and Latimer faces west with his head bowed and arms crossed.

The inscription on the base reads: 'To the Glory of God, and in grateful commemoration of His servants, Thomas Cranmer, Nicholas Ridley, Hugh Latimer, Prelates of the Church of England, who near this spot yielded their bodies to be burned, bearing witness to the sacred truths which they had affirmed and maintained against the errors of the Church of Rome, and rejoicing that to them it was given not only to believe in Christ, but also to suffer for His sake; this in the year of our Lord, MDCCCXLI'.

ST. PETER-IN-THE-EAST CHURCH

[St. Peter-in-the-East Church]

The church was first recorded in 1086, and is situated not far from the original East Gate of the city. The oldest part of the current building dates from the early 12th century. The crypt has a nave of 5 bays, and 8 sturdy Romanesque columns supporting the floor of the chancel above. The east window is noteworthy for its 16th century glass depicting the Four Evangelists. Sir John Betjeman described the church as follows: 'Like so much that is worth seeing, St. Peter's in the East is hidden away. It is in a peaceful walled enclosure made by St. Edmund Hall (26), Queen's College, and New College (190), down a little lane which is like what Oxford used to be before the petrol age … The church itself is like a village church

36

set down unexpectedly in a town'. Today it is not a church at all, having been deconsecrated and sympathetically restored and converted in 1970, to serve as the library of St. Edmund Hall. The tower became the book store with a Fellow's room above, the north aisle and west end of the church were also fitted out with book stacks, while the nave, chancel and Lady Chapel were furnished with reading desks. Nicholas Pevsner described the result as 'without any doubt the most interesting church of Oxford'. In the churchyard will be found the graves of Sir Edmund Rich of Abingdon (patron of St. Edmund Hall and former Archbishop of Canterbury), and James Sadler (the first English aeronaut).

TRINITY COLLEGE

[Top Left: The chapel whose roof provided the backdrop for the climatic scenes in *Fugue*, Top Right: Inside the chapel, and Bottom: The magnificent grounds of Trinity College]

Trinity College was founded by Sir Thomas Pope in 1555. He was a devout Catholic with no surviving children who saw the foundation of an Oxford college as a means of ensuring that he and his family name would always be remembered in the prayers and masses of its members. He came from a family of small landowners in Oxfordshire, trained as a lawyer, and rose rapidly to prominence under King Henry VIII. As Treasurer of the Court of Augmentations, he handled the estates of the monasteries dissolved at the Reformation, and amassed a considerable personal fortune. Later he became a discreet and trusted privy counsellor of Mary Tudor, and it was from Mary and Philip that he received Letters Patent and royal approval for his new foundation. The statutes of the college set out rules for a simple monastic life of religious observance and study. Within the walls of the College is a garden comprising an informal grove of trees, mainly elms, amongst which the members of the college could walk and meditate. In fact, Trinity College was not a new college at all, for in 1554 Pope merely purchased what remained of Durham College, a former monastic college which had fallen victim to the dissolution, and its simple buildings sufficed for the next hundred years. Pope died in 1559 and is the only founder of either an Oxford or Cambridge college to lie under a monument in his own foundation. Today the Old Library dating from 1421 is the only building that survives from the former Durham College.

In 1618, the then President undertook to build a cellar under the refectory but this collapsed, and as a consequence, the present Hall was constructed. The Civil War saw the College empty of scholars and all the College silver being given over to King Charles I to be turned into coin to pay the troops. By the end of the war the College was virtually bankrupt, although fortunes were to return thanks to one of the Fellows, Ralph Bathurst, who recognised a need to attract the aristocracy to Oxford. He had his friend, one Christopher Wren, design some luxurious accommodation for students (which included rooms for their servants) along what is today part of the Garden Quadrangle. The 2-storey building was completed in 1668. Soon, however, more accommodation was needed, so a second building was added in the 1680s. At the same time the garden became more formal, with an avenue of lime trees, a complex pattern of paths, obelisks and a maze. Indeed, the college has seen a gradual expansion of its buildings and increased student numbers ever since.

In the 18th century, Trinity College was at the forefront of reform and in 1789 introduced a simple form of examination, although women had to wait until 1979 to be admitted. Among the famous alumni are John Aubrey, Sir Richard Burton, Miles Kington, William Pitt the Elder and Terrence Rattigan.

ROCKET

SERIES 1 EPISODE 3

PREMIER: 28th April 2013   **AUDIENCE:** 7.1 million

LENGTH: 94 minutes   **DIRECTOR:** Craig Viveiros

GUEST STARS: Rosalind Halstead, Martin Jarvis, Maimie McCoy, Jenny Seagrove.

SYNOPSIS

Rocket is very much the 'town' episode of the series. It is set mainly within the confines of the British Imperial Electric Company's factory, where Her Royal Highness Princess Margaret, is making a visit to unveil the Standfast Mark II missile. The production site is presumably close to Cowley, since it is CS Bright's task at Cowley Road police station to provide security for the royal event. In reality this area is still the industrial heart of Oxford – the largest employer at that time would have been the car body manufacturing business of Pressed Steel (British Motor Corporation after 1965, and British Motor Holdings after 1966), which is today part of the BMW Mini plant.

During the royal visit one of the workers, Percy Malleson, is found murdered. There are motives and sub-plots aplenty. These include an Arab trade delegation which might be carrying out some industrial espionage, the fact that the company is in financial trouble and to survive will have to enter into an unpopular merger with a French concern, a demonstration by a group of anarchists, a suspicious German scientist working at the factory, and family tensions at boardroom level. It is Morse, though, who through his perseverance is able to reveal the truth behind the killing, but not before a second body is forthcoming.

This episode is the least satisfying of the series for a number of reasons. First there is the story, which breaks the Ronald Knox rules for murder mystery plotting in that it is not until after the second murder that the actual motive and suspect come to light. The clinching clue is kept from the viewer until just before the dénouement. In fact, it is not hard for those who are observant to identify the murderer from the opening titles, even before a crime has taken place. This is a case that does not really require the intellect of Morse to enable it to be solved.

Rocket also provides no new character insights into Morse himself, save that when at university another student, Alice Vexin, fancied him. This episode is more about the vanity of Bright and how he reacts under pressure. In addition to this there is a vital element for any *Inspector Morse, Lewis* or *Endeavour* episode missing – Oxford. Apart from a couple of establishing shots, a scene at a college, and another in Radcliffe Square **(222)**, Oxford is absent – this story is equally suited to Milton Keynes, or any other town for that matter, as is abundantly clear if you consider the fact that the vast majority of filming took place in London's Docklands, and in the county of Surrey.

SCENE BY SCENE

The opening titles, to the appropriate soundtrack of the *Chorus of the Hebrew Slaves*, affords glimpses of the factory **(42)** being prepared for the royal visit, Morse at home, a woman (Estella Broom) on horseback, workers arriving for the day shift, the factory office block along with introductions to the members of the board of directors (lead by Managing Director Henry Broom – played by Martin Jarvis who had such a key role in the *Inspector Morse* episode *Greeks Bearing Gifts*), Bright briefing his officers, and the Rudolph Hotel (undoubtedly a nod to the Randolph Hotel in Oxford) where the Arab delegation are staying.

Back in Oxford, Morse comes across the anti-royalist demonstration for the first and last time in this film, before there is a return to the factory for the royal arrival, tour and unveiling. Just as everything seems to have gone off successfully, it transpires that all is not well with the missile guidance system, or the proposed merger, and to top it all, Percy Malleson is found dead in a storeroom. He was a general fitter working on fuselage assembly, was not popular with his fellow workers, but more importantly as it soon becomes apparent, he was there to 'spy' on the workers, or as DI Thursday later puts it he was a "time and motion man".

All the employees need to be interviewed, and it is in the office block where the interviews are being conducted that Morse runs into an old friend from his college days, Alice Vexin, who just happened to be the person who found the dead body. It is clear that she still fancies Morse and would like to go out with him. Meanwhile one of the workers Morse interviews is Dr. Werner Volk, who is in charge of the aforementioned guidance system – as a disagreeable foreigner he immediately becomes a suspect. Soon a revolver is found in Malleson's locker, but why it is there remains a mystery until the end of the film.

It becomes apparent that the factory is not a happy place, with underinvestment, sexual harassment, and poor safety practices. Indeed, there has been a recent incident for which one of the workers, Lenny Frost, was held responsible and consequently lost his job. Frost blamed the late Percy Malleson for the loss – could this be a motive for murder? Not before time Malleson's flat is searched, and this is where Morse notices that the dead man wore handmade shoes from Cribb & Co., something that a factory worker could never have afforded. The trail takes Morse to the shoemaker, who is located in The Turl **(225)**. The premises

40

used for filming was the Oxfam charity shop which is adjacent to Duckers (since closed), the real-life bespoke Oxford shoemaker. This same shop, only appearing as different establishments, can be spotted in *Neverland* and *Coda*. The owner of the shoes is identified, however, the name is not Percy Malleson, but Eustace Kendrick, who Morse is told was involved with that "business with the Rix girl – it was in all the papers". This gives Morse an excuse for his first pub visit of the episode, where he meets Dorothea Frazil of the *Oxford Mail*. She informs him that on Coronation Day in 1953, a girl called Olive Rix went missing, and that Kendrick, being her boyfriend at the time, became the main suspect. He promptly fled the country and was never seen again. Olive's body was never been found.

Whilst all this is going on, Thursday interviews Crown Prince Nabil at his hotel, who because he is a foreigner becomes an instant suspect.

Morse manages to trace a cousin of Kendrick's, Marigold Proctor, and interviews her in Canterbury Quad at St. John's College **(192)** under the watchful gaze of Colin Dexter, making his cameo appearance as a don sitting on a bench in the background. It comes to light that Olive Rix had another boyfriend, and also that Kendrick has returned from South Africa, where he had fled in 1953. Wanting to clear his name, he joined the British Imperial Electric Company under the pseudonym of Malleson because he was convinced that it was somebody there who was responsible for Olive's death. The final part of this jigsaw puzzle is that Olive, at the time of her disappearance, was studying at an Agricultural College whose land just happens to be next to the family home of the Brooms **(43)**. It is at the Broom home that many of the subsequent scenes take place.

A sub-plot develops as Morse agrees to have a drink with Alice Vexin, and another when there is a near-miss accident back at the factory – an incident which causes the shop steward, Reg Tracepurel, to call a general stoppage. Morse gets his drink with Alice and more besides, as she is later seen in Morse's bed. Whilst Morse is enjoying himself, Lenny Frost is busy at the factory stealing technical papers relating to the Standfast missile gyroscopic system. But, to no avail, since he is electrocuted on his way out of the factory in what might be murder, or just another accident due to a leaky roof and an exposed electric cable. Suspicion once again falls upon Dr. Volk, whom it transpires, came to the company just after the end of World War II. Morse finds another clue which points in a different direction entirely, namely to the Arab delegation for whom Lenny Frost was now working.

Information on Olive Rix's other boyfriend comes to light via Alice Vexin. Following questions to the Broom family, it is revealed that Harry Broom was the other man in Olive's life. Further, it was Richard Broom who found her body the morning after her disappearance. Thinking that he was covering for his brother, buried Olive in the woods, without any qualms as to the possible consequences for Kendrick. Olive's remains are recovered, along with a piece of ceramic of unknown origin, but it is this item that will prove to be the crucial clue that cracks the case. For the moment, though, Bright wishes to close the investigation, and even though Morse and Thursday know full well that the death of Lenny Frost was no accident, they must keep quiet for lack of further evidence. Morse is despondent at the injustice, but back at his flat, has a distraction in the form of Alice Vexin, who stays the night. In St. John Street **(224)** Morse and Alice are seen leaving his flat, actually Rewley House **(203)** on the corner of Wellington Square **(226)**, together the next morning. However, by the evening, when they meet again in Radcliffe Square prior to going to the cinema Alice has changed her mind. She calls off the romance because she believes that Morse is not ready for a serious relationship.

Back in the boardroom, Henry Broom is being replaced as Managing Director by Estella Broom. Morse decides to go to the cinema anyway, and it is here while watching the Pathe newsreel of the royal visit, that he realises the identity of the murderer. Meanwhile Thursday has worked out what the piece of ceramic is. Between them they have established the motive, means and opportunity for the crime. All that remains is a return visit to the factory to arrest the culprit, which is done with a little subterfuge on Morse's part. The final scene has Bright promising to mention Morse's contribution, but only if the opportunity arises, when he reports on the arrest to the Chief Constable.

SILVERTOWN TATE & LYLE FACTORY

[The old Tate & Lyle works in Factory Road]

Silvertown, an industrial area of Newham south of the Royal Victoria and Albert Docks, was first developed in the 1850s around the rubber and telegraph works of S. W. Silver and Co. (thus the area's name). Later chemical and engineering plants, an oil refinery, and food and confectionery factories were forthcoming. Disaster struck in 1917 when there was an explosion in the Brunner Mond chemical works which resulted in the loss of 69 lives. A large part of West Silvertown was wrecked. In the 1970s the area was very much in decline, but the Thames Gateway regeneration brought Silvertown back to life, with a focus on residential complexes such as Britannia Village, Thames Barrier Park and Silvertown Quays.

Sugar has been associated with Silvertown since 1878, when Henry Tate opened a refinery here. In 1883, under two miles away in Plaistow, Abram Lyle started a sugar melting business. This was a new venture for him since up to 1865 his sole interest was in the shipping of products, including sugar, all over the world. Lyle knew that the sugar cane refining process produced a treacle-like syrup that was usually treated as waste, but which he felt could be refined to make a new saleable product – the result was Lyle's Golden Syrup, which today sell in excess of 1 million tins every month. The two companies merged in 1921, and at the time were responsible for the refining of around 50% of the country's sugar. Today the brand still exists, though since 2010 it has been under the ownership of American Sugar Refining.

THE HOMEWOOD

[Home of the Broom family in *Rocket*]

Esher is an outlying suburb of London being just 15 miles from Charing Cross. It is an ancient town having an entry in the Domesday Book of 1086 as Aissela and Aissele. Esher grew in importance when it became a stagecoach stop on the London to Portsmouth route. Famous inhabitants of the area have included Clive of India (who built Claremont mansion), George Harrison (who built a primitive recording studio at his house he named Kinfauns) and Maurice Gibb.

Just to the south of Esher and the Claremont estate, and beside the River Mole, is The Homewood (which became the Broom family home in *Rocket*). This extraordinary 20th century Modernist house is a masterpiece of design, set in the midst of a picturesque woodland garden. It was designed by the architect Patrick Gwynne for his family – his father, mother, sister and himself – and was completed in the early summer of 1938 at a cost of £10,000. To make way for The Homewood, an earlier rambling Victorian house had to be demolished. Gwynne's design, made when he was only 24 years-old, involved constructing the house on stilts (pilotis) with all the bedrooms and offices on one side of the building, and living and utility areas on the other (with the servants' quarters at one end). The house is open plan with the furniture, fittings and even the wallpaper being to Gwynne's specification. The property remained Gwynne's favourite project, serving as a living portfolio for his clients and students.

Gwynne lived in the house for the rest of his life, continuing to keep the building fashionably up-to-date until his death in 2003 e.g. turning the servants' quarters into a recreational area after World War II. The Homewood was given to the National Trust in 1999.

HOME
SERIES 1 EPISODE 4

PREMIER: 5th May 2013

AUDIENCE: 6.6 million

LENGTH: 98 minutes

DIRECTOR: Colm McCarthy

GUEST STARS: Kelly Adams, Louis Dylan, Jamie Glover, Edmund Kingsley, Poppy Miller, Guy Williams, Clive Wood.

SYNOPSIS

The final episode of the first series delves very much more into both DC Morse's and DI Thursday's past. It is January 1966, which means that the viewer can be treated to some superb photography of Oxford covered in snow. Morse is still on general duties and studying for his sergeant's exam, which he is due to take in just a few days. But before that, however, there is a night time hit-and-run incident with which to deal. As Morse is the only officer on duty when the call comes in, it is he who goes to investigate, and, as luck would have it, the victim, Professor Alistair Coke Norris, is a don at Baidley College, which in 'Morseland' can only mean one thing – murder.

Almost immediately it comes to light that Professor Coke Norris was at odds with the other fellows at Baidley over the sale of a piece of College land, Booth Hill, for a large development scheme. This inevitably leads to a corruption scandal involving the College, the City council and local gangland villains who are operating out of an Oxford nightclub, the Moonlight Rooms. To add to the plot the main villain, Vic Casper, is known to Thursday from when he served as a junior officer in London. Emotions run high as a personal feud ensues between the two men since Thursday is convinced that Casper is at the centre of events. Meanwhile, Morse has his own problems with which to deal. His father is dying back in Lincolnshire. Despite being away for part of the investigation, it is Morse who, once again, gets to the truth and solves the case, but not before he has taken a bullet in the line of duty. The plot can be best summarised by two quotes from Sherlock Holmes. The first is directed to Thursday – 'There is nothing more deceptive than an obvious fact'. The second sums up Morse's contribution to the case – 'It may seem to point very straight to one thing, but if you shift your own point of view a little, you … find it pointing in an equally uncompromising manner to something entirely different'.

SCENE BY SCENE

The opening titles begin with workmen erecting an advertising board on Booth Hill in the snow, before quickly focussing on Professor Coke Norris teaching at

Baidley College – actually Keble College **(49)**, Morse undergoing firearms training, Judy Vallens at Baidley College, Georgina Bannard as a cigarette girl at the Moonlight Rooms, a lorry being stolen from a truck stop (supposedly on the Botley Road), Professor Coke Norris arranging papers relating to Booth Hill in his study, a glimpse of Colin Dexter as one of the College Fellows at the meeting to discuss the Booth Hill development, someone being beaten up outside the Moonlight Rooms, and Morse about to go off duty but receiving the telephone call about the hit-and-run incident in Link Side. At the scene Morse is immediately suspicious that there is no broken glass, or the like, from the vehicle involved.

In quick succession there is an establishing shot of Oxford showing the Radcliffe Camera **(222)**, Jolyon Frobisher, Master of Baidley College, discovering that his car has been vandalised, and the dead man's wife, Millicent Coke Norris, getting off a train. It is supposed to be Oxford station, but was actually filmed at Horsted Keynes station on the Bluebell Line in West Sussex **(52)**. Morse is seen picking up Fred Thursday at home **(245)** and giving Joan Thursday a lift to work due to a bus strike. On the way, Fred pops into a tobacconist in Holywell Street **(212)**, which in real life is a sweet shop called The Alternative Tuck Shop. At the mortuary further suspicions arise when Dr. DeBryn reveals that the body has no injuries to the lower limbs, something that would normally be expected if hit by a vehicle. A briefcase is discovered in a street neighbouring the location of the body, and the ownership is soon traced to Professor Coke Norris. Further confirmation is implied since Millicent Coke Norris is now at the police station to report that her husband is missing.

Morse interviews both Jolyon Frobisher (learning that dead man maintained a London mews flat), and Dr. Ian Kern, a friend of the late professor. A visit to see Dorothea Frazil of the *Oxford Mail*, sheds light on the Booth Hill development and, allegations of possible intimidation by the developers. Meanwhile, the stolen truck has been found, minus its cargo of cigarettes. This leads Thursday to ask his 'grass', Albert Gudgeon, for information on any possible gangs operating in Oxford. This, in turn, leads Morse and Thursday to the Moonlight Rooms, the exterior of which was shot at the Regent's Park College building in Pusey Street **(220)**, where they meet the new boss, Vic Casper, who Thursday knows from his London days. Vic says that he is retired, and introduces them to his son, Vince Casper, who runs the club.

Just as the case gets going, Morse's sister Joyce calls the police station to say that their father has been taken ill. Morse is given leave of absence to go home to Lincolnshire, but it is actually to a cottage just outside of Hambleden **(231)** in Buckinghamshire. Once he arrives at home, it becomes clear that Morse's relationship with his father has never been a close one, though he seems to have been proud of his son in his own way. While there Morse takes the opportunity to visit his mother's grave, which is actually located at the redundant All Saints Church in the grounds of Shirburn Castle **(250)**. He also manages a visit to the local public house with his sister before she sees him off at the station (Horsted Keynes once again) the following day.

Back in Oxford at the police station, the exterior of which is now Prytaneum Court in Green Lanes, London **(246)** Morse discovers a link between Professor Coke Norris and the Moonlight Rooms, and Strange discovers that the Master of Baidley has checked his car into a garage to have its windscreen repaired. Dorothea Frazil grills Jolyon Frobisher, and later in the episode has her offices at the *Oxford Mail* turned over by two men. Thursday tries unsuccessfully to elicit information on Vic Casper from Morris Cubitt, one of the employees at the Moonlight Club.

Meanwhile, Morse is following a different line of enquiry altogether as he interviews Judy Vallens at her student lodgings. He manages to track her down via a telephone number written on the inside of a matchbook from the Moonlight Rooms which was found in the possession of Professor Coke Norris. It transpires that she shares the accommodation with Georgina Bannard, who worked at the Moonlight Club, but has suddenly vacated the flat. Morse suspects an affair and visits Mrs. Coke Norris – at home in Catte Street **(211)** – to ask about Judy Vallens, Georgina Bannard and Booth Hill. He learns that the land was originally gifted to the College by the Coke Norris family. This is the reason why the professor objected to the development, despite being in line, along with all the other college Fellows, for a considerable amount of money from the project. Next Morse grills the Master of Baidley in a heated exchange.

To summarise events thus far, there is the usual lunchtime meeting at a local public house – the King's Arms on this occasion **(51)**. At the nightclub, Casper's son tells Cynthia Riley, Vic Casper's girlfriend, that he thinks that Vic has gone soft. Very soon afterwards a warning wreath of flowers arrives at Thursday's home. At the Town Hall Morse interviews a planning officer, Mark Carlisle, who has no sympathy with the current tenants on the Booth Hill land.

The trail now takes both Thursday and Morse to the Moonlight Rooms, but for different reasons. Morse is there to enquire about Georgina Bannard, while Thursday arrives to declare war on Vic Casper. Morse notices that Joan Thursday is also there dancing with DS Jakes, but diplomatically keeps this information to himself for fear that his boss would not be pleased at the news.

The next day Morse has another heated exchange with the Master of Baidley, this time over the 'frighteners' being put on Dorothea Frazil. Frobisher subsequently

47

makes a formal complaint about Morse, which comes to the attention of CS Bright.

The body of Georgina Bannard is found out in the country, and in her pocket is a matchbook from the Moonlight Rooms. The location of the body is actually once again in the grounds of Shirburn Castle, just a few metres from where Constance Morse is buried.

This leads Morse and Thursday to Vic Casper, who denies knowing anything about the death, but Cynthia Riley recognises a photograph of the dead girl who she knows as Judy Vallens, not Georgina Bannard. At last the threads of the case are coming together, and upon further questioning, Judy Vallens comes clean and reveals that Georgina Bannard, a known prostitute and also her girlfriend, had 'entertained' Mark Carlisle at the London flat of Professor Coke Norris. Further, Carlisle had boasted about the money that he was about to make from the Booth Hill development if only it wasn't for the interference of Professor Coke Norris, information that Judy Vallens decided to pass along to the late professor.

Mark Carlisle is confronted and urged to cooperate with the police enquiries. Morse is sent to search the London flat and finds a left luggage ticket, and that Professor Cope Norris kept a car in London. Morse also discovers some background information on Thursday and his career in the Capital. Back in Oxford, Joan Thursday walks down Holywell Street **(212)** by New College **(190)** and ends up sitting on a bench on the ramparts of Exeter College **(179)** overlooking Radcliffe Square **(222)**. It is here that she is approached by one of the gangland members while having her lunchtime sandwich.

In Radcliffe Square, on the Catte Street side **(211)**, Morse interviews a taxi driver, whom he has traced from a receipt, about the journey Professor Coke Norris made just prior to his demise. It turns out that he was taken to Oxford railway station (Horsted Keynes once again), which is where Morse now goes to retrieve the case the professor deposited there at the left luggage office. It contains evidence of every bribe made by Baidley College to Oxford City Council, something Bright does not wish to pursue. Over another drink, Thursday warns Morse not to get involved with the gangland element of the case, and also sheds light on an incident in his past of which he is not very proud.

Later, Dr. Kern shares some College gossip with Morse, that the Master had a spare key to Professor Coke Norris' London flat, and was in the habit of secretly letting Fellows have use of it for various illicit purposes. Thursday visits the Moonlight Rooms and offers Vic Casper a truce, but again the gangland boss reiterates that he is retired. On his way out Thursday learns from Vince Casper that Joan Thursday was there with a policeman, whom the former assumes to be

Morse. Threats are made against Joan unless Thursday hands over the Booth Hill documents.

However, before he can confront Morse there is news that Morse's father has taken a turn for the worse. Thursday sees Morse off from the station (rather strangely on a steam train that seems to be reversing out of Horsted Keynes station). During the journey Morse examines some papers which solve the case for him. With his family being threatened, Thursday decides to take matters into his own hands, and retrieves an old (wartime) revolver from his garden shed.

The climax to the episode starts at the Moonlight Rooms as Thursday confronts Vic Casper at gunpoint. Thursday has it wrong though, as becomes apparent when Morse turns up. He has not gone to Lincolnshire but returned to Oxford, and elucidates just who is responsible for bribing Mark Carlisle – an arrest is made.

Morse also knows by now who is responsible for the two murders. In fact, by the time the second arrest of the episode is made, the body count will total three for Dr. Kern is also to become a victim. It is at this point that Morse receives a bullet wound to the leg. Part of the reveal, which in hindsight should be obvious to the viewer as all the clues were there from the start, includes mention that Professor Coke Norris was not the victim of a hit-and-run incident, but murdered out in the country with the body being brought back and dumped in Oxford to make it look like an accident. The location used as that where the Professor Coke Norris is murdered is once again Shirburn Castle. The motive for the murders was both love and money.

The case concluded, Thursday drives Morse to his parents' house where he is in time to spend a few hours with his father, who subsequently dies peacefully in bed overnight. Morse has missed taking his DS's exam, and in the final scene is told by a doctor that the bullet wound received might cause him to limp from time to time in middle life (thus giving an explanation to the limp that John Thaw had in real life when he played *Inspector Morse*).

KEBLE COLLEGE

Founded in 1868, and named after John Keble, one of the leaders of the Oxford Movement, Keble College was built with money raised mainly by public subscription. The College was established to be 'open to the less affluent and inculcating the Christian virtues of poverty and obedience'. Within two years of Keble's death the fund stood at £35,000 which enabled the purchase of the 4.5-acre site from St. John's College **(192)**. On the 25th April 1868 the foundation stone was laid, this being the first new college in Oxford since Wadham in 1612.

The college was to be different in style from all others, and for this reason William Butterfield, a member of the Oxford Movement himself, was made the architect. It was constructed of red, blue and white bricks (with the blue and white forming patterned bandings) in the Victorian Gothic style. The result came in for great criticism, not least from the architectural historian, Nikolaus Pevsner, who said that the college was 'actively ugly'. The Oxford tradition of 'staircases' was replaced with undergraduate rooms along corridors, and a don's quarters at the end. The chapel, which has never been consecrated, was built as a result of a donation made by William Gibbs, whose fortune had been made from guano. Other buildings, such as the hall and library, were also possible only due to generous benefactors, but even so the college was intended to be even larger than it is today as evidenced by various raw ends of buildings which remain visible.

[The chapel from Liddon Quadrangle]

Keble might have become a theology college if not for the first Walden, Edward Talbot, who encouraged the admission of students reading the widest possible range of subjects. It was not until the 1930s though that undergraduates no longer had to first be a member of the Church of England. This did not apply to Fellows and the Warden who still had to be in Holy Orders – those restrictions were finally lifted in 1952 and 1969 respectively.

The most famous work of art in the College is Holman Hunt's *The Light of the World*, which hangs in the side-chapel. Hunt, however, was so angry when the College started charging visitors to see it that he painted another version, which hangs in St. Paul's Cathedral in London.

THE KING'S ARMS

[The King's Arms is always busy, especially on graduation days]

Buildings were first erected at No. 40 Holywell Street **(212)** in 1268 by the Augustinian Friars who owned the site until 1540. On 18th September 1607 the buildings became the King's Arms public house (in honour of King James I) and contained many lodging rooms, a large stable, and a back courtyard. It was soon a popular place for plays, and although parts of the original inn still remain, in the early 18th century the south frontage and rear wing were rebuilt, with a staircase and a stone floor and oak-beamed cellar being added. The west front was added in the late 18th century, and by 1771 this public house had become a coaching inn on the London to Gloucester run. Wadham College converted the upper floors into student's rooms in 1962.

THE BLUEBELL RAILWAY

[Platform 2 at Horsted Keynes station became the departure point for
Morse on his way home to see his sick father]

The Bluebell Railway, the world's first preserved standard-gauge steam-operated
passenger railway dates back to 1877, when an Act of Parliament authorised the
construction of a line from Lewes to East Grinstead, sponsored by local
landowners. The following year another Act allowed the London, Brighton and
South Coast Railway to buy and run the line. The Lewes and East Grinstead
Railway had six stations, but except for Barcombe they were situated close to the
residences of the sponsors. Sheffield Park station, for example, was built for the
use of the Earl of Sheffield. Only Barcombe station was within easy reach of a
village. The line was intended to be double track throughout, but from Horsted
Keynes to Lewes only a single track was laid, with passing loops at the stations.
From 1882, when it was opened, the line was rarely profitable, and in 1955 it was
closed by British Railways.

Local users challenged the decision, pointing out that the 1877 and 1878 Acts
imposed a duty on the line to provide four passenger trains each way every day,
stopping at Sheffield Bridges, Newick, and West Hoathly, with through
connections at East Grinstead to London. British Railways reopened the line in
1956, with trains stopping at the stations specified, but following a public enquiry
the relevant section of the Acts was repealed, and in 1958 the line was finally

52

closed. In 1959 the Bluebell Railway Preservation Society was set up, with the aim of operating a commercial service over the whole line, using an ex-Great Western diesel railcar, but the plan was unsuccessful, as the society was unable to buy the whole line.

A more modest proposal was adopted: that the section between Sheffield Park and Horsted Keynes should be preserved as a tourist attraction, using vintage stock and operated by volunteers. In 1960, the line was opened from Sheffield Park to Bluebell Halt, just short of Horsted Keynes, where the station still served the electrified line to Ardingly. Three years later British Railways closed that line, allowing the Society to take over Horsted Keynes station. Little by little, sections of the original line were purchased and re-opened. The extension from Horsted Keynes to Kingscote was completed in 1994, and the line from Kingscote to East Grinstead opened in 2013. There are currently plans to extend the line southward, eventually connecting it with the main line at Lewes.

For film and television producers, one of the most appealing aspects of the Bluebell Railway is that the various stations have been restored to represent different historical periods. Sheffield Park is quintessentially Victorian, Horsted Keynes embodies the era of the Southern Railway between 1922 and 1948, and at Kingscote we find a British Railways station of the 1950s. This was a dilemma for *Home* since Kingscote would be the correct style of station, but is clearly not large enough to represent that of a city like Oxford, and so Horsted Keynes was chosen, despite being painted in the wrong colour scheme for Western Region.

The many films in which the Bluebell Railway has featured include *The Innocents* (1961), John Betjeman's *Metro-land* (1971), Ken Russell's *Savage Messiah* (1972) and *Lisztomania* (1975), *A Room with a View* (1985), *The Wind in the Willows* (1996), *102 Dalmatians* (2000), *Miss Potter* (2006) and *The Woman in Black* (2012). It is also a favourite location for television dramas, such as *The Adventures of Sherlock Holmes*, *Miss Marple*, the 1999 version of *The Railway Children*, *Foyle's War*, *Tess of the D'Urbervilles* (2008), and most recently *Dancing on the Edge* (2013).

The Bluebell Railway is still run largely by volunteers. Its collection of more than thirty steam locomotives – the largest on any preserved line in the country, and second only to the National Railway Museum – is complemented by almost 150 carriages and wagons, most of them dating from before 1939. Prospective visitors should check the railway web site (www.bluebell-railway.com) for details of special events.

TROVE
SERIES 2 EPISODE 1

PREMIER: 30th March 2014   **AUDIENCE:** 7.0 million

LENGTH: 89 minutes   **DIRECTOR:** Kristoffer Nyholm

GUEST STARS: Jessie Buckley, Nigel Cooke, Beth Goddard, Jamie Parker, David Westhead.

SYNOPSIS

The second series of *Endeavour* starts 4 months after the events of *Home* in which DC Morse received a bullet wound to the leg. He has been on light duties in Witney, but now returns to general duties at Cowley Road police station where attitudes toward him have improved, especially that of CS Bright and DS Jakes. This is one of the few episodes where Morse admits that he has it wrong, and subsequently apologises wholeheartedly to Bright, DI Thursday, and Jakes.

There are three backdrops to the investigation that is to follow. First there are celebrations to commemorate the 900 years since the Battle of Hastings, second there is a by-election taking place, and finally there is a beauty contest – all will become entwined and integral to the plot.

On Morse's first day back, a procession to mark the historic battle is marred by Kitty Batten, daughter of Barbara Batten (who is standing as a candidate in the by-election), who fires a gun, loaded with red paint, at Diana Day, the beauty queen in the parade. Around the corner the body of an unknown man falls from a building onto a car – is it suicide or murder? Also included in the plot is Bernard Yelland, who has come to Oxford in search of his apparently runaway step-daughter, Frida Yelland. Soon there is even more police work to be done, when part of the second Wolvercote Trove is stolen from Beaufort College. The only weak element in the script is the introduction of Freemasonry, which, although well done, is a very easy plot device and target for those who are not initiated into such matters.

SCENE BY SCENE

The episode begins with a shot of the garage belonging to Eric Fisher & Sons at Shotover, which looks more like a location from the *Inspector Morse* episode the *Promised Land*, set in Australia, than one in East Oxford. Next there are establishing shots of Morse doing a crossword (having a flash back to when he was shot in *Home*), at his medical examination, Miss Great Britain, Diana Day, opening Burridges' Spring into Summer fashion collection, museum artefacts from the time of William the Conqueror, Bernard Yelland listening to the radio, Barbara Batten at a by-election meeting, Kitty Batten planning her attack on Diana Day, and private detective, John Pettifer, writing some numbers (98018) on a notepad. These numbers will become the central clue in the investigation that follows – a clue that only Morse will be able to understand.

Before the plot gets underway, Morse picks Thursday up from home **(245)** on his first day back on duty. They drive to the police station via Oriel Street **(62)** and Merton Street **(216)**. Meanwhile the '900 Years of History' parade is taking place in Broad Street **(210)**, and this is where Kitty Batten climbs onto a float and fires red paint from a starting pistol at Diana Day in an act of protest against beauty pageants. At the police station Bright welcomes Morse back to work with some warmth and regard for his welfare. From here on in this series the exterior shots of the police station are that of Prytaneum Court in London **(246)**. Inside, Bernard Yelland is asking for help in tracing his step-daughter. Just around the corner from Broad Street in Brasenose Lane **(209)** a body lands on a parked car just after a traffic warden has placed a parking ticket on the windscreen – this is odd given that this has been a pedestrian zone for many years with no road markings to indicate that cars may traverse the street, let alone park there in unmarked bays. A notebook lying on the ground close to the body later disappears. Morse is called to the scene and meets up with PC Strange who reveals that he has failed his PS's exam by just 3 points. When Morse and Dr. DeBryn go onto the roof to see from where the body has fallen they are actually in Alfred Street **(61)**, nowhere near Brasenose Lane.

Back in Broad Street, the parade has come to an end by the Bridge of Sighs **(182)** where Dorothea Frazil of the *Oxford Mail* is interviewing Diana Day, and her manager, Val Todd.

Morse finds some receipts in the dead man's pocket. This leads him to the garage and motel in Shotover where the deceased was staying. Here Morse finds out that he drove a large white American car, and in his motel room Morse retrieves a notepad (which will be so vital later in the episode). He also spies a postcard of the adjacent, now closed, Caplins Funderland holiday camp. Following this visit it is time to report back to Thursday at lunch, which is usually taken at a public house – The Royal Standard of England in Forty Green **(229)** in this instance. Thursday has been busy himself that morning cautioning Kitty Batten, and also speaking to her parents, Captain Archie Batten and Mrs. Barbara Batten. The Battens have come to the police station to ask for leniency for their daughter. Bright is willing to overlook the incident (maybe because of the Battens' social position and their sponsorship of the police 'widows and orphans' fund). Later by the entrance to Christ Church College **(62)** in Oriel Street, Barbara and Kitty Batten have words.

For his return to Oxford, Morse has now moved lodgings to Park Town **(218)**, and here the viewer is introduced Monica Hicks, a nurse, who will become a regular feature, and love interest, in this series.

The following day starts with the discovery that there has been a robbery of 11th century items at Beaufort College – the scenes were actually filmed at Merton College **(187)**. It is here that Dr. Matthew Copley-Barnes, a character who will reappear in the *Inspector Morse* episode *The Infernal Serpent*, is interviewed about the theft. He reacts arrogantly to the police questioning, but Morse puts him in his place. The missing items constitute the bulk of the finds from the second Wolvercote Trove (which will resurface literally in the *Inspector Morse* episode *The Wolvercote Tongue*). While walking in the grounds and discussing the case, Thursday and Morse pass Colin Dexter sitting on a bench making his usual cameo appearance. Morse also meets Dorothea Frazil at the porter's lodge. Soon afterwards the American car belonging to the unidentified dead man is found, and according to the log book the owner lives in London. Morse will head for the Capital to follow up on this lead, but not before his duties take him to Chipperfield Studios where he meets Tony Frisco, and Val and Muriel Todd, at a publicity shoot for Diana Day.

In London, Morse discovers that the registered address for the car is the premises of Pettifer, Confidential Enquiries, in Soho. In Pettifer's empty office Morse is mistaken for Pettifer himself, and is first coshed, and later beaten up when he does not know the combination to Pettifer's safe. Thursday is soon in London to bring Morse back to Oxford. The safe is opened and various documents found, including a file labelled Muriel Todd. Thursday also sees justice is done to the thugs who beat up Morse, but not to the unknown person who coshed him. It seems that Pettifer was a private investigator who was not above blackmailing the people he was supposed to be investigating.

Next day Morse is at the beauty pageant being held at a lido **(60)** where he and Thursday question Muriel Todd about her involvement with Pettifer. She admits to hiring him to look into her husband's relationship with Diana Day, but says that Pettifer found no trace of any infidelity. The Rudolph Hotel, last seen in *Rocket*, makes a brief appearance as where Diana Day is staying.

Back at the police station Morse finds a clue in the form of a pawnbroker's ticket hidden in the inside band of Pettifer's hat. He visits the pawnbrokers, which is located in Turl Street **(225)** – it is actually Norah's Antiques and is adjacent to the shop used for Cribb & Co. (shoemaker) in *Rocket*, the jewellers in *Neverland* and the florists in *Coda*. Morse retrieves a silver item inside of which are photographic negatives of the entrance to a stream that runs under a portion of the City, including Beaufort College. On film the viewer sees a fake entrance in Addison's

Walk in the grounds of Magdalen College **(184)**. The scenes that follow are not of any subterranean river, but the Hornsey Wood Reservoir at Finsbury Park in London **(59)**. The body of Frida Yelland is soon found there wrapped in a curtain. Morse, Thursday, and Jakes are soon seen walking in front of the New Building of Magdalen College just prior to a lunchtime drink back at The Royal Standard of England, where Thursday warns Morse about his drinking habits. Morse opens a box (which he had obtained from Bernard Yelland earlier in the episode) that once belonged to the deceased girl – it contains a bundle of letters along with some professional photographs which she had sat for at the studio of one Justin Delfarge.

Logically enough the next stop is the studio of Justin Delfarge, then to Val and Muriel Todd again for further questioning. Later, on reading the correspondence in the box, Morse finds a letter of condolence written during World War II to Frida's mother, by her father's then commanding officer, Captain Archie Batten. A further investigation of the stream under Beaufort College yields one of the pieces belonging to the Wolvercote Trove, presumably dropped by the thief.

At another visit to the pub Strange asks Morse's advice about whether he should join the Freemasons – Morse replies that it is hard to serve two masters.

Morse is convinced that Dr. Copley-Barnes is involved in the murders and says as much to his face, while Thursday is the one to make the breakthrough needed when he notices that some photographic pictures on the wall at Beaufort College where done by Justin Delfarge. A raid on his studio recovers the remainder of the Wolvercote Trove. However, Delfarge escapes and there follows a car chase down New College Lane **(217)**, Queen's Lane **(221)**, and then emerging from near the Undercroft of Christ Church College **(62)** into Broad Walk **(200)** and finishing in the River Cherwell (literally). Morse gives his theory about the murders and theft – at this stage he is wrong and expresses anger at his bosses for not agreeing with him. Even so, both Thursday and Bright are very lenient towards Morse. He soon returns to Eric Fisher & Sons, where he finds the room in which Frida Yelland was murdered. Her luggage is found floating in the adjacent pond, and in the case are some beauty pageant photographs.

It is at the beauty contest held at the lido that Morse realises that all the main suspects are Freemasons. Back in Oxford, Barbara Batten wins the by-election with Kitty Batten now showing support for her mother.

Subsequently, Morse sets a trap at the motel, having worked out that the five numbers refer to the identity of a Masonic lodge (this is incorrect, however, since lodge numbers are only four digits long). When all the suspects are gathered at the motel, Morse reveals that the motive for the murders, and the subsequent cover

58

up, revolve around incest and bigamy. Arrests are made, including that of the person who coshed Morse in London.

Here, Morse is warned by the murderer that he will be making a dangerous enemy of the Freemasons, a theme that is returned to in the *Inspector Morse* episode *Masonic Mysteries*. Morse and Thursday have a final drink at The Royal Standard of England, and the episode closes with the missing notebook from the Pettifer crime scene being handed over to a mystery person within the confines of a Masonic lodge.

HORNSEY WOOD RESERVOIR

[Victorian industrial architecture at its best – the magnificent
Hornsey Wood Reservoir]

The East London Waterworks Company was established in 1807 at Old Ford where the River Lea supplied water to a works spread over 30 acres. The company, whose motto was 'Thou, too, shall become one of the honoured founts' (taken from Horace), expanded rapidly, taking over both the Shadwell Waterworks Company and West Ham Waterworks. By 1815 they had entered into an agreement with the New River Company that gave the concern a monopoly in East London. With this expansion, a new water intake was needed higher up the River Lea. The solution presented itself with the purchase of the Hackney Waterworks in 1830, which made it possible to cut a canal from Lea Bridge, across Hackney Marsh, to Old Ford.

In 1861 a new reservoir was constructed at Walthamstow, but disaster was to strike in 1866 when there was a cholera outbreak which necessitated the closure of the Old Ford works. As a consequence, a new supply line was laid between the River Thames at Sunbury Lock, and reservoirs at Finsbury Park (the East and West Reservoirs which today form part of the Woodberry Wetlands), a distance of some 19 miles in total.

An expansive overflow space was also needed. This was provided close by, beneath Finsbury Park itself, and was completed in 1868. More formally known as the Hornsey Wood Reservoir, it could hold up to 5 million gallons of water. When the reservoir was originally excavated, the spoil was used to build up the north-east section of the park. There used to be tennis courts on top of the reservoir. In 1884 disaster struck again in the form of eels, some of them 45 centimetres in length, which invaded the water pipes. The Old Ford site was sold in 1892, and the company absorbed into the Metropolitan Water Board in 1902.

Today, although disused, the reservoir comes under the auspices of Thames Water. It is not open to the public, but has been featured in films such as *Sherlock Holmes* (2009) and *Skyfall* (2012).

TOOTING BEC LIDO

[The Tooting Bec Lido where the beauty pageant was held in *Trove*]

Tooting Bec Common is an open space of over 200 acres located between Balham and Streatham in South London. Until the death of his friend Henry Thrale in 1781, Samuel Johnson was a frequent visitor to Thrale's house which overlooked the Common. The avenue of oak trees which line Dr. Johnson Avenue are thought to have been planted in 1600 to commemorate the visit of Queen Elizabeth I. Facilities on the Common include nature walks, wildlife areas, tennis courts, sports pitches, an athletics track, and most prominent of all, the Tooting Bec Lido.

It was built in 1906 by 400 unemployed workmen, and at 90 metres by 33 metres, with a capacity of 1 million gallons of water, is one of the largest open-air swimming pools in the country. In 1931 an aerator, or fountain, was added to help pump the water around the pool and keep it clean, and in 1936 a café was opened. Apart from the entrance being moved to the shallow end in 2017, and a pavilion being constructed on the site of the former entrance, the lido looks much as it did when first opened. The alternating bright red, green, and yellow doors of the changing cubicles make it easily recognisable when used for filming in such productions as *Snatch* (2000), and the television series *Luther* in which there was a shootout at the pool.

ALFRED STREET

[Alfred Street is one of the few still cobbled roads in Oxford]

It is known that this narrow street, running between the High Street and the junction with Blue Boar Lane and Bear Lane, was in existence in 1220. At that time it was called Venella Sancti Edwardi after St. Edward's Church, which until 1500 stood on the west side of the lane. It later became Vine Hall Street after a hall of that name belonging to Christ Church College **(62)**. Later still in the 17th century it became part of Bear Lane, after the public house of that name which still stands at the end of the street. It is not known why it was ever renamed Alfred Street, though it is speculated that it has a connection with King Alfred who has been credited with the foundation of nearby University College.

ORIEL STREET

[19th century print of Oriel Street]

The earliest known record of this street is from 1220 when it was known as Shidyerdestret, and later Sidyerd Street. By 1728 it had become Sched (or Writers') Street, possibly because books that had been printed in nearby Magpie Lane were sold here at the sign of the St. John the Evangelist's Head. Around 35 years later it was known as St. Mary Hall Lane, and only after that academic hall had been incorporated into Oriel College in 1902, did it become Oriel Street (although there are reports of locals calling it Oriel Street in the mid-19th century).

Oriel derives from La Oriole, the French form of *oratoriolum*, the name of a house given to Oriel College by King Edward III in 1329. Coaches used to drive down this narrow street as a back way to the Angel Inn in High Street. There is a large 'real tennis' court situated behind the stuccoed houses facing the College, and also a tunnel under the road built in 1986 connecting St. Mary Quadrangle and O'Brien Quadrangle.

CHRIST CHURCH COLLEGE

Christ Church was the 13th Oxford college to be built and remains one of the largest, though its founding was a complex process. Originally the site was occupied by the Augustinian Saint Frideswide's Priory which was dissolved in 1524 during the reign of King Henry VIII. At that time the area around the priory was occupied by houses, a hospital, churches, the Oxford Jewry, and Canterbury College (the home of the monks of Christ Church, Canterbury). Under the direction of Cardinal Wolsey demolition began in 1525 but the priory church was largely unaffected save for the westernmost bays being destroyed, since the remainder of the building was to be incorporated into the new Cardinal College. By the time of Wolsey's fall from power in 1529, three sides of the Great Quadrangle were virtually complete, although only the foundations of the planned chapel were in place. The hall and kitchen were completed in 1529 and have remained intact ever since. King Henry VIII took over the buildings and endowments of Wolsey's foundation and renamed it King Henry VIII's College. This name only lasted until 1546 when he designated the former priory church as

Christ Church Cathedral of the new Henrician diocese of Oxford, and as the chapel to the new college of Christ Church.

[Christ Church College, looking towards the Great Hall]

Major additions have been made to the buildings through the centuries. Wolsey's Great Quadrangle was crowned with a gate-tower designed by Sir Christopher Wren, and to this day the bell in the gate-tower, Great Tom, is rung 101 times every night at 9 o'clock Oxford time (which is 5 minutes behind that of Greenwich) in honour of the 100 original scholars of the college plus the one added in 1664. In former times this also signalled the closing of all college gates throughout Oxford.

The Great Hall was the work of two of the greatest craftsmen of their time: the mason Thomas Redman, and the glazier James Nicholson. It is reached via a wide stairway enhanced by the most delicate fan tracery dating from around 1640, although the current stairs only date from 1805. The Great Hall itself is dominated by the large hammerbeam roof, richly carved and gilded. Among the notable portraits upon its panelled walls are those of Lewis Carroll and John Wesley. It is interesting to note that King Charles I held his Parliament here during the English Civil War.

Christ Church has produced many famous people, including 13 British prime ministers (the two most recent being Anthony Eden, 1955-1957 and Sir Alec Douglas-Home, 1963–1964), which is more than all the other Oxford colleges put together, and more than any Cambridge college (and only two short for the whole of the University of Cambridge). Even Albert Einstein had a 5 year research studentship here from 1931.

[The Great Hall is recognisable to any Harry Potter enthusiasts]

The college is the setting for parts of Evelyn Waugh's *Brideshead Revisited*, as well as being an inspiration for Lewis Carroll's *Alice's Adventures in Wonderland*. More recently it has been used in the filming of Philip Pullman's *The Golden Compass*, and perhaps most notably has featured in the Harry Potter series as Hogwarts (although the Great Hall was deemed too small, for filming, with a replica one and a half times the size being built in the studio).

NOCTURNE
SERIES 2 EPISODE 2

PREMIER: 6th April 2014

AUDIENCE: 6.9 million

LENGTH: 91 minutes

DIRECTOR: Giuseppe Capotondi

GUEST STARS: Desmond Barrit, Nell Tiger Free, Daniel Ings, Susy Kane, Simon Kunz, Emily Renée.

SYNOPSIS

It is July 1966 and there are World Cup references throughout this episode as the England football team make it to the finals. DC Morse, however, shows no interest in the games despite having 'England' in the office sweepstake. While it seems that most are watching the matches on television, at the Oxford University Museum of Natural History (71) – no stranger to the odd murder in the *Inspector Morse* and *Lewis* series – a group of girls from Blythe Mount School (70) are present when Adrian Weiss, a specialist in heraldry and genealogy, is killed. Later there is the death of a Blythe Mount schoolgirl, which is most certainly connected to the first murder, but how? It is left up to Morse to delve into the history of Shrive Hill House, where the school is located, and find a connection. He discovers a 100-year-old murder mystery along with a bastard child whose fifth-generation descendant is set on claiming what they regard as rightfully theirs. This episode, which has both a supernatural and an Indian theme running through it, is one of the darkest of the series given that one of the victims is a schoolgirl.

SCENE BY SCENE

The opening titles include shots of the murder scene in 1866, Cowley Road police station with detectives eagerly watching the football on television, the group of schoolgirls on their visit to the Oxford University Museum of Natural History, inside of which the viewer is introduced to Nahum and Tabby Gardiner, Terrence Black, and Colin Dexter making his cameo appearance. By the time the producer's name appears the murder of Adrian Weiss has already occurred.

DI Thursday is at home (245) trying to watch the football on television when Morse arrives with news of the murder at the Museum. He and Morse travel to the Museum by car via Merton Street (216). What appears to be the first clue, a katar (a type of Indian dagger) is soon found, but it will transpire that this is not the murder weapon. The dead man's pocket watch is found to be missing suggesting that the motive for the crime may have been robbery.

Very soon Morse is at the private school interviewing the seven schoolgirls who were on the Museum visit (having not gone home for one reason or another for the summer holidays), along with their teacher, Miss Victoria Danby, and head mistress, Miss Bronwen Symes. While he is there some one places a note in Morse's jacket pocket with the words 'SAVE ME' written in capital letters.

Two suspects come to light in the form of father and son Wilf and Billy Karswell, who look after and live in the school grounds. That night there are pranks, or maybe something supernatural, going on at the school.

Two further suspects, who were also at the Museum at the time of the murder, are Americans Mr. and Mrs. Gardiner. Morse interviews them the next morning, but they do not seem to be involved as they are apparently just on holiday in Oxford. In Brasenose Lane **(209)** Morse also talks with Daisy Weiss, Adrian's niece, about the missing fob watch. It is interesting to note that unlike in the previous episode, *Trove*, there are no parking metres or any signs of cars, with or without bodies on their roofs, in the street. It is here that Morse learns that Adrian Weiss does private commissions for those wanting a coat of arms designed, or genealogical research done. This is a little inaccurate for it is only one of the three Kings of Arms that can officially assign a coat of arms (or armorial bearings/achievements as they should be called).

In an aside to the main story, PC Strange asks Morse to make up a foursome with him, and two girls, that Saturday night for a visit to the pub and cinema.

A return to the Museum reveals that the katar had been bequeathed to the Museum by the Blaise-Hamilton family in 1879. They had made their money through a tea plantation in India. Back at the police station **(246)** Thursday recognises the name from an historic crime, and points Morse in the direction of the *Illustrated Police News*. This gives Morse the excuse to seek the help of Dorothea Frazil of the *Oxford Mail*, who he meets at The Royal Standard of England **(229)**. The newspapers from July 1866 cover the story of the five murders (3 children, the governess and nursemaid) that took place at Shrive Hill House, now Blythe Mount School. The bodies were discovered by Samuel Blaise-Hamilton, and the only child to survive was Charlotte, whom it was later assumed was the perpetrator of the multiple bludgeonings with a croquet mallet. Samuel had her committed to an asylum and she died there childless. It is for this reason, perhaps, that all surviving photographs and pictures of Charlotte have been defaced with her face being removed. Meanwhile at the school there are more scary goings on during the night.

Next day Thursday and Morse visit the College of Arms and ask Robin Ballstrode, one of the Pursuivant of Arms, about Adrian Weiss. He is able to tell them that

Weiss had recently undertaken a commission on behalf of an American couple who hoped to find possible descendants of their son. He had died during World War II while serving in England, after having married an unknown local girl who they think may have been pregnant at the time of his death. By the end of the episode Morse will trace their granddaughter, so there will be one happy ending at least. The reuniting of grandparents and granddaughter takes place on the raised section of Exeter College **(179)** overlooking Radcliffe Square **(222)** at exactly the same spot where Joan Thursday ate her lunch in *Home*.

Just as there is an *Ipcress File* connection in *First Bus to Woodstock*, here there appears to be a James Bond one, for when Thursday and Morse arrive at the College of Arms they are met by Robin Ballstrode who apologises for the fact that Sir Hilary (one of the Heralds) is not available to see them as he is on holiday. This must be a direct reference to Sir Hilary Bray, whose identity Bond adopts in *On Her Majesty's Secret Service* to infiltrate Ernst Stavro Blofeld's Piz Gloria stronghold. The homage does not quite work for the book was published in 1963, and the film dates from 1969. There is an establishing shot of the roof of the College of Arms, with St. Paul's Cathedral added in the background, though no actual filming took place here. A computer generated composite image had to be used since today, unlike in 1966, there are many skyscrapers that would be seen in any shot of the area.

On their return from London, Thursday and Morse report to CS Bright who has just received a communication that one of the schoolgirls, Bunty Glossop, has gone missing during the night. Strictly speaking, because it is outside of Oxford the investigation should fall under DI Bart Church at 'county' (where Morse had been assigned light duties after the events of *Home*), so there must be collaboration between the two police forces. Jointly the police officers conduct interviews at the school. A musical clue, in the form of a Chopin Nocturne (op. 9 no. 1 in B flat minor) that was being played just before Bunty went missing comes to light. Of the schoolgirls, only the unpopular Shelly Thengardi – of Indian extraction – would be capable of playing it on the piano. On searching the girls' dormitory, Morse finds a book about the Blaise-Hamilton murders with certain keywords and passages underlined. All the girls are asked to write down 'SAVE ME' multiple times, but analysis of their handwriting does not reveal who wrote the note to Morse.

A search is made of the disused part of the school. Miss Danby is afraid to enter the area believing it to be haunted by the ghost of Charlotte Blaise-Hamilton, Morse, however, is not deterred, and just before he falls through some rotten flooring (poor Morse seems to be required to have one injury per episode) he sees a girl (too small to be Bunty Glossop) dressed in Victorian clothes and holding a croquet mallet. Morse is convinced that this is not some apparition, supernatural event, or trick of the light.

Morse's attention now turns to the book about the murders where he learns that when the bodies were found a music box was playing the same Chopin nocturne heard the previous night. He concludes that somebody is trying to recreate the scene from 100 years ago.

Back at his flat, Morse's injuries are tended to by nurse Monica Hicks, a character who was introduced as a possible love interest for him in *Trove*. He invites her out for a drink on Saturday night, forgetting that he has already promised to make up a foursome with Strange that evening. The inevitable happens later in the episode as Morse cancels his date with Monica. She then sees Morse down the pub in the company of another woman – the female part of the group meant to be Morse's date, Joan Thursday, who gives Morse some good advice about the fair sex in general. The advice will not be followed by Morse, who for the rest of the episode will remain without female companionship.

Morse next makes contact with Stephen Fitzowen, the author of the book about the Shrive Hill House murders, who it transpires was contacted by Adrian Weiss shortly before his death. DS Jakes has made progress on the case, and has a tip off as to who has the stolen fob watch from the dead man. He later arrests housebreaker Ossie Lloyd, although this lead will turn out to be a false start for whereas Lloyd took/found the watch, he has nothing to do with the murder. Meanwhile Morse interviews the Gardiners who still seem to have no motive. Later Thursday and Morse go to see Fitzowen who gives them a magic lantern show and a lecture about the Victorian murders. Within his talk the real motive for the crimes, both past and present, is revealed albeit well hidden.

A search is made of the Weiss home, where Morse uncovers details of the special commission he was working on at the time of his death. There is a file relating to the Blaise-Hamilton family, along with a design for a coat of arms, within which are certain heraldic clues that will prove vital in solving the case. Next stop is the Museum again, where Morse requests any documents held about the Blaise-Hamilton family from Terrence Black. Among them is an accounts ledger that also contains a vital clue for Morse to interpret.

That night Miss Danby is frightened by more strange events going on at the school. She follows pupil Edwina Parish into the music room where another girl in Victorian dress is playing the piano, but before Danby can enter the door slams shut in her face and remains locked preventing entry. The next morning Edwina Parish is missing. By the time Morse arrives, the school is under lock down by county. The most unnatural thing about this episode is that despite two girls going missing nobody seems to have made any effort to contact the parents. Suspicion falls on both the headmistress and Billy Karswell. Wilf Karswell lets slip that there has always been a Karswell at Blythe Mount, but Morse corrects him since he has been told that 100 years before it was the Pigstock family who managed, and lived in, the grounds.

Fitzowen turns up with sound and photographic equipment to patrol the school that night. He is there in search of the supernatural. Morse, Church, and Thursday are on hand when the lights go off and unusual things start to happen. In the chaos that ensues, the body of pupil Maud Ashenden is found. She was supposed to be away from school for the summer holidays, but had secretly remained hidden there teaming up with Bunty Glossop and Edwina Parish to 'haunt' the other pupils and staff as a prank. It is revealed that Maud was the one who wrote the note placed in Morse's pocket. This murder affects Dr. DeBryn most, and he instructs Morse to "find this piece of work" for him personally.

The photographs and sound recording taken by Fitzowen reveal nothing, but an interview with Edwina is more fruitful. She recognised the killer as the person she had seen at the Museum during the school visit. In fact, it was the same person she saw kissing Miss Danby at there.

This new suspect is interviewed, but no motive can be established. But, it is now that Morse manages to piece together all the parts of this particular jigsaw puzzle. From examining the coat of arms that Weiss was preparing he realises the significance of one of the heraldic devices, the bar sinister, denoting a bastard. This is actually wrong for since 1912 the bar sinister has been replaced by a tessellated border so would not have been appropriate for Weiss to use. The murderer is the illegitimate descendent of Samuel Blaise-Hamilton, who had arranged for the Pigstock family to raise his bastard child. It was boy, Robert, who had been responsible for the murders of 1866. This is partly proven by the fact that the murderer is wearing an heirloom, a distinctive ring passed down the male bloodline from father to son. With the prospect of a change in the law on inheritance as it relates to illegitimate children, the killer thinks that he has a chance of claiming Shrive Hill House which he regards as rightfully belonging to him.

There is a twist in the story though. During his genealogical investigations Weiss had discovered a second descendent of Samuel Blaise-Hamilton, Miss Bronwen Symes, and that is why Weiss had to die. It is now clear that it was actually Symes who the murderer was trying to kill the night of Maud's death, and that that the murderer will need to try again.

Thursday, Morse, Strange, Bright, Church, and Jakes all converge on the school, and between them corner the killer, who conveniently falls through the same hole in the ceiling that Morse did earlier in the episode. But whereas Morse's fall only resulted in cuts and bruises, this time it is fatal.

Just as the case is solved, and the episode closes, there is one unnecessary scene. It is discovered that the family ring opens up to reveal a Masonic device, thus following on the theme from *Trove*, and hinting at a Masonic involvement, and possible cover up.

REDDAM HOUSE

[Entrance to 'the second palace of Berkshire' (after Windsor castle)]

There is documentary evidence that the village of Winnersh has been in existence since the late 12th century, its name coming from two Old English words, 'winn' meaning a meadow or pasture, and 'ersc' denoting a stubble field or park. The area remained largely undeveloped until the coming of the railway in 1849, although the station, which takes the village name, was not opened until 1910.

Today Winnersh is more of a small town with a population of over 7,000 and 2 railway stations, the second, Winnersh Triangle, serving an industrial estate.

It was in 1830 that John Walter, the then owner of *The Times*, bought 5,000 acres of land near the village and set about building a mansion, which when completed in 1874, was one of the largest country houses in England. The bricks for building came from clay on the estate at what is now California Country Park. A dam was also constructed around the site, which was then flooded to form Longmoor Lake. In 1921 the Royal Merchant Navy School, actually an orphanage for those children who had lost parents at sea, moved into the mansion. By 1961 the number of orphans had reduced in line with the smaller British merchant fleet, and as a consequence the school started to accept fee-paying scholars. The name was changed to Bearwood College around this time. In 2009 there were 374 pupils, of whom 85 were boarders.

In 2010, the school was in a dispute over unpaid rent with the landowners (The Royal Merchant Navy School Foundation), and furthermore was having to fight to stay out of special measures. It was taken over in 2014 by a South African educational trust and renamed Redddam House, and within a very short time was rated outstanding by the Independent Schools Inspectorate.

The college has appeared in several films and television productions such as *Lord Mountbatten: The Last Viceroy* (1986), *Restless* (2012), an episode of *The Sweeney* and 2 episodes of *Midsomer Murders*.

OXFORD UNIVERSITY MUSEUM OF NATURAL HISTORY

The University Museum of Natural History came about as a consequence of a meeting held in 1849, which resolved that a building should be erected to bring together all 'the materials explanatory of the organic beings placed upon the globe'. It was not until 20th June 1855 that the foundation stone was laid, and five years later that the building was complete. Almost immediately it was a place of controversy since the British Oxford Association decided to meet there, and it is recorded that on that occasion the fundamentalist Bishop of Oxford, Samuel Wilberforce, argued with Professor Thomas Huxley about Darwin's theory of evolution.

The architect was Benjamin Woodward of the Dublin firm of Sir Thomas Deane, Son and Woodward. He produced a fine Gothic structure much influenced by John Ruskin's *Stones of Venice*, as clearly evident in the Museum's design. It is approached through an elaborately decorated portal, carved in marble, which opens into a large square court divided into three main aisles by iron pillars supporting a glass roof. The stone columns of the arcades are also exhibits – each being hewn from a different British rock. The wrought-ironwork embellishing the spandrels between the arches of the main aisles 'is formed into branches', in the words of the Museum guide, 'with leaves, flowers and fruits of lime, chestnut, sycamore, walnut, palm and other trees and shrubs, and the leaves of many different plants are incorporated in the capitals. The carved stone capitals of the columns and piers of the arcades represent a series of plants, often with birds and animals too, and are remarkable in that the stonemasons, including the colourful, mercurial O'Shea brothers, conceived as well as executed the designs themselves, on the basis of actual specimens provided by the Botanic Garden'. The O'Sheas, eventually, fell out with the dons, exasperated by their interference, but not before they had carved likenesses of members of the Convocation between parrots and owls. Although these were ordered to be obliterated, they are still visible in part.

**[The University Museum of Natural History
within which is the Pitt Rivers Museum]**

[The museum interior equals that of any cathedral]

Francis Skidmore was paid to start the wall-frescoes and complete the carvings, but money ran out so the building was never finished as planned. Soon after opening, the departments of astronomy, geometry, experimental physics, mineralogy, chemistry, geology, zoology, anatomy, physiology, and medicine all moved here. The building soon proved too small for all this, so it became principally a home for the scientific collections. There are four curators who are also involved in teaching and research activities. Today the Museum holds the collections of the explorer, William Burchell, the geologist, William Buckland, as well as a collection of osteological and physiological material from Christ Church College **(62)** and a huge collection of insects (over 3,000,000 specimens) and crustaceans presented to it by the Reverend F. W. Hope.

SWAY

SERIES 2 EPISODE 3

PREMIER: 13th April 2014   **AUDIENCE:** 6.6 million

LENGTH: 89 minutes   **DIRECTOR:** Andy Wilson

GUEST STARS: Rob Jarvis, Tim McMullan, Cécile Paoli, Adrian Schiller, Matthew Wilson, Max Wrottesley.

SYNOPSIS

In the autumn of 1966 Oxford is in the grip of a serial killer, or so it seems. Vivienne Haldane, the wife of an academic, is found strangled in her home. She is the killer's third victim. None of the murdered women are known to each other; the evidence points to a killer who preys on married women, removes their wedding and engagement rings, and has intercourse with them prior to strangling them with a particular brand of stockings, *Le Minou Noir*, which is only on sale at the Oxford department store Burridges. The prime suspect is Joey Lisk, who is not only the wholesaler of the stockings, but also knows at least one of the victims. However, as with all his investigations, the case is not that simple and will require all of DC Morse's detective powers to find the killer.

This episode provides the viewer with much more than a murder mystery for it also delves deep into the past of DI Fred Thursday. It visits themes of love – lost, found and lost again – as well as sexual prejudices that were prevalent at the time.

SCENE BY SCENE

As ever, the opening shots introduce all the varied elements of this story: a blind piano tuner, Talfryn Pugh, establishing shots of Oxford – the Radcliffe Camera **(222)** and New College **(190)** in this case, Morse typing up a document entitled 'Towards 'Thames Valley' – an appraisal of the proposed amalgamation' authored by CS Bright, while his colleagues are working on the first two strangulations, Vivienne Haldane getting ready for a date (but not with her husband Rufus who is seen giving a tutorial), and Burridges department store (actually two quite separate locations – **(80)** and **(81)**). As the staff leave the store it is a misty night as demonstrated by the headlights of the ubiquitous double-decker bus **(176)** that has appeared in almost every episode to date. It passes along Catte Street **(211)**, and onboard are Vivienne Haldane along with most of the Burridges' staff travelling home from work. Meanwhile, Morse, bored of his general duties, takes the file on the strangulations home with him to study. Finally, we see Vivienne being killed in a car. Her body is found by a postman next morning on the floor of her home (the front door was conveniently left open with part of the body visible from the doorway).

This episode is different from all others to date, since the viewer joins the investigation part way through the case, i.e. there have already been two murders, with the third having taken place by the end of the title sequence. Also, although there is the usual dose of classical music, *Lacrimosa* from Mozart's Requiem, it is interspersed with a haunting jazz piece (rather reminiscent of the theme from the *Ipcress File* and certainly John Barry-esque) for much of the episode.

Thursday and Morse are soon at the scene of crime and join Dr. DeBryn who confirms that Mrs. Haldane was strangled with a silk stocking (not hers), and that she had had intercourse a couple of hours prior to her death. It is at this point that Morse makes the connection that all three women were married, but that none have been found wearing their wedding or engagement rings. In his opinion it must be same killer each time.

Later, after Bright has agreed to release Morse from general duties, there is an establishing shot of All Soul's College **(82)**, strange since seconds later Thursday and Morse are seen walking around the cloisters of New College and interviewing Rufus Haldane. He reveals that he and his wife lived apart. Consequently, he knows little about the company she kept, though he did know that she was prone to periodic affairs.

Next the viewer is introduced to Joey Lisk buying a suit at Burridges. He looks not unlike Michael Caine in the 1966 film *Alfie*, and certainly has the same attitude towards women, regarding them as no more than sexual objects. Back at Cowley Road police station **(246)** there is a briefing following which Morse visits Burridges to enquire about the stockings used to strangle the victims. Mrs. Luisa Armstrong in the hosiery department is able to identify the brand, *Le Minou Noir*, and it transpires that they are a new line with few sales to date. It is now that Norman Parkis, an impaired stockman, reports that there is a discrepancy in numbers with regard to that particular item.

The lunchtime drink between Thursday and Morse is taken at The Royal Standard of England **(229)** where Thursday reveals that he is about to celebrate his 25th wedding anniversary (meaning that he was married during World War II), and encourages Morse not to let time slip by and remain single all his life. Meanwhile, Win and Joan Thursday are shopping at Burridges and talking about the forthcoming anniversary and how to commemorate it.

Back in Catte Street at the bus stop, Win and Joan help the blind piano tuner onto a double decker (the same one as in the opening titles). One of the passengers already onboard is Colin Dexter making his usual cameo appearance. Morse makes another visit to Burridges, and this time meets Monica Hicks, his neighbour and possible love interest who was introduced in *Trove*. She is looking for a new mattress. Morse apologies for standing her up in *Nocturne*, and to make amends invites her out for a drink. They are mistaken for a couple and invited to try out a mattress by a store assistant.

In the women's department the very attractive assistant, Gloria Deeks, receives a rose from an admirer in the internal pneumatic tube mail system. Morse is actually at the store to see the manager, Brian Quinbury, and Luisa Armstrong about the stocking sales – only 19 pairs have been sold, but 5 of these were to non-account holders and so cannot be traced. Mrs. Haldane was one of the account holders and among other items she purchased are a pair of cufflinks which she had had engraved. Alan Burridge, the new proprietor of the store, drops in and assumes that Morse is there to investigate a case of pilfering from the store. To complete the scene, Thursday arrives and on his entering the room Luisa Armstrong faints. The viewer will soon find will that they knew each other during World War II. The extent of their relationship isn't clarified, albeit there will be hints of infidelity on Thursday's part, but it is certainly apparent that they cared about each other greatly.

Next there is a clue, in the form of a chalk-like substance, possibly plaster, found on the clothing of one of the victims as noted by Dr. DeBryn. Action moves to the pub, by coincidence The Royal Standard of England once again, where Joey Lisk tries chatting up Gloria Deeks at the bar. Window dresser and friend, Charles Highbank, who is openly gay, and also happens to be drinking at the pub, tries to protect Gloria from Lisk's advances, but is told by the latter that his sort should have been "strangled at birth". An argument ensues which prompts Norman Parkis, also in the bar, to tell the bully to "pick on someone your own size". In return he is called a "freak show" by the unpleasant Lisk, who exemplifies the attitudes held by some at that time. Shortly afterwards Gloria is seen getting into an unknown passing car in Brasenose Lane **(209)**.

Morse has dinner with Monica Hicks before escorting her back to Park Town **(218)** where they both reside in flats on the same floor, and, although he will have to wait until his next date on fireworks night, he does eventually end up in bed with her.

Thursday finds some wartime photographs of Luisa and goes to visit her flat in King Edward Street **(213)**. Here he explains that during World War II he had last seen her lined up against a wall in Italy, and had thought that she had been killed by a German firing squad who were there to punish the villagers for hiding British soldiers. He had seen her fall to the ground, but as Luisa goes on to explain she was only wounded and was found the next day when the British troops arrived in the village. In fact, the incident only happened because she, and her fellow comrades, had been betrayed by a German informer.

The next morning on a hunch, Morse visits the first crime scene and finds a single cufflink engraved with the initial 'A', which it seems was missed when the area was searched originally. At Burridges, Miss Deeks does not turn up for work, but, just when the viewer has concluded that she is the 4th victim, she arrives having been delayed due to a domestic incident involving her cat and goldfish. Morse visits Lisk at his warehouse, and confirms that Burridges is the sole retailer with stock of *Le Minou Noir*. On further questioning, Lisk has unsatisfactory alibis for the nights of the various murders.

Morse and DS Jakes are tasked with visiting the Burridges' account customers who purchased *Le Minou Noir*. When they get to the home of a Mrs. Shears, they find the front door open and her strangled body in the bath. On the wall there is the symbol for infinity written in chalk – is this a message from the killer to indicate that the killings will continue indefinitely?

As an aside Morse is called in by the Burridges' store detective, Mr. Jellicoe, himself a retired police officer, who has caught a shop lifter. The person under arrest is none other than Win Thursday, but when she discloses that Jellicoe had offered her a fine instead of being arrested it is clear to Morse that Burridges has a corrupt employee. Jellicoe, who had been planting merchandise on unsuspecting women in order to blackmail them, is subsequently dismissed. Following this incident Morse takes Win to The Royal Standard of England for a drink. That evening Fred Thursday and Luisa Armstrong are also in the same pub having a heart-to-heart conversation over drinks. Subsequently she goes to see Charles Highbank for another heart-to-heart, and is warned by him not to be careless and lose the rekindled love that she has found for Thursday.

Morse recognises a connection, in that each of the victims has a piano that might have been tuned recently. He goes to interview Rufus Haldane at New College (St. Saviour's in the screenplay) and once again he is of no help, exhibiting little knowledge about such domestic matters.

During the night, just as Talfryn Pugh is passing Burridges, he hears a noise, but being blind does not see the unfortunate Norman Parkiss falling to the floor in one of the display windows. He has been stabbed to death during an apparent attempt to rob the store – the recently sacked Jellicoe is an immediate suspect. Morse thinks otherwise, especially when Dr. DeBryn identifies the scene of crime as being the hosiery counter (right next to a basket containing the stock of *Le Minou Noir*).

During various Burridges' staff interviews Morse discovers that (a) Gloria Deeks' husband is currently serving a 3 year prison sentence and (b) that one pair of *Le Minou Noir* stockings unaccounted for was taken by Mr. Lee, a manager, who finds it is more comfortable for his leg at the point where it fits into his prosthesis. Morse also tracks down the blind piano tuner, who confirms that he had visited two of the victims, and smelt the same after shave and French cigarettes at each home. In another turn of events, the single cuff link that Morse found, is identified as being part of an 'alpha and omega' set purchased by Mrs. Haldane for her mystery lover – the alpha had been retrieved from the first scene of crime, but who would be the 'omega' victim?

It is now fireworks night, and while Morse is busy missing the bus in Catte Street with Monica Hicks, whom at last he kisses, Thursday is several streets away with Luisa returning the photographs he had found earlier in the episode – they talk, after which she asks Fred to hold her and then never see her again.

There is revelry all around Oxford that evening, and from a parked car in Brasenose Lane, Gloria Deeks emerges followed by Joey Lisk who is on the verge of raping her. Luckily PC Strange is on hand and makes an arrest.

Lisk is interviewed, and he seems to be the strangler for (a) he knew the first three victims and admits to seeing each of them on the nights they died, (b) he smokes French cigarettes and wears the after shave identified by Pugh, (c) as the wholesaler he has access to *Le Minou Noir* and (d) the missing 'omega' cuff link is found at his house. While completing the paperwork Morse discovers Luisa's name in Lisk's address book and goes to see her.

Meanwhile, Monica Hick's has her new mattress delivered and Morse is eager to help her try it out that evening! It is only now that he works out the significance of an earlier clue, when he notices a number '4' in chalk on his coat and on the wall outside Monica's flat. The number has come from the mattress packaging, and is used to identify the order for deliveries for Burridges. Hence the 'infinity' symbol at Mrs. Shears' home was, in fact, a number '8' on its side, left there from where her recent delivery from Burridges had rested against the wall. Some detective works reveals that each victim had recently had such a delivery from Burridges.

Thursday celebrates his wedding anniversary with a party, and makes a heartfelt toast to his wife. He is soon to be interrupted by Morse who informs him that they have arrested the wrong man. The person they are looking for is a Burridges' employee. A search of the home of their new suspect reveals the wedding and engagement rings for all the murdered women. Furthermore, Morse thinks that his next move will be against Gloria Deeks, given that Lisk has been arrested while he was with her. He is right, and Thursday and Morse arrive at her house just in time.

Was the culprit a mad man? No, it was a simple case of revenge in that Lisk had had an affair with the killer's wife, and as a consequence he had strangled 4 innocent women in order to frame Lisk for murder. In addition, he was responsible for the death of his own wife, and the murder of Norman Parkiss – who had to die when he caught the killer stealing more *Le Minou Noir* from the stock. He used the stockings, and planted the 'alpha' cuff link, in order to point suspicion at Joey Lisk.

There is a final sad twist in the story when Strange, rather diplomatically, informs Morse that Luisa Armstrong has committed suicide in her flat. She has left a note for Thursday, which explains that it was she that had been the German informer all those years ago – a fact she could no longer live with, having met Thursday again. There is an establishing shot of the Bridge of Sighs **(182)** before the action moves to the Coroners' Court, actually the Old Warden's Lodgings of Merton College **(83)**. After the inquest Morse gives Thursday her note and shares a drink with him at the pub (The Royal Standard of England once again). Later Morse reads the note while sitting on a bench in the cloisters of New College as the closing titles role ending this bittersweet episode.

JACKSONS CORNER

[Jacksons Corner circa 1920]

In September 1875 Edward Jackson founded the department store that bears his name. At its height there were 7 branches, though the flagship store was always located on King's Road, Reading, and this location became known as Jacksons Corner. Originally the shop was a gentlemen's outfitters, but later it expanded into a department store selling clothes for women, lingerie, shoes, knitting supplies, craft supplies, textiles, and school uniforms.

By 1994, however, the company had contracted to just Jacksons Corner, and on Christmas Eve 2013 that store also closed ending an era for Jacksons of Reading. Stepping into the store was like stepping back in time with the establishment being the very last in the country to still employ a Lamson pneumatic tube system to transport cash and documents around the building. A customer's cash and ticket of sale would be sent by the assistant to the cash office, where the purchase would be recorded, a receipt was then issued and returned to the assistant, along with any change, in another capsule. It may have been antiquated, but the system did have the advantage of avoiding any thefts from tills on the shop floor.

In *Sway* the system is used for an altogether more romantic purpose i.e. the sending of a rose to one of the shop assistants! Although exterior shots for Burridges department store were all shot at Randalls store in Uxbridge (see below) good use was made of the school uniform department at Jacksons Corner, which was transformed into the ladies' department, for all the interior filming in the episode.

RANDALLS DEPARTMENT STORE

[The last days of Randalls in Vine Street]

For 123 years Vine Street, Uxbridge, was home to Randalls, a family-run department store established in 1891. The shop had a Grade II listed Art Deco exterior, but in January 2015 the current owner, Sir John Randall, was forced to close citing online shopping, lower footfall, and pressure on margins from bigger rivals as the chief reasons. The site has since been redeveloped by Inland Homes. However, a small consolation is its television appearance in *Sway* where the outside can be seen in the establishing shots for Burridges department store from where the Le Minou Noir brand of stockings, used to murder three women, had apparently been purchased. Interior shots were filmed at Jacksons Corner store in Reading (see previous entry). Randalls can also be seen in an episode of the television comedy series *Only Fools and Horses*.

ALL SOULS COLLEGE

[The Twin Towers as seen from Radcliffe Square]

The College of the Souls of all the Faithful Departed, as it is formally known, is unique to Oxford University as being the only college comprised entirely of

Fellows, i.e. there are no undergraduates (although in the past there were a limited number whose purpose was to provide the Fellows with household servants). It operates a system whereby any recent graduate, or postgraduate student, may apply to become a Fellow by taking what has been described as 'the hardest examination in the world' followed by an interview. All Souls College has a financial endowment of over £420 million making it one of the wealthiest colleges in Oxford, though because it is so exclusive its income is modest.

The College was founded in 1438 to commemorate the victims of the Hundred Years' War, and was originally only open to those in Holy Orders. Among buildings of note are the Codrington Library, endowed in 1710 by a wealthy slave and plantation owner from Barbados, which contains around 185,000 items with an emphasis on law and military history books. The chapel has remained largely unchanged since its construction in 1442, save for a renovation in the mid-19th century. Christopher Wren, who was a Fellow of the College, produced a sundial for the College which was originally on the south wall of the chapel, but was later moved to adorn the central entrance to the library. The most prominent feature of the College when viewed from Radcliffe Square **(222)** are the twin towers along the east range of the Great Quadrangle. These were constructed between 1716 and 1720 to the design of Nicholas Hawksmoor, who instructed that they should be 'Gothic exteriors with classical interiors' to match the chapel and rest of the buildings.

OLD WALDEN'S LODGINGS

[The Old Warden's Lodgings]

To the north of Merton Street **(216)**, and belonging to Merton College **(187)**, are the Warden's lodgings. These were built in 1908 to the design of Basil Champneys, but changing styles of living have made such a large and grandiose building outdated, and so the College constructed a more modest accommodation for the Warden at the south-east corner of the street. The building was vacated in 1947 and today houses the college library. It is a Grade II listed building.

NEVERLAND

SERIES 2 EPISODE 4

PREMIER: 20th April 2014   **AUDIENCE:** 6.6 million

LENGTH: 91 minutes   **DIRECTOR:** Geoffrey Sax

GUEST STARS: Oliver Lansley, Vince Leigh, Paul Ridley, Louis Ashbourne Serkis, James Wilby.

SYNOPSIS

The end of the 2nd series is very much an end with a beginning, for in it one of the main characters will be shot, maybe fatally, while another finishes up in prison, leaving the viewer to ponder whether this is the end for DI Thursday and DC Morse, or just the setting of the scene for what will follow in the next series? It is an episode that deals with the unpleasant joint truths of police corruption, and child abuse, a theme that has been covered many times in various dramas, and, although, it is not perhaps as gripping as a series like *Line of Duty*, it is gripping enough for most.

As usual there are several strands to the story, beginning with Tommy Cork, a boy with a brutal father, who is reported missing from his home. Next there is the discovery of the body of a journalist, Eric Patterson, on a railway line, and not much later, the body of an escaped convict, George Aldridge, who only had a month of his sentence left to serve. There is, of course, a connection between them, and in this case it is the disused correctional facility for boys, Blenheim Vale, which has been designated as the site for the new Thames Valley Police headquarters. Add to this the possibility of shady property dealings, corrupt police and civic officials and the ensemble is complete. Given the Freemasonry references throughout this series, and the theme of police corruption in this episode, it is surprising that more is not made of the allusions to Masonic involvement here. If there is a flaw with this episode it is that (a) the ultimate villain in this story is not hard to guess and (b) that there are just too many coincidences linked to Blenheim Vale around which the plot revolves. It is undoubtedly an episode with very dark themes, and one to which the police authorities originally objected, causing the original ending to be reshot at short notice.

SCENE BY SCENE

The opening scenes consist of George Aldridge in prison **(89)** holding his rosary beads (which will be a vital clue later in the story), an establishing shot of Oxford – Brasenose College **(177)**, Colin Dexter sitting on a bench talking with an unknown woman, the exterior of Cowley Road police station **(246)**, Dr. Henry Portmore giving a lecture on the Knights of the Round Table, Fred Thursday taking a medical examination from which he will learn that he has high blood pressure – something that CS Bright thinks might curtail his police career, Tommy Cork playing near his home, a choir (including Morse) singing in Brasenose College chapel, and Eric Patterson climbing the stairs of the town hall **(91)** to attend a charity gala in aid of the police widows and orphans. It is at the gala that property developer, Josiah Landesman, Alderman Gerald Wintergreen, and CC Rupert Standish are introduced to the viewer.

Next up is a variety show at which there is a ventriloquism act – Benny (Topling) and Clyde. The theatre used was the Kenton Theatre in Henley-on-Thames **(92)**. There are brief shots of Aldridge absconding from prison, Morse at his Park Town flat **(218)**, and of the Thursday residence **(245)**. It is at the latter that it is noted that Morse is wearing a new scarf from Burridges (something that will later prove detrimental for him). Morse is soon on the trail of Tommy Cork, who he finds looking after some dogs in a caravan beside the canal. He is taken to Cowley Road police station where everybody, including Bright, is nice to him, but as the boy says he has been brought up to believe that all policemen are bastards.

The next morning the body of Eric Patterson, who was apparently drunk at the time he died, is found beside the permanent way on the up line (towards London) between Oxford and Bristol. In real life this scene was shot at the Buckingham Railway Centre **(237)**, a location that last made an appearance in *Fugue*, making this the 2nd dead body to be found here. Over a drink down the pub, The Royal Standard of England **(229)**, Morse learns from Dorothea Frazil of the *Oxford Mail* that the dead journalist was onto a big story, and had just interviewed Alderman Wintergreen. Following a visit to Dr. DeBryn, Morse and Thursday discuss the case while walking in Turl Street **(225)**.

Back in Park Town, Morse and Monica Hicks are now living together like a married couple. Also acting like a married couple are DS Jakes and DI Chard, the latter having been introduced in *Sway*. Morse goes to look for engagement rings in The Turl – at the same shop (Oxfam) which served as the bespoke shoemakers in *Rocket*, and will also appear as a flower shop in *Coda*. Thursday eats his sandwiches alone at the pub, while Morse has lunch with Josiah Landesman (Kingston upon Thames County Hall once again) where he discovers very little, but is later, as he is leaving, introduced to ACC Clive Deare who is about to have lunch with Bright.

Meanwhile Tommy Cork has gone missing again. Morse searches the caravans where he fled the last time, and although he is not present, Morse discovers evidence that George Aldrich had shared a meal there with him. Close by, Morse finds the body of Aldrich who has been beaten prior to drowning. It is during his post mortem that the significance of a tattoo, 'A41', on Aldrich's arm is revealed by Morse – it stands for 'all for one' part of the motto of 'The Three Musketeers'. Further there was a cryptic message, including the letters/numbers 'A41' in the personal advertisements of the *Oxford Mail* that Aldridge had read in prison. Maybe it was this coded message that prompted him to escape. Another connection is found when Morse looks into the background of Aldrich and finds that he spent time as a youth at Blenheim Vale. Finally, Morse remembers that it is Landesman Holdings that is redeveloping Blenheim Vale, and it was Josiah Landesman that Eric Patterson went to see just before his death.

At the prison there is a mystery, in that unidentified police officers have already taken Aldrich's personal possessions by the time Morse arrives. However, a clue remains, a theatre poster that will later take Morse and Thursday to see Benny Topling. The entertainer has obviously been frightened by something and insists in only answering questions through his dummy. Records show that he was also a Blenheim Vale boy. Topling says that if Thursday and Morse want to know the extent of the terrible things that went on at Blenheim Vale that they should seek out Dr. Fairbridge, who was there to look after the medical welfare of the boys.

Before that, though, Morse needs to visit the disused Blenheim Vale **(90)** where he sees an unidentified woman laying flowers by a tree in the grounds. It is then time for another update between Morse and Thursday at the pub, where the latter hints that he might retire soon. That night Morse contemplates giving up being a detective and becoming a teacher. Next morning the *Oxford Mail* runs the headline 'FARNLEIGH ESCAPEE FOUND DROWNED' which is seen with interest by both Dr. Fairbridge and Alderman Wintergreen.

Walking in Radcliffe Square **(222)** Thursday talks with DI Church about police gossip and learns that Wintergreen might well be a corrupt official. They end their walk in Brasenose Lane **(209)**. At the same time Morse goes to interview Landesman who is playing golf with Standish, Chard, and Alderman Wintergreen. Again, he learns very little and returns to Holywell Street **(212)** to visit a solicitors' office (located at No. 15 and adjacent to No. 17 where Pamela Walters lived in *Girl*). Morse is here to see Nicholas Myers, a junior clerk, since it is from his office that the cryptic personal add in the *Oxford Mail* originated. He is of little help.

At the town hall Thursday interviews Alderman Wintergreen (back from his golf) about possible corruption, something that the civil servant denies. At another pub meeting between Morse and Thursday, the former has worked out that the rosary beads are assembled to form a piece of Morse code which reads 'All for one and one for all'. This infers that the newspaper advertisement in the personal column was a call for the 'musketeers' to meet as one of them was in need of help.

Next morning Alderman Wintergreen's body is found stabbed to death in his office. Jakes is particularly shocked by this turn of events. It is only now, after having been approached by Deare, and asked to report any irregularities directly to him, that Thursday and Morse believe that corruption is afoot, and that it probably runs deeper than anybody suspects.

An interview with Dr. Fairbridge is interrupted by a telephone call and reveals nothing on this occasion. His daughter, Angela McGarrett, though, is more helpful. She finds a photograph of some of the Blenheim Vale boys with whom she used to play as a child. Sitting on a bench, close to the sundial in the front quadrangle of Brasenose College, they discuss the various boys. One of them is Nicholas Myers.

In a second interview Myers tells of an incident involving revenge on an abuser when a gang of boys led by 'Big Pete' set their abuser's car alight – shortly afterwards 'Big Pete' disappeared. It was Alderman Wintergreen who was the abuser, and it was him, and his Blenheim Vale connections, that Eric Patterson was investigating at the time of his death. To complete his story Myers had just recently had visits from both the police and Patterson. This had prompted him to place the personal advertisement in the newspaper.

Morse next visits the home of another Blenheim Vale boy, Dr. Henry Portmore, who happens to live with his wife only a mile from Blenheim Vale in the former home of Dr. Fairbridge. He has an archaeological dig going on adjacent to Blenheim Vale, but this is just a cover since his real intention is to try to find the remains of 'Big Pete', who he believes is buried there. His dig, however, has recently been closed down by the council. There is a further connection, Dr. Portmore's wife, Hilary, had a brother, who was at Blenheim Vale. Later this brother had had a breakdown and hanged himself from a tree in the grounds. It was Hilary that Morse had seen on his first visit to Blenheim Vale laying flowers at the base of a tree.

Bright will not entertain the possibility of police corruption or conspiracy theories. Indeed, he points out that Blenheim Vale had been investigated at the time by Deare himself, and that nothing untoward had been found (outside of that which may happen 'at any minor public school').

PC Strange has a sighting of Tommy Cork just as he is bundled into a car and abducted. Strange finds out that the registration plate of the car he saw Tommy in is that of an unmarked police vehicle. It is now clear that Tommy is in danger since he was apparently a witness to Aldridge's murder. Morse contacts Deare to outline his suspicions. They arrange to meet, but while he is waiting for Deare to turn up a police officer shoots at Morse. He is lucky to escape alive (and surprisingly, given previous episodes in this series, uninjured). Meanwhile, Thursday receives a similar call, and is told to meet Deare at Blenheim Vale. There is a third call to Dr. Fairbridge in which he is asked to kill Tommy.

Morse returns to Cowley Road police station, and, realising that Thursday is in danger, tries to summon officers to go with him to Blenheim Vale. Strange says that he cannot assist since he has received orders from on high that no officers should respond to any request to attend Blenheim Vale due to a 'county' operation. Morse also visits the pub (The Royal Standard of England again) to ask Jakes for help, but he breaks down as he reveals to Morse that he too was one of the Blenheim Vale boys in the photograph.

Morse goes alone, and finds an armed Thursday – who also knows full well that it is a trap. They talk, and Morse reveals which police officer is behind most of the killings and cover up. However, the murder of Alderman Wintergreen was by another – someone whom he abused. While waiting for the inevitable showdown, Morse recites the last verse of *The Remorseful Day*, just as he does in the last episode of *Inspector Morse*. A gun is fired, one of our heroes falls to the floor, while the remaining one finds out that he has just been framed for the murder of Standish. Before he too is killed, the culprit is shot dead by the person responsible for the death of Alderman Wintergreen. They then turn the gun on their self. The cavalry arrives in the shape of Strange, Bright, and others. Tommy is found alive, and the episode closes with one officer in prison having been framed for a crime he did not commit, and another fighting for his life in hospital. Finally, the remaining Blenheim Vale boys are seen at the archaeological dig, armed with shovels, now united in their quest to find the body of their leader.

HMP KINGSTON

HMP Kingston, near Portsmouth, dates from 1877 and was built, as were many prisons of the time, in a radial configuration with the centre providing a panoptical vision of all the wings. From 1965 the establishment was designated to hold just those serving life sentences, and hence it had a unit exclusively for elderly male prisoners.

However, in 2003, following a damning report, it was re-designated as a general category B and C prison, with the elderly prisoner unit moving to HMP Norwich. In March 2013 the prison closed altogether, and as of 2019 there are plans afoot for the development of 183 new flats along with a shop and restaurant.

The prison offered a print shop which produced all the paperwork, such as the various letterheads and forms, for the prison service as well as taking on outside work. In addition, there was a motorbike shop where inmates could get a qualification in mechanics, and also a bicycle shop where old bicycles got a makeover before being given to charities.

[Left: Main entrance to HMP Kingston, and Right: Langleybury Mansion presents a rather sad prospect for potential buyers]

LANGLEYBURY MANSION

Langleybury was originally a country house at Abbots Langley (now better known for the nearby Leavesden film studios where the Harry Potter film series was produced) dating from around 1711 when Robert Raymond, then Solicitor General and later Attorney General and Lord Chief Justice of England and Wales, bought the estate. In 1720 he demolished the original house and built the mansion that exists today. Evidence of his residence is still visible in the form of a griffin in a crown, his personal cipher, built into the stonework. In turn the house was owned by the Filmer, Whittingstall, and Loyd families, but in 1947 the whole estate was sold to Hertfordshire County Council who converted it into a school.

A modern school building was erected adjacent to the main property in the 1960s so that the mansion could be used as teacher accommodation. The school closed in 1996, and apart from a short spell as offices for Social Services, it has remained empty and in a state of ruin.

It was, therefore, the perfect location for the television production of *Hope and Glory* starring Lenny Henry that was set in a school under threat of closure. As a film location, it is described as being suitable for those needing an array of dressable rooms, wood panelled spaces, and a selection of staircases where a Victorian dilapidated feel is required.

KINSTON UPON THAMES COUNTY HALL

[County Hall]

The King's Estate, or Kingston, has always been of strategic importance because at one time the River Thames was fordable here. Until 1750 a wooden bridge, dating back to pre-Conquest times, was the only structure to cross the river above London Bridge. The current stone bridge dates from 1828. Fishing was also important to the area and explains why there are three salmon embodied in the Kingston coat of arms. Other industries past and present have included brewing, malting, tanning, milling, boat building, aviation, chemicals, engineering, plastics, printing, and refrigeration.

The royal connection with the borough dates back to a charter granted in 1200 during the reign of King John. In 1628 King Charles I gave the town a charter for a market, forbidding any other market within a 7 mile radius.

Buildings of note include Kingston Grammar School (founded by Queen Elizabeth I in 1561), and the Market Hall built in 1838 to the design of Charles Henman. The latter was also the town hall until 1935 when it was replaced by the Guildhall designed by Maurice Webb. Close by is another civic building, the County Hall, opened in 1893. It serves as the administrative centre for Surrey County Council, and befitting its status, is adorned by a clock tower and various sculptures. The original building has been extended several times (1930, 1938, 1963 and 1982) and today forms two quadrangles. In July 1944 it was unfortunately hit by a V1 flying bomb, which destroyed the Ashcombe block (subsequently rebuilt in 1953).

A major function of the County Hall was as a court and jail. However, since the opening of a new court next door several decades ago, the existing rooms have remained empty or converted to offices. Today the 'Old Court House' may be hired out for weddings and other events, and is often to be seen in television productions where a court or prison cells are required. In *Neverland* it was the

91

main hall with its mosaic floor, committee rooms, and offices that were used as the location where Alderman Gerald Wintergreen works, and where the Police Widows and Orphans benefit at the beginning of the episode was held.

THE KENTON THEATRE

[The proscenium arch was rebuilt and painted by renown local artist John Piper, who also designed sets for some of the productions]

The Kenton Theatre's claim to fame is that it is the fourth oldest working theatre in the United Kingdom, situated in the heart of Henley-on-Thames. It was founded on 7th November 1805 and is staffed and run by volunteers. It has not always been used for theatre work though, since it closed between 1813 and 1935 during which time it became variously a non-conformist chapel, a school, a church hall, and a store for theatrical scenery. The auditorium capacity is 240 persons.

Among those who have tread the boards here are Celia Johnson, John Mortimer, Anthony Newley, Kate Winslet, Diana Dors, and Jeremy Irons.

RIDE

SERIES 3 EPISODE 1

PREMIER: 3rd January 2016   **AUDIENCE:** 6.8 million

LENGTH: 88 minutes   **DIRECTOR:** Sandra Goldbacher

GUEST STARS: Samuel Barnett, Ben Mansfield, Hilton McRae, David Oakes, Jemima West.

SYNOPSIS

After the climax of the 2nd series in April 2014, there could be very few who did not believe that both DI Thursday and DC Morse would return for a new series. The only surprise was that the viewer would have to wait nearly eighteen months for that return. *Ride*, then, picks up a few months after the events of Blenheim Vale as seen in *Neverland*. Thursday is back at work, while a rather despondent Morse (and who could blame him given the way he was treated in previous series) wants nothing more to do with the police force, his former colleagues, or even his friends. He is to be found living alone in a shack beside a lake **(240)**, rather akin to *Death in Paradise* only without the sunshine. The story has elements of *The Great Gatsby*, and also *The Dark Knight*, intertwined within it. The plot though, does break Ronald Knox's 'Rules of Murder' No. 10 in that 'twin brothers, clones, doubles may not appear unless the reader has been prepared for them'.

It is while Morse is residing at his lakeside dacha that he is befriended by an unhappy millionaire, Joss Bixby, along with Bixby's circle of hedonistic friends. Meanwhile, at a funfair on Cowley Green, a young girl, Jeannie Hearne, goes missing. Her dead body is found the following day in the woods close to where Morse is now living, and it seems likely that Morse's new friends are involved in some way. If further proof were needed Joss Bixby seems also to be found dead, but then reappears the following day, prompting the question who was murdered, and why? The conundrum can only be solved by Morse, who will come to realise that his future lies in being a detective again, and that the funfair is central to cracking this particular case.

SCENE BY SCENE

The title sequence shows the board of enquiry pronouncement/cover up concerning the Blenheim Vale case, and the home of Joss Bixby. The exterior is actually Waddesdon Manor **(99)**, the former home of Baron Ferdinand de Rothschild, while the interior is Halton House **(96)**, which in real life was the former home of another family member, Alfred Freiherr de Rothschild. Next comes the establishing shot of Oxford and a double decker bus **(176)** – the one seen in so many episodes already – passing the Sheldonian Theatre **(204)**. Jeannie Hearne is the conductor. Finally, in this sequence the viewer sees one Harry Rose being released from prison, and a funfair **(101)** – including a magician who goes under the title of The Great Zambezi, and a ghost train ride on which Jeannie Hearne is a passenger.

It is the first day back at work for Thursday, and there is the shot of him leaving home **(245)** and making his way with DS Jakes to the woods by Lake Silence (Black Park) where the body of Jeannie Hearne has been run over several times by an unidentified car.

Morse is living at the lake in a shack. He is visited by his neighbour, and friend, Anthony Don, who invites him to go for a drive to see Bruce Belborough who lives on the other side of the lake. On the way they pass the crime scene in the woods, but Morse does not want to stop when he sees his former colleagues. Anthony Don was a flatmate of Morse's during his college years, and was chronologically first introduced in the 1989 Inspector Morse episode *Deceived by Flight* (in which he is murdered). Belborough's magnificent house is actually Minley Manor in Hampshire **(102)**, and it is here that Morse runs into Belborough's wife, Kay, who is a model, and Elva Piper, a professional tennis player.

Back at Cowley Road police station **(246)**, Jeannie Hearne's mother is reporting her daughter's disappearance. She had last been seen at the funfair with Albert Potter, a mechanic at the bus depot where she worked. Another establishing shot of Oxford, taken from the tower of the University Church of St. Mary the Virgin **(206)** and showing both Brasenose College **(177)** and Exeter College **(179)**, precedes an interview with Potter who is working on 'that' bus, which seems to have broken down in Market Street **(214)** just outside the entrance to the covered market.

The story then moves to the fictional Carlisle College – actually Exeter College with Colin Dexter inside the chapel attending a service – where a student, Gerald Ashbourne, has been found dead in his room. It will later be revealed that he died from taking what Dr. DeBryn calls Chinese heroin, a new variety to Oxford. In the meantime Morse has returned to the woods and the original scene of crime, where he finds a clue in the form of a golf scorecard. Thursday goes to seek out Morse at his flat in Park Town **(218)** and runs into Monica Hicks, who gives him his new contact details, but warns Thursday that Morse does not want to be found.

Morse attends a stereotypical 1960s party held at Joss Bixby's house (again the outside being Waddesdon Manor and the interiors being Halton House). Bixby is a man intent on holding the land speed record, just as Donald Campbell was in

1967. He invites Morse to watch him put his hydroplane, the vehicle in which he hopes to obtain the land speed record, through its paces. Later that evening Morse and Thursday meet at his lakeside shack, but Thursday fails to persuade Morse to come back off suspension and help with the case. Morse, however, does give Thursday the golfing scorecard clue.

Bixby offers Morse a job as his 'corner man' to keep Bixby out of trouble. He also wants to make him a present of a red Jaguar (what else?) that Morse admires in his collection of sports cars. Morse notices that one of the cars has been vandalised with the inscription 'Numbers 32:23' which has been scratched on the paintwork. It is a warning that Bixby has sinned and that his sin will find him out. That night, Morse visits the funfair with his new friends, and finds another clue which he hands over to the newly promoted PS Strange who is also present. The following night Joss Bixby is throwing a masked ball to which Morse is invited. Thursday, who has found a 'JB' casino chip from Joss Bixby's Belvedere Club in the handbag of the late Jeannie Hearne, is also there to interview Bixby.

At the ball there is tension between Bruce Belborough and Joss Bixby. Morse dances with Kay Belborough who seems distressed. Harry Rose, 'king of the one-armed bandits', makes an appearance and talks with Morse. Thursday warns Morse about keeping such bad company. Morse gets a kiss from Kay Belborough, who also reveals that her husband had a fancy woman who worked on the buses. Elsewhere Bruce Belborough is losing heavily (£75,000) at cards and accusing Joss Bixby of running a crooked game.

Back in his shack, Morse hears a gunshot and on investigation finds the body of what appears to be Bixby in the lake. If it weren't for a car seen in the woods prior to the death the logical assumption would be that Bixby had committed suicide by blowing his brains out. It is Morse who identifies the body from Bixby's lucky gambling chip that he always carried. This death that prompts Morse to go back to active duties.

Morse takes 'our favourite' double-decker bus back to Oxford which is seen passing down Holywell Street **(212)**. At Cowley Road police station he meets CS Bright who is clearly happy to see him return and says that he "can't change yesterday but a better tomorrow … for all of us". Now officially on the case, Morse interviews Potter and is suspicious that he won a cuddly toy at the shooting gallery when he is not a good shot. His suspicions take him to the funfair where he interviews Clem Skivett who runs the shooting gallery. He is then off to discuss his findings with Thursday over his usual sandwich lunch. However, instead of this scene taking place at the pub, they sit on a bench in Radcliffe Square **(222)**. It is also here that Thursday thanks Morse for his help in the Blenheim Vale case – a loyalty that he says he will never forget.

Thursday and Morse return together to the funfair to talk with The Great Zambezi. They also try to find his mute assistant for an interview. In the assistant's caravan they find a cuddly toy, like the ones given away at the shooting gallery, stuffed with Chinese heroin. It is now clear that Jeannie Hearne was involved with the drugs scene in Oxford as a courier. What is more, she was also making a bit on the side by retaining some of the heroin, which she sold on to students like Gerald Ashbourne. At the centre of it all is Harry Rose as distributor, via his empire of one-armed bandit halls.

The viewer soon finds that Bixby has been in love with Kay Belborough for many years, and a twist ensues when Bixby turns up alive and well. He explains that the person found in the lake was, in fact, one Roddy Farthingale who had lost a lot of money gambling and had decided to take his own life. By coincidence he was also a student at Carlisle College, and knew Gerald Ashbourne very well. A search of his College room reveals that he also had a drug habit. Very soon afterwards a shotgun is found in the lake, but it is determined that the weapon could not have been used in a suicide owing to its length, and, therefore, Farthingale must have been murdered.

Finally, Morse works out what has been going on, and returns one last time with Thursday to the funfair for the dénouement – the case has revolved around a love affair and a mistaken identity between twin boys, one of whom had had his name changed to Joss Bixby. Was he the one whose body was found in the lake, or was he the one who had tried to frame his friend for murder? It transpires that the fate of the twins had been decided long ago on the toss of a coin. An arrest is made, but the story ends in tragedy as the remaining twin is killed. The final scene has Thursday and Morse in a churchyard following the funeral of that last twin. The location is same as that used in *Home* for the resting place of Constance Morse, supposedly in Lincolnshire but actually at Shirburn Castle **(250)**.

HALTON HOUSE

Halton is a small village in the Vale of Aylesbury, about two miles from Wendover and five from Aylesbury itself. The Wendover arm of the Grand Union Canal flows through the village on its course from Wendover to Marsworth lock, near Tring.

The area is dominated by RAF Halton, a training station with a grass airfield used for glider training. The base had a large military hospital employing thousands of people, which was closed in 1995. The buildings have since been demolished in favour of the Princess Mary Gate housing scheme.

In 1913 Alfred de Rothschild, who owned the Halton Estate, invited No. 3 Squadron of the Royal Flying Corps to use his land for summer manoeuvres, the first flight being recorded on the 18th September. At the outbreak of World War I Rothschild offered Lord Kitchener the use of the estate for the British Army, and by 1916 the area was covered in tents, with some 20,000 troops in training. That same year, the RFC moved its air mechanics school from Farnborough to Halton, and in 1917 the school became permanently housed there in workshops constructed by German prisoners of war.

[Halton House doubles as the home of Joss Bixby]

Alfred de Rothschild died in January 1918, and the War Office seized the opportunity to purchase the whole estate on behalf of the RAF, which would come into being in the April of that year. The price paid was £112,000; clearly a bargain, for included in the sale was the family residence, Halton House (one of several houses owned by the Rothschilds), built in 1883 in a French style.

It had been the scene for Alfred's sparkling weekend house parties, which attracted the cream of British society. Today it is the Officers' Mess. In fact, there had been a house on the site since the 11th century, at which time it belonged to the Archbishop of Canterbury. In the mid-16th century, Thomas Cranmer sold it to Henry Bradshaw, the Chancellor of the Exchequer. In 1720 it was in turn sold to Sir Francis Dashwood, and in 1853 it became the property of Lionel de

97

Rothschild. The house was uninhabited and in ruins when the estate, comprising some 1,500 acres, was given to Alfred de Rothschild who demolished the house. The new building that sprang up in just three years is very much influenced by nearby Waddesdon Manor (see next entry), the home of Baron Ferdinand de Rothschild, Alfred's brother-in-law. Although not as large, it does have many of the same architectural features, such as classical pediments jutting out from mansard roofs, spires, gables, and a giant cupola. In fact, it was described as looking somewhat like a giant wedding cake. The inside was furnished in what is known as *le style Rothschild*, i.e. 18th century French furniture, boulle, ebony, and ormolu, complemented by Old Masters and fine porcelain.

**[The main atrium where Morse attends
the party given by Joss Bixby]**

In 1919, Lord Trenchard established the No. 1 School of Technical Training at RAF Halton, where it remained until 1993 when it was moved to RAF Cosford. During World War II the base was host to 112 and 402 Squadrons of the Royal Canadian Air Force.

Today the establishment is the gateway to the RAF and, although it no longer trains aircraft engineers, it does provide 9 weeks of basic training before recruits continue on their individual trade training. In October 1997, RAF Halton was honoured with a Queen's Colour in recognition of its outstanding contribution to training over many years. The Trenchard Museum, which is dedicated to the history of the base, is open to the public on Tuesdays.

Halton House has featured in a number of television and film productions including *Jeeves and Wooster, Evita* (1996), *An Ideal Husband* (1999), *The World Is Not Enough* (1999), *What a Girl Wants* (2003), *The Queen* (2006), *Flyboys* (2006), and *The King's Speech* (2010). It even appeared briefly in *Downton Abbey* as the house which Sir Richard Carlisle takes Lady Mary to view as their prospective marital home.

In *Ride,* the main atrium becomes the scene of the very 1960s party held by Joss Bixby to which Morse is invited as a guest of glamorous tennis player Elva Piper. Interestingly the Rothschild connection is subtly emphasised by the exterior shots of Bixby's residence, which do not show Halton House, but the larger Waddesdon Manor (see below), the seat of Alfred de Rothschild's brother-in-law, Baron Ferdinand de Rothschild.

WADDESDON MANOR

To call Waddesdon Manor a country house is something of an understatement – it is actually a neo-renaissance building in the style of a French chateau, as found in the Loire Valley, with a large estate around it. Ornate luxury comes to mind when looking at the magnificent large mansion, not a surprise considering that it was built for Baron Ferdinand de Rothschild. His chosen architect was Gabriel-Hippolyte Destailleur.

It may look old-fashioned on the outside, but on the inside, it incorporates the most modern innovations of the 19th century, such as a steel frame, which permits the layout of the upper floors to be totally different from that of the lower floors. It also has hot and cold running water in its bathrooms, central heating, and an electric bell system as well as electric lighting. The Manor housed an extensive French 18th century collection of fine art as well as English and Dutch paintings, some of which were passed on to the British Museum as the 'Waddesdon Bequest' after the Baron died in 1898.

99

[Waddesdon Manor in bloom]

The gardens were landscaped extensively, under the guidance of the French landscape architect Lainé. This was no mean feat as the hilltop was barren. Several fully-grown trees were planted, some so big it took sixteen horses to move them to their new location. It is regarded as one of the finest Victorian gardens in Britain. Queen Victoria invited herself to view the park, but is reported to have been more fascinated by the new invention of electric lighting that had been installed – it is said that she spent ten minutes switching a chandelier on and off. While some collections were bequeathed, new generations of Rothschilds have added to the fine art and furniture collections, and they continue to be a draw for visitors.

The grounds and property have been owned by the National Trust since 1957, but continue to be administered by a Rothschild family trust as a semi-independent operation, an unprecedented arrangement – normally the National Trust administers a property itself once it takes ownership, and former owners tend to be no longer involved. James de Rothschild bequeathed the Manor and its contents along with 200 acres of grounds and the largest ever endowment to the National Trust – £750,000, however, Eythrope and the rest of the Waddesdon estate remain in the Rothschild family's possession. The Rothschilds tended to reside around the borders of Hertfordshire and Buckinghamshire, an area unofficially known as

'Rothschildshire'. At one point they owned 7 large country houses and 30,000 acres of land in the area, and further afield another 40 great Rothschild properties across Europe. The current baron, Jacob Rothschild, 4th Lord Rothschild, has overseen a major restoration and introduced new collections there.

On 10th June 2003, approximately 100, irreplaceable and priceless, French gold snuff boxes and bejewelled trifles were stolen from the house, none of which has thus far been recovered. There is still a reward for information leading to their recovery.

Films that made use of the stunning house and gardens include *Carry On Don't Lose Your Head* (1966), *Never Say Never Again* (1983), *An Ideal Husband* (1999), *The Tenth Kingdom* (2000), *Daniel Deronda* (2002), *The Queen* (2006) starring Dame Helen Mirren, where it stood in for Buckingham Palace gardens, and *Downton Abbey* where it fleetingly becomes Haxby Hall. It also appears, along with Halton House (see previous entry) as the home of Joss Bixby in *Ride*.

CARTERS STEAM FAIR

[Carters Steam Fair in Bath – every ride is recommended with the exception of the Ghost Train where Jeannie Hearne was last seen alive]

John and Ann Carter began their steam fair back in 1977 with the purchase of the Jubilee Steam Gallopers, which during the 1980s travelled with them around the country to steam rallies and the like. They soon became specialists in vintage fairground rides, and their restoration, as they added more rides to their collection.

In 1999 they found a new yard that could house the fair during the winter months, and from which they could host training courses in the art of signwriting and fairground art. Today Carters Steam Fair, still a family firm, is the largest travelling vintage fair in the world. The family are the custodians of an incredible collection of rides and side stalls which date from the 1890s to 1960s. One of the features which makes Carters Steam Fair unique is the decoration of its engines, rides and transport with consistently superb signwriting, lining, and traditional fairground decoration created by Joby Carter.

MINLEY MANOR

[Minley Manor is built in the French Gothic style]

The Grade II listed house known as Minley Manor was built between 1858 and 1860 by Henry Clutton for the banker (and one-time MP for Northampton) Raikes Currie. The manor was constructed of red brick with stone dressings in an asymmetrical French Gothic style with very tall roofs. The interior was more Jacobean and classical than Gothic. Robert Toswill Veitch was commissioned to lay out the gardens.

In 1870 a fire destroyed the south portion of the house and clock tower, and it was only from the drafting in of dragoons from nearby Sandhurst, that the main part of the house survived. In 1886 the chapel and orangery were added, while in 1896 other modifications were made. In 1936 Bertram Currie sold the house and 2,500 acre estate to the War Office, which subsequently used it as the Senior Wing of the Staff College at nearby Camberley. After 1971 it became the Officers' Mess for the Royal Engineers at Gibraltar Barracks, but it closed in 2013, and was subsequently sold in 2014 for around £5 million to a private investor. It has appeared on film in *Mosquito Squadron* (1969), *Let Me Go* (2017), *Crooked House* (2017) and *The Nutcracker and the Four Realms* (2018).

ARCADIA
SERIES 3 EPISODE 2

PREMIER: 10th January 2016   **AUDIENCE:** 7.2 million

LENGTH: 89 minutes   **DIRECTOR:** Bryn Higgins

GUEST STARS: Charles Babalola , Max Bennett, Richard Dillane, Gala Gordon, Elizabeth Hopper, Chris Larkin, Genevieve O'Reilly.

SYNOPSIS

By the time *Arcadia* takes place in the summer of 1967, it is as if the events of the past two episodes had never happened. Morse is back at work and must look for connections involving a number of incidents –a fire in a Jericho flat that kills artist Simon Hallward, the blackmailing of a local supermarket called Richardsons (note the lack of an apostrophe in the name), and the subsequent kidnapping of the owner's daughter (Verity Richardson). He must also explore the possible involvement of the followers of Gideon Finn (who is the leader of a nearby hippy commune), and a political activist, Cuthbert Mukamba, who is protesting against Richardsons possible participation in the import of illegal goods from Rhodesia.

The main character, and hero of this episode, is not DC Morse, but DS Peter Jakes who is about to leave the series on a high. His place in the regular cast is taken by WPC Shirley Trewlove, who is introduced in this episode as a hardworking, efficient and intelligent officer. *Arcadia* is very much a 'town' episode, which suffers a little for its lack of Oxford college interest. Indeed, given the settings and characters it might be more at home having taken place in Midsomer.

SCENE BY SCENE

The episode opens with Simon Hallward in his studio flat in Upper Fisher Row **(111)**, then moves to Richardsons supermarket **(110)** and the shop manager, Ivor Maddox, to a glimpse of the Richardsons' home **(108)**, and finally to a gang of students in formal attire bullying two black gentlemen who are waiting for a bus in Holywell Street **(212)** close to New College **(190)**. The latter flee and as they are chased by their tormenters, they pass the collapsed body of Lorraine Figgis who is on her way home having just shopped at Richardsons. One of the harassed men is thrown in the River Cherwell at the end of Broad Walk **(200)** close to where the car chase scene involving Justin Delfarge finishes in *Trove*. Meanwhile, in hospital, Lorraine Figgis dies from an unknown cause, which Dr. DeBryn will later reveal to be arsenic poisoning. Before that, though, there is a party that Ivor Maddox is holding at his home at which Annette and Leo Richardson are present. Leo tells Ivor to "deal with it" referring to the current blackmail threats against his supermarket. Morse has an early run-in with the Richardsons, since on their way home from the party their car is stopped, and Leo Richardson is arrested on suspicion drunken driving. He has friends in high places, however, and since the new road safety act has not yet become law, he will not be charged.

In Jericho the following morning, there is a fatal explosion in Simon Hallward's studio flat. Morse is immediately suspicious that there has been foul play because the alarm clock on Hallward's teasmade was set to 5am – rather too early in the morning. He brings this point to the attention of DI Thursday and Jakes at their normal lunchtime meeting at The Royal Standard of England **(229)**. Morse has also found out that Hallward had dropped out of arts college the previous summer, and joined the hippy commune out at Boar's Hill. He and Thursday visit the commune **(112)**, known as House Beautiful, where they are met by Ayesha and Gideon Finn. The latter confirms that Hallward left the commune after last year's harvest, as he was not ready spiritually to join the group fulltime.

Meanwhile back in Oxford, Richardsons is under siege from some protestors led by Cuthbert Mukamba. Inside the supermarket somebody has added glass to the baby food jars. Fortunately, nobody is badly injured by this action, and later a blackmail note is found.

Morse moves into his new flat – a basement one this time in Wellington Square **(226)** only a few paces from his previous residence in Rewley House **(202)**. Next morning Morse picks Thursday up at home **(245)**, where Win Thursday gives her husband a bloater paste sandwich for lunch. Morse's first call of the day is to an artist's space that Hallward was renting at Osney. Here it becomes clear that he is the blackmailer. Among the evidence are some bloater paste jars that have been infused with arsenic. Realising that his superior might be in danger Morse goes to The Royal Standard of England and stops Thursday having his lunchtime sandwich just in the nick of time. As a consequence, the supermarket is closed by order of the police, while investigations continue into all the products for sale on the shelves. Jakes reveals that he has resigned from the police force, and will be off to America for a fresh start with his girlfriend, who is expecting his child.

At the home of the Richardsons it is revealed that several blackmail notes have been received over the previous month, but that each has been ignored by the management. Morse meets Dorothea Frazil, of the *Oxford Mail*, at The Royal Standard of England for a drink and learns that when the firm was founded in 1843 it was called Maddox and Richardson, but that there was a falling out between the families during World War I. This rather points to a similar plot in the Inspector Morse episode *The Sins of the Fathers*. Morse is called away to the Richardsons' home when Annette Richardson reports that there might be an intruder in the house, but it is a ploy to seduce Morse – or is it? In the morning the daughter, Verity Richardson, is missing from her room and it seems she has been kidnapped. A ransom telephone call is received, and the sum of £100,000 is to be dropped off in a holdall at a specified location. Morse volunteers to be the courier.

The subsequent scenes are straight out of *Dirty Harry*, with Morse even dressed in a similar style to Clint Eastwood in that classic 1970s film. The initial call is supposed to be from a telephone box in Merton Street **(216)** – and indeed the call comes to a fake prop telephone box situated outside Corpus Christi College in Merton Street. From here, Morse has to get to another telephone box in New College Lane **(217)** in just four minutes. Here there is a slight problem as there are two telephone boxes in that street. It is also around a third of a mile by the most direct route, so Morse will have to run at around 5 mph and travel via Magpie Lane, along Catte Street **(211)**, past the Radcliffe Camera **(222)** and under the Bridge of Sighs **(182)** to reach his destination. He does not get off to the best of starts, and takes a much longer route running down Merton Street, in the opposite direction to that he should take, before proceeding up Queen's Lane **(221)**, with Thursday and Jakes not far behind in the Jaguar. Morse passes the first telephone box (the wrong one as it happens), then passes up New College Lane, under the Bridge of Sighs, and quite inexplicably is next seen in Brasenose Lane **(209)** on the other side of Radcliffe Square **(222)**. He finally answers the telephone call in a box in Radcliffe Square cited against the south wall of the Bodleian Library **(197)**. From here, he is instructed to go to a bench by Broad Walk **(200)** in Christ Church Meadow. The most obvious route would be to retrace his steps to Merton Street and then go down Grove Walk **(111)**, but there is a major flaw in the plot here, since all the gates giving access to Christ Church Meadow are locked at dusk each evening, and this scene takes place long after the sun has set. It really isn't Morse's evening, as on arrival at Broad Walk he is coshed and the ransom money taken from him.

In the morning as Morse is nursing his wound, he reveals that he placed some aniseed balls in the bag containing the ransom money. As a consequence sniffer dogs are called in to track the holdall. They soon find the empty bag abandoned, and it is Morse and Jakes who continue the search on foot until they come to a disused chalk and flint works, which in a former life had been used to excavate materials for the relaying of the Botley Road after World War II. They find an entrance to an abandoned network of tunnels – suspiciously it has a new padlock on the door. In reality this entrance is entirely fake and located at Shirburn Castle **(250)**. The tunnels in the following scenes are those of the Hellfire Caves at West Wycombe **(109)**. They discover Verity locked in a chamber with some sort of a bomb primed to explode. She is rescued just in the nick of time before the device detonates, and for a while the viewer is concerned that Jakes may have been killed – but he too escapes unharmed.

Morse later discovers that the explosion was set off from outside the cave so, Verity was never in any real danger. He thinks that the culprit may be Maddox seeking revenge against the Richardsons. Morse interviews Ivor Maddox, a Quaker, who assures him that there are no ill feelings on his part towards his boss. He also thinks that he has confirmed his suspicion that the teasmade in Hallward's studio was the trigger for the explosion and fire that killed him, and gives a demonstration to his superiors, but it fails. However, Morse was on the right lines, and it is left up to Trewlove to work out later in the episode that the experiment only failed because Morse conducted the demonstration outdoors.

Presently the trail takes Morse to a Quaker meeting house **(107)**, where he interviews Prudence Maddox and gets some background information on the Richardson family, including the fact that Verity does some voluntary work for Amnox (a local Oxford charity which appears to be a cross between Oxfam, itself founded in Oxford in 1942 by a group of Quakers, and Amnesty International). There is an establishing shot of Oxford taking in The Radcliffe Camera, Brasenose College **(177)** and Exeter College **(179)**, before Morse visits the offices of Amnox where he meets Marion Brooke, a character who has a central role in the Inspector Morse episode *Masonic Mysteries*. Marion suggests that they take lunch, and the two are seen walking along Grove Walk. She provides a clue, which leads Morse back to Annette Richardson.

Morse notices a discrepancy on the tape recording of the ransom demand, which necessitates a further visit to House Beautiful. He also visits Verity in hospital and picks up yet another clue in the form of a 'get well' card from Cuthbert Mukamba. Strangely, that card has been torn in half. While being interviewed along Broad Walk, Mukamba reveals to Morse that he had been the cause of Verity having an abortion (something still illegal in Great Britain in April 1967 when this episode is set). As they walk, they pass Colin Dexter sitting on a bench talking with a woman. Meanwhile a baby is taken from a pram parked outside Richardsons supermarket. The culprit is Ayesha, who takes the baby back to the commune at House Beautiful.

Morse now has all the information at hand to work out who did what to whom and why. The climax takes place at House Beautiful where he reveals the identity of the murderer, who then commits suicide. Thursday expresses distain for almost everyone involved.

The episode ends on a happier note as Jakes is recommended for the Queen's Police Medal by CS Bright. His farewell party takes place at The Royal Standard of England, but when he steps outside to say goodbye to Morse (who does not want to join in the celebration) it is clearly the Lamb and Flag public house **(202)** in Oxford. Jakes and his financé depart from Broad Street on a coach that passes the Sheldonian Theatre **(204)**, as the couple head off into the sunset for their new life in America.

JORDANS MEETING HOUSE

[Jordans offers a place of quiet contemplation for all]

The Quakers have had a significant presence in the Chilterns since the 17th century. Indeed, there are records of gatherings being held at Old Jordans farm, close to the present Meeting House, from 1659. Among those prominent in the early years were William Penn (the founder of Pennsylvania), George Fox and James Naylor. In 1671, William Russell, the owner of Old Jordans, sold a parcel of land that became the Quaker burial ground, and this is where William Penn, along with his immediate family, are buried. With the Declaration of Indulgence the fear of meetings being disrupted and members imprisoned ceased, and groups like the Quakers were given the right to build their own places of worship.

Hence in the summer of 1688 a piece of land adjacent to the burial ground was purchased, and within 3 months the meeting house was constructed from locally-sourced materials. The original entrance was via the caretaker's cottage. In 2005 there was a devastating fire, which destroyed the roof and the 20th century extension. The opportunity was taken to build a new centre that could be used for conferences and meetings of all kinds. Today the Meeting Hose remains a much-loved place of worship and quiet contemplation in the simple tradition of the Religious Society of Friends, just as it has for over 300 years.

[The interior of Jordans is stark, and without ornamentation]

SHRUBS WOOD

Located in Chalfont St. Peter, Shrubs Wood is a privately owned, Grade II listed, Art Deco country house that was built between 1933 and 1934. It was designed by Erich Mendelsohn and Serge Chermayeff, who during their short partnership were only involved with one other building project – Cohen House in Chelsea. Although Art Deco, the building is unique as a Modernist interpretation of a traditional English country house, and is notable for its exterior, staircase, and integrated furniture. The property was called Nimmo House until 1949 when it

108

was purchased and renamed by Bridget D'Oyly Carte (who was head of the D'Oyly Carte Opera Company of Gilbert and Sullivan fame).

[Shrubs Wood makes a perfect location for the home of the Richardsons]

Belonging to the 1930s, it is no surprise to find that Shrubs Wood has appeared in such productions as *Poirot*, *Agatha Christie's Marple* and *Midsomer Murders*.

HELLFIRE CAVES

[Left: Entrance, and Right: Main passageway in the Hellfire Caves]

West Wycombe is inextricably associated with the country mansion called West Wycombe Park **(151)**, built between 1740 and 1800. It was conceived as a pleasure palace for the decadent 18th century libertine and dilettante Sir Francis Dashwood. The mansion is set within a landscaped park, containing many small temples and follies which act as satellites to the greater temple, the house. The park is unique in its consistent use of classical architecture from both Greece and Italy.

However, there is another monument to Sir Francis Dashwood nearby – the Hellfire Caves which extend around a quarter of a mile, and are directly beneath Saint Lawrence's church and mausoleum. Within the Caves are a series of chambers with names such as the Entrance Hall, Steward's Chamber, Whitehead's Cave, Lord Sandwich's Circle (named after John Montagu, 4th Earl of Sandwich), Franklin's Cave (names after Benjamin Franklin), the Triangle, Miner's Cave, the Banqueting Hall, and finally the Inner Temple where meetings of the notorious Hellfire Club were held. The Club was dissolved in 1766 amid rumours of black magic, satanic rights and orgies being performed here. In *Arcadia* this is where kidnap 'victim' Verity Richardson is held.

MARY ROSES TOY SHOP

[A toy shop in Watford became the location of Richardsons supermarket]

In the normal way Watford would not be an obvious place to double for Oxford, but in *Arcadia* the Charter Place shopping centre did exactly that when, shortly before demolition, it became the home of Richardsons supermarket. Although, on the screen the concrete exterior looks very much like a typical 1960s shopping centre, Charter Place was not actually opened until 1976. The premises that was used was the old Mary Roses Toy Shop which was set dressed to become a supermarket.

110

Charter Place was never that popular with shoppers, and for many years had been marked out for redevelopment. Capital Shopping Centres had been the first company to express interest in the location, but after 5 years of disagreements over planning they pulled out in favour of London & Regional, who in turn did likewise in 2011. A third company, Henry Boot, then tried and failed to develop the site, and finally Capital Shopping Centres, now rebranded as Intu, expressed a renewed interest. The site was finally acquired from Watford Borough Council in 2013, and demolished in 2015. The result is a £100 million, 1.4 million square foott, shopping and leisure complex, comprising 16 new stores, 10 restaurants, and a 9 screen IMAX cinema, as well as a public square that can host street art, music shows and other public events.

GROVE WALK

[Grove Walk with Merton College Chapel to the right]

Grove Walk is a private pedestrian right of way (which is also known as Merton Grove and Grove Passage), that runs on land belonging to Merton College **(187)** between Merton College and Corpus Christi College, and linking Merton Street **(216)** to Merton Field **(200)** at Dead Man's Walk. It is gated at both ends, and locked at dusk. In 1701, Corpus Christi College tried to buy the land, but were rejected. The name is thought to have derived from an orchard that may have one time have been present in the south-western corner of Merton College. Originally the thoroughfare ran over Merton Street and incorporated what is now Magpie Lane, which up until 1927 was called Grove Street.

UPPER FISHER ROW

Occupational communities were a feature of towns of the past. Fisher Row runs southwards from Hythe Bridge Street to Quaking Bridge beside Castle Mill Stream. The residents here have long been connected with boats and fishing.

During the 17th century there was a row of fisherman's houses, and later the area attracted bargemen and canal boatmen after the opening of the Oxford Canal in 1790. Upper Fisher Row is an extension of Fisher Row, which runs northwards from Hythe Bridge Street towards Sheepwash Channel.

[Upper Fisher Row]

BRAZIERS PARK

The house was started in 1688, and modelled on the Gothic style of Strawberry Hill near Twickenham. The architect was Daniel Harris who worked on behalf of Isaac Manley, an ex-naval officer who had served with Captain Cook on his first *HMS Endeavour* voyage in 1768. He rose to become a Rear Admiral in 1809, and had been the commander of *HMS Apollo* when it captured the French corvette *Legere* in 1796.

Charles Kingsley visited Braziers Park and met Frances Eliza Grenfell, who was living here in 1839. His visit must have had a profound affect, for Kingsley since he used his experience as a basis for the meeting of Argemone and Lancelot Smith in his first novel *Yeast*, and in 1844 he married Frances Grenfell in Bath.

112

**[Given its history Braziers Park was rather typecast
as the hippy commune, House Beautiful, in *Arcadia*]**

In 1906 the house later passed to the Fleming family, at which time Valentine Fleming made substantial changes to the building. His son, Ian Fleming (of James Bond fame), briefly lived in the house as a child., but in 1911 it was sold to Sir Ernest Moon. When Moon died in the house it was sold to Norman Glaister who was to set up the School of Integrative Social Research which is still active at Braziers Park today. Currently the Grade II listed country house and estate is home to a secular intentional community of around 20 persons, some of whom live communally, and run a variety of educational courses.

In 1967, Mick Jagger came to stay with Marianne Faithfull, who at the time was Jagger's girlfriend. In her autobiography she describes Braziers Park as a 'mixture of high utopian thoughts and randy sex'!

PREY

SERIES 3 EPISODE 3

PREMIER: 17th January 2016   **AUDIENCE:** 6.9 million

LENGTH: 89 minutes   **DIRECTOR:** Lawrence Gough

GUEST STARS: Rob Callender, John Draycott, Peter Forbes, Ben Lambert, Darrell D'Silva, Stefanie Martini, Amy McCallum, Milo Twomey.

SYNOPSIS

This is neither a 'town' nor 'gown' episode, but very much a 'country' adventure. It starts with the disappearance of a Danish *au pair* with evidence pointing towards a cast of suspects who might be involved. These consist of a biologist, a 'jobs-worth' caretaker, an equally officious park keeper, and a family of aristocrats at Crevecoeur Hall, close to Wytham Woods. This has echoes of the Inspector Morse episode *The Way Through the Woods*, in which Karin Eriksson, the 'Swedish Maiden', goes missing, with the 'woods' in question coincidentally also being Wytham Woods.

As a murder mystery this episode is disappointing, since the culprit responsible for the killings around the Crevecoeur Hall estate and Wytham Woods, is unbelievable but not surprising. It is very much a case of Occam's Razor, in that if it looks like a tiger, and acts like a tiger, then it probably is a tiger. However, at one point there is a possibility of the plot veering off and taking the direction of one of the (worst) Sherlock Holmes stories, *The Adventure of the Veiled Lodger*. It is all pretty straight forward, the only mystery being the back story to the plot, and that is left for DC Morse to solve.

What this episode lacks in plot is more than made up for in its characterisation and sheer drama, which is superlative. The viewer is made to feel that Morse, DI Thursday, and CS Bright are all in real danger during the final climatic scenes. If the hero of *Arcadia* was the now departed DS Jakes, the person here to be most admired is Bright. The viewer is introduced to information about his past which results in a new found respect for this up until now 'cold fish' of a policeman. There is also sympathy for Thursday, who begins to face up to his own mortality as the audience learns that the bullet lodged in his chest is too close to his heart to attempt any form of surgery, and will probably kill him one day. He is running out of time and seen to be vulnerable emotionally, in failing health, and exhibiting anger above professionalism in his police work. For the first time in their relationship Morse is disappointed in his superior and mentor. As Thursday puts it, in a very touching scene with his son, Sam, there is never enough time to say the things you mean.

Of lesser significance there is also some character development between Morse and Strange, the latter having the rank of DS (and therefore now senior to Morse) still wanting to be a 'matey' and not wishing his elevated standing to get in the way of their friendship. Thursday senses the possible friction to come as well, and tells Morse that he is far better than merely sergeant material, and is, in fact, more qualified to be a DI – Morse is aware of this and reveals that he has already applied for his DS's examination.

SCENE BY SCENE

The opening titles afford glimpses of Crevecoeur Hall (123) and its maze, around which a baby in a pram is being pushed by Julia Mortmaigne (a scene which will be repeated in the climax to this episode). The viewer is also introduced to the rest of the Mortmaigne family (who own Crevecoeur Hall), to the more modest home of Dr. Hector Lorenz where Ingrid Hjort works as an *au pair*, to the officious park keeper (Mr. Hodges) at the University Parks (121), to Dr. Lorenz at work in his laboratory, to a bird watcher (Dr. Moxem) in the woods, and finally to Ingrid Hjort doing the ironing (including some handkerchiefs which will become a vital clue in the episode). There is also a woman on a ventilator in hospital, which it will later be revealed is one Sandra Jordan. Meanwhile at Raimer College, Ingrid Hjort is called out of her Spanish lesson by the caretaker, Mr. Turnbull, to take a private telephone call. After night school the students walk across University Park with their tutor, Mark Bryden, to The Royal Standard of England (229) for a drink. It is here that Ingrid's absence is first noticed, for she has said that she left her purse at the College and has returned there to collect it. She is, in fact, waiting at a nearby bus stop rather like Sylvia Kane in the Inspector Morse episode *Last Bus to Woodstock*.

Morse goes to pick up Thursday at home (245) the next morning, and informs his superior of the missing *au pair*. At the police station (246) Dr. Lorenz, who works in wildlife conservation, arrives to report the disappearance of his au pair, Ingrid. Morse's first call is to Raimer College where he meets Turnbull and interviews Mark Bryden. He says that Ingrid has a boyfriend who works as a groundsman out at Crevecoeur Hall. His name is Philip Hathaway, which fits perfectly with the *Lewis* series, since in the episode entitled *The Dead of Winter* Sergeant Hathaway says that he grew up at Crevecoeur Hall where his father was in service.

Logically enough, the next port of call is Crevecoeur Hall itself, where Morse meets Philip Hathaway who claims that he doesn't know Ingrid that well. He also meets Geoff Craven the land agent, and brother and sister Guy and Georgina

116

Mortmaigne. Back in Oxford, Thursday is suspicious that the Ingrid Hjort case is similar to that of a previous unsolved disappearance, that of Sandra Jordan back in 1963 – exactly four years ago to the day.

The following scenes are straight out of the 1975 Steven Spielberg film *Jaws*, and portrays a group of youths punting, then around a camp fire, with two of them going off to take a late-night swim. Just as in the film the male (Ricky Parker) falls over, but the female (Cassie Watkins) makes it to the river, only to apparently be dragged under by something unknown (though it certainly isn't a shark in this instance!).

The next day there are some establishing shots of the Bodleian Library **(197)** followed by Morse revisiting Raimer College to interview Turnbull, who it transpires has an interest in taxidermy. He also interviews the park keeper who says he did not see Ingrid on the night of her disappearance. As the two walk and talk Colin Dexter can be seen sitting on a bench talking with a woman.

Later that day a call comes in from Cassie Watkins who is concerned about Ricky Parker. Morse interviews her on High Bridge (often referred to as Rainbow Bridge) at University Parks, while WPC Trewlove searches the banks of the River Cherwell. In the water close to the bridge, she discovers the severed arm of Ricky Parker. This is a twist on the *Jaws* theme for in that film it was the female swimmer, Chrissie Watkins (note the similarity to the name Cassie Watkins) who was killed, while the male survived. As Dr. DeBryn is on holiday it is a Professor Kemp, a Home Office pathologist, who is sent to examine the arm. He pronounces that it is most likely a boating accident, though Morse and Trewlove have their doubts.

At Dr. Lorenz's laboratory, some mammal samples have gone missing. It will later be divulged after some detective work by Trewlove that the only sample missing is that of some animal musk. Thursday and Morse discuss the case, including the fact that a bird watching academic, Dr. Moxem, has also been reported missing in the Wytham Woods area. They walk and talk as they pass through the Bodleian Library Quadrangle from Radcliffe Square **(222)**. Thursday and Strange interview Hodges, who confirms that he was the last person to see Ingrid Hjort when she flagged his car down saying that she had lost her purse. In the event he gave her a lift to Wytham Woods.

Morse is at Wytham Woods searching for Dr. Moxem when he meets Julia Mortmaigne. In fact, these scenes were all done at Black Park **(240)** not too far from where Morse had his lakeside shack in *Ride*. Morse finds the bird spotter's tent in disarray. Reinforcements are called in and it is Trewlove who finds a clue

117

in the form of one of Dr. Lorenz's monogrammed handkerchiefs. The inference at this stage is that Ingrid must have borrowed the handkerchief.

That night Strange visits Morse at his Wellington Square **(226)** basement flat and brings him an LP as a gift, and a signal that he hopes that their friendship will remain strong. They end up at The Royal Standard of England where Morse keeps to his usual beer, while Strange now drinks lager.

Tension builds as in the garden of a house near Crevecoeur Hall a toddler plays, a dog barks and a tethered goat is slain. It doesn't take a genius to work out that all the deaths and disappearances are connected, and that it is the work of a large animal. Strange suggests that it might be the fabled 'Beast of Binsey'.

Next there is an establishing shot of the University Church of St. Mary the Virgin **(206)** in Radcliffe Square, to herald the return from holiday of Dr. DeBryn, who arrives by coach in Catte Street **(211)**. Morse meets him and sets the doctor to work immediately. He disagrees with Dr. Kemp's assertion, and says that in his opinion the severing of Ricky Parker's arm looks more like the work of a big cat.

A hunt is organised to capture the mysterious animal which it is assumed is loose in Wytham Woods (Black Park once again). It is now that Bright tells the story of how, when he was in India in the Colonial Police, he was called upon to deal with a tiger that had been terrorising villagers. The man-eater was dealt with, but not before Bright's partner was killed.

The hunt is not successful, although the mutilated body of Dr. Lorenz is found by Philip Hathaway (who is very nearly shot having been mistaken for the animal). For the moment Morse suspects that the killings are not random, and that it may be a straight forward murder made to look like the work of a savage animal. It is Guy Mortmaigne who now reveals that there are plans, about with which Dr. Lorenz had been advising, to turn Crevecoeur Hall into a wildlife park. In addition, he divulges that there have been wild animals at Crevecoeur Hall in the past, and that six years ago Georgina Mortmaigne had been attacked by one of them (a Bengal tiger called Brutus). He assures the police though, that no such animals are there now since they were all put down, or repatriated back to the wild. Craven, in a scene that takes place at St. James the Less Church at Dorney **(119)**, confirms this and tells Morse that the person who had been in charge of the animals was an estate worker called Goggins who was subsequently sacked – he will try and find a current address for him.

Hodges is re-interviewed by Thursday and Strange. The park keeper now adds to his previous story saying that after he dropped Ingrid Hjort off at Wytham Woods he heard a scream and went to investigate.

In an aside, Morse finds a book entitled *The Leopard Men of West Africa* about a cult who went around killing people using a ceremonial steel claw. He also finds some slides of a recent Mortmaigne family safari. Part of the case is cleared up when Turnbull finds Ingrid's missing purse at the college and hands it over to Morse (albeit with some Masonic overtones). In another interview Mark Bryden reports that Ingrid was the mistress of Dr. Lorenz, and that it was he who called her at night school on the evening that she went missing.

Strange's enquiries bear fruit. He learns that Hodges' alibi for 1963, when Sandra Jordan was attacked, is false. Thursday is convinced that Hodges is responsible for the attacks on both women. He searches Hodges' workplace and finds a pair of women's underwear. At the subsequent interview Thursday becomes angry and attacks Hodges, who then confesses to the crimes. Bright shows sympathy for his colleague, but also reprimands him severely, though he is still willing to cover up his actions if needed. Thursday hands over his warrant card, but Bright refuses to accept it from an officer with 30 years of service.

Information comes in as to Goggins' last known address, which just happens to be a shack in the woods on the Crevecoeur Hall estate. Here Thursday and Morse find the (very small) enclosure where the Bengal tiger (Brutus) has been kept. They also find pieces of Ingrid Hjort's clothing, and handkerchiefs belonging to Dr. Lorenz infused with animal musk. Morse pieces together the clues and identifies who is responsible – the motive revolves around unrequited love and jealousy.

More importantly at this point in the episode is the fact that the murderer has led the tiger back to the maze beside Crevecoeur Hall in which Julia is walking with her baby. Craven and Guy Mortmaigne, both of whom have guns, enter the maze. Morse is already inside, and soon Thursday and Bright are also at the scene. Bright exhibits excellent leadership. All three policemen are unarmed. Tension again rises as Craven is mauled by the tiger. Morse finds Julia and her baby at the centre of the maze and tries his best to protect her. Guy has a chance to kill the tiger but his gun jams. Luckily, Thursday is on hand to save him, but who will save Morse, Julia and her child? It is Bright who is now the man of action. He kills the tiger just in the nick of time, though he does have sympathy for the dead animal.

ST. JAMES THE LESS

Standing serenely to the immediate west of Dorney Court is the exquisite parish church of St. James the Less, which has stood on the same yew fringed patch of ground since the 12th century. Indeed, there is archaeological evidence to suggest there were buildings here that were pre-Conquest. At some point the nave has been rebuilt and the floor level raised (most probably to alleviate flooding from the nearby River Thames – the name Dorney means 'island of the bumble bee' indicating that the area was frequently surrounded by water).

At the west end of the nave is a Norman font with decorative designs of *fleur-de-lys* and doves carved into the stonework around the basin. It occupies a central spot beneath an ancient oak gallery which is home to the church organ. The tower is Tudor, and being the highest point in Dorney, commands excellent views over the vicinity. The Garrard Chapel was added in the late 16th century as a mortuary chapel, and within it is an ornate monument to Sir William Garrard and his wife Elizabeth. The style is typical of the early Jacobean period, with the couple kneeling and facing each other, while their numerous children (7 boys and 8 girls) are arrayed in prayerful attitude across the base of the tomb. Five of the children carry skulls indicating that they died in childhood.

[The tower and south porch]

The south porch, which is the main entrance to the church, is made of ancient red brick dating from 1661, when it was built to commemorate the birth of Lady Anne Palmer, the daughter of Barbara Villiers, Countess of Castlemaine (and mistress to Charles II), and Roger Palmer, Earl of Castlemaine.

UNIVERSITY PARKS & HIGH BRIDGE

[Part of the beauty of the Parks are the variety of different trees that have been planted over the years. It is close to this spot where, sitting on a bench, Colin Dexter made his cameo appearance in *Prey*]

The land upon which the University Parks (which today although a single parcel of land is always referred to in the plural) is first mentioned in the Domesday Book of 1086, where it was described as 'thirty acres of meadow near the wall, and a mill'. The wall and mill in question are Holywell Manor and Holywell Mill respectively, which were given to Merton College **(187)** by King Henry III in 1266. Sir John Peshall, writing in 1773, described 'a neat Terras Walk made round part of a large field, called the Park, adjoining to the north-east end of the city, extending about a mile, which serves for a pleasant and wholesome walk'. During the Civil War the Royalist troops used to exercise here, and later in 1685 King Charles II exercised his dogs in the Parks whenever he stayed in Oxford.

[High Bridge, close to where Trewlove finds the body of Ricky Parker]

The name Parks plural stems from the fact that from 1853 the University acquired further land, until in 1864 the area comprised some 91 acres, stretching from North Lodge (built in 1865 in what was originally called Rome), down a wide path bordered by trees past Lady Margaret Gate to the lily pond (constructed in 1925). From here the path runs beside the River Cherwell to High Bridge (more commonly known as Rainbow Bridge) and on to South Lodge by Linacre College, skirting the Science Area to Keble gate in Parks Road. There is another path from South Lodge that forms the southern boundary passing Parson's Pleasure (a place where traditionally men bathed in the nude) to King's Mill Gate. There is a cricket pavilion, designed by T. G. Jackson, and built in 1880 to accompany the first-class cricket ground that has been used by the Oxford University Cricket Club since 1881. The Parks are closed at dusk each day, and also on one complete day a year in order that the Parks remain private property and do not become a public right of way.

ROUSHAM HOUSE & GARDEN

[The imposing front of Rousham House]

Bicester has a history going back to Saxon times. It has been a popular market town for hundreds of years, and more recently is perhaps better known for its designer outlet centre. In 2014 it was announced that Bicester would become a new garden city with around 13,000 new homes to be built, and in October 2015 a new railway service from Oxford Parkway to London Marylebone via Bicester was opened. It was heralded as the first pioneering railway project linking a major city and London in over 100 years, and with a journey time of less than an hour, twice an hour, between Bicester Village and London, it places the area firmly within the London commuter belt.

Rousham, around 7 miles to the west of Bicester, and its landscape garden, is a place of pilgrimage for students of the work of William Kent (1685– 1748). It represents the first phase of English landscape design and remains almost as Kent left it, one of the few gardens of this date to have escaped alteration, with many features which delighted 18th century visitors to Rousham still in situ, such as the ponds and cascades in Venus' Vale, the Cold Bath, the seven arched Praeneste, Townsend's Building, the Temple of the Mill, and, on the skyline, a sham ruin known as the Eyecatcher.

The house, built in 1635 by Sir Robert Dormer, is still in the ownership of that family. Kent added the wings and the stable block. The south front is almost as Kent left it, but for the replacement of the octagonal glazing with plain glass. This was unfortunately carried out by the architect St. Aubyn when he added the north side of the house in 1876. Kent made alterations to the interior of the house, which retains some 17th century panelling and the original staircases, furniture, pictures, and bronzes. Not to be missed when visiting, is the walled garden with its herbaceous borders, small parterre, pigeon house, and espalier apple trees. A fine herd of rare Long-Horn cattle are also to be seen in the park.

In the *Lewis* episode *The Dead of Winter,* Rousham House played the part of Crevecoeur Hall, the home of the Mortmaigne family. It transpires that the place is familiar to Hathaway since his father was once the estate manager, so the young Hathaway grew up here. Indeed, a love interest from that time, Scarlett Montmaigne, the lord's daughter, is still a resident, as is another old friend, Paul Hopkiss who is now the butler. *Prey* links very nicely with the *Lewis* story, in that it introduces the viewer to Hathaway's father, Philip, and makes good use of the same location.

Rousham House appears to be a very dangerous place to live, for there is a tiger on the loose in the grounds. The climax of this episode takes place in a giant maze where a tiger is stalking its prey. The visitor may be disappointed, however, for if you visit Rousham House not only are there no big cats to be found, but the maze doesn't exist. It was cleverly superimposed into the grounds on the north side of the house.

[The closest thing to a maze in the gardens of Rousham House today]

CODA
SERIES 3 EPISODE 4

PREMIER: 24th January 2016   **AUDIENCE:** 6.4 million

LENGTH: 90 minutes   **DIRECTOR:** Olly Blackburn

GUEST STARS: Robbie Carpenter, Samantha Colley, Mark Heap, Conor Lovett, Tom McKay, Tom Mothersdale.

SYNOPSIS

The final episode of series 3 is deceptive, for what appears to be a very straight forward 'town' plot involving Oxford gangland rivalries is, in fact, far more subtle, having a 'gown' dimension as well. At first the viewer may think that the story has elements from the 1971 Michael Caine film *Get Carter*, but that would be a false assumption. It is June 1967 and Harry Rose, a gangland boss, dies. The question is who will fill the vacuum left by his absence? The heirs apparent seem to be the Matthews brothers, Peter and Cole.

DC Morse and DI Thursday are called to investigate the death of Cedric Clissold, a garment factory owner, who is killed during a wages snatch. Loyalties are tested when Thursday hits an informant, much to the disapproval of Morse, though DS Strange seems not to be bothered by such actions. It leads to Thursday being suspended from duty. With his health problems related to the bullet lodged close to his heart, the rest from work should do him good.

In another strand to the story Morse's former tutor, Felix Lorimer, asks him to look into a bingo caller, Paul Marlock, who is seeing Lorimer's estranged wife, Nina. It will soon become evident that Marlock also has his eye on Joan Thursday. Morse discovers that Marlock consorts with the Matthews brothers. In addition he is told by Nina that she believes that Lorimer killed Clissold.

The investigation leads Morse to the bank where Joan Thursday works. Unfortunately, the bank is the target for armed robbers who take hostages, including Morse and Joan, who try to hide their identities. It is Morse who eventually works out the details of the murder, and comes to realise that he is merely a part of someone else's plan to conceal something.

SCENE BY SCENE

The opening titles mirror that of the Inspector Morse episode, *The Promised Land*, only this time it is Thursday, Strange, and other police officers who stake out the gangland funeral of Harry Rose in order to observe the mourners present. In both episodes it was Kensal Green cemetery that was used as the location for filming **(129)**. Morse is absent as he is taking his DS's exam, something he seems to have no difficulty in completing given that he finishes early. He decides to use the remaining time to complete a crossword. The viewer also gets a glimpse of Paul Marlock at work in the bingo hall, and the staff of the Wessex Bank going about their duties. Dorothea Frazil, of the *Oxford Mail*, makes an appearance at the funeral where there is a minor altercation on the steps of the chapel between Peter Matthews' wife and the widow. Back at the bank the payroll for Clissold Fashions is handed over to Cedric Clissold. He leaves the bank as Joan Thursday returns (late) from her lunch break. The bank, supposedly in Cross Street, is actually in Merton Street **(216)** and part of Merton College **(130)**. On his way back to the factory in his car Cedric is killed in a smash and grab raid – supposedly in Holywell Street **(212)**. Clues appear: a small carbon copy book is missing from the crime scene, the boot of Clissold's car contains a selection of pornographic films, and the dead man has an outdated Chinese take away menu in his pocket with one of the food options circled in pen.

That night Morse attends an open-air concert at his old *alma mater*, Lonsdale College, but actually filmed at Exeter College **(179)**, where during the interval he meets his old tutor, Dr. Lorimer, who invites Morse over to see him the next day at 10 o'clock. The eagle-eyed viewer might also recognise the back of Colin Dexter's head at the concert – he is present as a cello player in the orchestra.

As an aside Thursday sees his son, Sam, who has joined the army (a fact that will feature in the episode *Colours*), off on the coach, which departs from Market Street **(214)**. Following this Thursday goes to see his informant, Bernie Waters, whom he roughs up in order to extract some information about the wages snatch. Waters will subsequently make a formal complaint leading to Thursday's suspension.

Morse goes to see Felix Lorimer at college, who is now chairman of the 'Greats' examination board. He asks Morse for help because he suspects that his wife, Nina, who is asking for a divorce, has gotten mixed up with the wrong sort of person, Paul Marlock, and that she may be in physical danger. Nina is seen walking through Radcliffe Square **(222)** on her way to view a house for sale, which by chance Morse is also viewing. Morse learns that her boyfriend is indeed Marlock. To investigate further Morse takes WPC Trewlove to the bingo hall that evening so he can observe Marlock at work. He is a little surprised to see that Joan Thursday is also at the bingo hall.

The next day takes Morse to the Wessex Bank to talk about his overdraught. While there, he warns Joan not to get involved with Marlock. Morse next goes to see Nina at her workplace, a flower shop, to warn her off Marlock. The building used is actually the Oxfam shop in Turl Street **(225)**, which has already featured as different establishments in *Rocket* and *Neverland*. Unexpectedly, in the conversation that ensues, she accuses her husband of the murder of Clissold. It transpires that apart from fashion, Clissold was also involved in the making of pornographic films, one of which featured Nina. Felix had found out and had asked Cedric to destroy all the copies of that film. Clissold had refused, and in return he had threatened to put Felix in a book of names that he kept.

Morse reports back to Felix, finding a clue in the form of some betting slips in his desk draw, and advises him to 'let it go'. On his way out of College, Morse bumps into another old friend, Jerome Hogg, who indicates that Felix, in his new position, has been lowering the academic standards by awarding degrees to those who do not deserve them.

It is now the turn of Strange and Morse to visit Bernie Waters. Strange treats him in the same manner as Thursday, and warns Morse not to interfere when he is 'questioning' a suspect. He also reminds Morse who is the senior officer.

Following an establishing shot of Exeter College, the action moves back to Merton Street and the Wessex Bank the following morning. Morse goes to see Thursday at home **(245)** to discuss the case. The conversation centres around Clissold's notebook in which he kept all the names of those who had bought his blue movies. There is a degree of animosity between the two men as Thursday tells Morse that maybe it is time for him to move on, since as he puts it 'everything in its season'.

Morse asks Howard Fordyce, the manager of the Cross Street branch of the Wessex Bank, for access to Clissold's safety deposit box. He also spots a clue in the bank manager's office in the form of a photograph of his son who has recently graduated from Lonsdale College. Inside the box is Clissold's notebook, but before any further investigating can take place, the bank is held up at gunpoint by the Matthews brothers (with the help of other gang members).

Things do not go as planned though. From a telephone box in Radcliffe Square an anonymous caller tips the police off to the bank raid. Matters escalate when the get away vehicle, parked outside the bank, speeds off without the robbers, but not before the driver shoots a policeman (not fatally). Armed police seal off the area and CS Bright takes charge of the situation. The hostages are locked up in the bank vault, while the robbers' demands for transport and safe passage are arranged by the police. To pass the time Morse turns his attention to cracking the code in Clissold's notebook. The Chinese menu found earlier in Clissold's jacket pocket holds the solution. It soon becomes apparent that the book contains a list of horse racing gambling debts, and not, as thought earlier, the list of those purchasing pornographic films.

Thursday volunteers to help at the bank siege, but being suspended, he is refused permission. Bright does, however, return his gun to him, which was found after the events at Blenheim Vale as seen in *Nocturne*. Inside the bank it transpires that Marlock had been asking Joan questions about the bank's routine, and so indirectly she might be partly responsible for the robbery. One of the bank employees, Ronnie Gidderton, in order to curry favour with the robbers tells them that Morse is a policeman. It does not improve his situation though – he is shot in the chest since the robbers 'hate a grass' even more than 'policemen who lie'. For his part the only bargaining chip that Morse possesses is that he now realises that somebody has set the robbers up, so if they kill him, they will never know who is behind the whole affair. Thursday telephones the bank and speaks to Cole, but his threats are not taken seriously, since the robbers hold the trump card in that they know that Joan is Thursday's daughter. At home, Thursday, who is anxious to be involved in the rescue of his daughter, has a coughing fit and brings up the bullet that has been causing his recent health problems.

A coach comes to take the robbers and hostages away, but with an armed Trewlove as the driver, and other armed officers just around the corner, they do not get far. Cole and Peter are not among those on the coach since they have remained in the bank with Morse and Joan Thursday as hostages. They try escaping out the back of the building, but Fred Thursday and Strange are on hand to prevent it. In the shootout that follows, Peter and Cole are both wounded. For a moment it looks as if Thursday is going to finish the job and kill Cole outright, but with Bright and his daughter both present he does his duty and has Strange arrest Cole instead. Part of this sequence relies on whether Cole's gun had discharged all of its bullets – a scene reminiscent of the Clint Eastwood film, *Dirty Harry*.

Morse has been duped regarding the notebook. During the confusion accompanying the robbery, it has been switched for a blank one by Nina, who was also a hostage. Morse is not quite so stupid though, he had already removed the carbon copies and so still has the evidence he needs for a conviction. Morse outlines the people responsible, and the real reasons, for Clissold's murder as he and Thursday walk down Holywell Street. More arrests are made and Morse is thanked by Thursday for his actions to save Joan at the bank shoot out – they have regained a mutual respect for each other, and are friends, again.

The episode ends on an uncertain note as Morse has flashbacks concerning Joan for whom (he now realises) he has genuine feelings. On her part she has been very much affected by what has happened at the bank and decides to leave home. She sneaks off early the next morning, and is followed by Morse who pleads with her in Walton Well Road **(131)** to stay. He fails.

KENSAL GREEN CEMETERY

[The Doric porch of Kensal Green Cemetery]

All Souls Cemetery was the first of the great commercial cemeteries to be opened in London. The General Cemetery Company was founded in 1830 and in the following year purchased 54 acres of land in Harrow Road for £9,400. A competition was run to design the chapel and entrance gates. It was won by H. E. Kendall with a Gothic design, but the chairman of the company insisted that it should be a Greek Revival construction and his will prevailed. Hence the Anglican Chapel has a Doric porch and flanking colonnades. Beneath the chapel are extensive catacombs served by a hydraulic lift.

Among the good and the great buried here are Sir Marc Isambard Brunel along with his son Isambard Kingdom Brunel, Anthony Trollope, W. M. Thackeray, W. H. Smith, Wilkie Collins, and Charles Blondin. The cemetery is open to the public and tours are given at certain times of the year by the Friends of Kensal Green Cemetery.

The location can be seen in many a feature film including, *Look Back in Anger* (1959), *Villain* (1971), *Theatre of Blood* (1973), *The End of the Affair* (1999), *Sherlock Holmes and the Case of the Silk Stocking* (2004), and *Lady in the Van* (2015).

FACULTY OF PHILOSOPHY BUILDING (OLD)

[The Wessex bank – Not such a safe place to put your savings]

Up until 1976 it was the Faculty of History who occupied No. 10 Merton Street. The building had been designed between 1938 and 1939, though not constructed until 1954 to 1956, by Sir Hubert Worthington using squared rubble for the elevation, and oak for the doors, trim, tables, and chairs. The standout feature of the building was the large library, which the Faculty of Philosophy had desires on for themselves. They proposed a lending library for undergraduates and graduates alike, with the incorporation of philosophy books in the Social Studies Library in Wellington Square **(226)**. The faculty of Philosophy would use the reading room on the upper floor that looks out over Merton Street **(216)**, and the Fellows' Garden of Merton College **(187)**, but partition off the northern reading room to provide a lecture room and stack room. The Powicke Room, which after the departure of the Faculty of History became the Ryle Room, on the ground floor was designated a seminar room.

By the 2000s the department was in need of more space, so in 2005 the University of Oxford sold No. 10 Merton Street, with a 10 year buy back lease. The Faculty of Philosophy was moved to the old Radcliffe Infirmary building, which was being refurbished. No. 10 Merton Street was vacated in 2012, and was taken into the central site of Merton College. It presently offers accommodation for the Academic and Development Offices on the ground floor, and the New Library on the first floor. At no time has it ever been a bank, except during the filming *Coda*.

WALTON WELL ROAD

[The fountain at the junction of Walton Well Road and Longworth Road]

It is not known with certainty which well is indicated by the road name since it could equally be Aristotle's, Brumman's or Brimmanes Well, though it is presently thought that Aristotle's Well was Wolward's Well and that Brumman's is Walton Well. In 19th century maps of the city made before 1885 the well is incorrectly ascribed to Aristotle. It was at this time that a fountain was put on the site 'by the liberality of Alderman Ward'.

The narrow road which led over the canal to Port Meadow was the subject of frequent arguments between the city and the Abbess of Godstow Abbey. She complained that the City had encroached upon the road, and even built a house on it in order to keep a watchful eye upon the street.

131

[Where Morse pleads with Joan Thursday not to leave home in *Coda*]

The houses along the road were built between 1873 and 1897 with many being designed by H. W. Moore. No. 2 was the home of the ironmaster at the nearby Eagle ironworks, owned by W. Lucy & Co., while on the south side of the street is 'Elijah Terrace' – a row of eight terraced houses which have carved panels telling the story of Elijah.

132

GAME
SERIES 4 EPISODE 1

PREMIER: 8th January 2017   **AUDIENCE:** 7.6 million

LENGTH: 88 minutes   **DIRECTOR:** Ashley Pearce

GUEST STARS: Chris Fulton, Adam James, James Laurenson, Robert Luckay, Abram Rooney, Tristan Sturrock, Ruby Thomas.

SYNOPSIS

The 'game' of the episode title is chess which appears in various guises throughout this story, but is only a backdrop for a series of murders, that only Morse will be able to unravel. Although the audience had to wait a year for series 4 to be produced, the events follow on just 2 weeks after those of *Coda*. It is an unhappy time for most – Joan Thursday has left home leaving her parents, and DC Morse for that matter, bereft. To add to Morse's woes, through no fault of his own, he has failed his DS's examination because his paper was lost before it could be marked.

Despite all this, crime continues in the not so quiet city of Oxford, and there will be four murders to be solved in this episode. They begin with that of Dr. Nielsen, a researcher on a computer project at the appropriately named Lovelace College, who has been missing for some weeks having said he was going fishing. His state-of-the-art computer is about to be pitted in a game of chess against Russian master, Yuri Gradenko. Soon two more bodies will be found in separate incidents at the East Cowley Baths. The first might well be an accident, but the second is rather more unusual since the victim was a non-swimmer. It is the link between the three corpses that is the key to solving this mystery, which has more to do with the game of deception than with the game of chess, since it is the result of a family secret that has been kept hidden for many years. Of course, Morse will discover the connection, with a little help (principally from WPC Trewlove who knows a thing or two about chess moves, Dr. DeBryn who knows a lot about most things, and DS Strange who does some basic police work), but not before there is another victim.

SCENE BY SCENE

The title sequence includes shots of the East Cowley Baths – actually shot in Swindon **(143)** and London **(137)**, Morse at a concert inside the Sheldonian Theatre **(204)**, various flashbacks to *Coda*, Edison Smalls at work at the local pumping station – the Kempton Steam Museum **(138)**, Professor George Amory introducing Jason (the Joint Computing Nexus or JCN for short) – a thinking machine which will shortly try to win against Gradenko at chess, and a book reading and signing at the Katz Bookshop. Finally, the body of Dr. Nielsen is seen floating under the bridge in Addison Walk within the grounds of Magdalen College **(184)**, just before the usual establishing shot of Oxford – in this instance the Radcliffe Camera **(222)** and the University Church of St. Mary the Virgin **(206)**.

First off, Morse goes to pick up DI Thursday at home **(245)** and subsequently drives him along Turl Street **(225)** and then down Holywell Street **(212)** stopping outside New College **(190)** so Thursday can visit the tobacconist. Morse continues alone to somewhere 'near Magdalen College', but really Binsey **(249)**, where Dr. DeBryn is examining Dr. Nielsen's body. In fact, the body lies very close to where Morse first met Dr. DeBryn, who was at that time examining the body of Miles Percival in *First Bus to Woodstock*. This location isn't that satisfactory, for clearly it isn't anywhere near Magdalen Bridge, or even central Oxford, as mentioned in the screen play. Due to the stones in his pockets, to weigh down the body, it would appear that Dr. Nielsen has committed suicide (though the viewer knows better, of course).

Back in Oxford, Morse drives down Turl Street again and ends up at Lovelace College, which is actually St. Catherine's College **(141)**, where he informs Dr. Amory of his suspicions that the body found in the river is that of Dr. Nielsen. He also searches Dr. Nielsen's office. The next scene is at Cowley Road police station where Morse is informed by CS Bright that he has failed his DS's examination because his paper has been lost. Not far away at the East Cowley Baths, the body of Miss Palfrey is found in cubicle No. 2 of the slipper baths, while elsewhere an unknown person is seen handling a plaster cast death mask.

It is lunchtime and instead of the normal visit to the pub, Thursday can be found in melancholy mood on a bench feeding his sandwich to the ducks along Broad Walk **(200)**. Dr. DeBryn provides a clue in the form of an unknown oil-like substance found on the face of Miss Palfrey. This leads Morse to Miss Palfrey's home where he meets Tessa Knight, a journalist from the *Oxford Mail*. Here he verifies that she had a bathroom of her own, so why she would go all the way to East Cowley to use a public bath is a mystery (never explained).

At Lovelace College, Jason is acting erratically and needs to be reset. Dr. DeBryn provides another clue to Morse, when he notes that Dr. Nielsen was using the wrong fly for his fishing. Meanwhile at the baths, Morse discovers a crucifix hanging on the back of the door of cubicle No. 2, along with the word 'DENIAL' written on the mirror, which only becomes visible when steamed up (rather akin to a scene from the Alfred Hitchcock film *The Lady Vanishes*).

134

The following morning Professor Yuri Gradenko arrives at Lovelace College by car, being driven via Turl Street. Introductions are made, and Morse renews his acquaintance with Dorothea Frazil of the *Oxford Mail*. The chess game begins, and Morse is introduced to the mystery writer Kent Finn, who invites him around to his house that evening. Morse is presently called back to the baths when the body of Edison Smalls his found drowned in the pool. His locker (E4) is opened, and inside is the key to the adjacent locker (E5), which contains yet another locker key (F4). When this locker is opened it is found to contain some empty envelopes. Trewlove will later recognise the sequence as chess notation for the King's Gambit opening. There is also the mystery of how Smalls could gain access to the baths when they were closed. Upon exploration an unsecured service hatch is discovered, which leads via the boilers to the baths. Edison's parents reveal that he couldn't swim, and also that he was a keen chess player at the local youth club. Dr. DeBryn's examination of the body concludes that although drowned, the victim certainly wasn't killed in the pool given that the water in his lungs shows no sign of chlorine. There were, however, traces on his face of the same oil-like substance found on Miss Palfrey.

Another establishing shot of the Radcliffe Camera takes Morse back to Lovelace College, where Jason wins the first game of chess against the Russian. At the celebration reception that follows, Morse interviews Dr. Pat Amory (daughter of Professor Amory), Yuri Gradenko who tells Morse that according to letters received by him from Dr. Nielsen all was not right within the computing group, Dr. Broderick Castle (a good chess related name and a member of the computing research group) who remains tight-lipped, Dr. Bernard Gould (another member of the computing research group) who confirms that Dr. Nielsen had argued with the group over possible misappropriation of funding money, and finally Tessa Knight (another chess related name) who is looking for a story to print in the newspaper. She provides a vital clue in that Miss Palfrey used to work for a doctor's family out at Binsey, where she had had an affair with the doctor, but Tessa does not know the doctor's name.

That night Morse visits the disused railway station that is home to Kent Finn, where he notes two things that he will later think are clues (albeit they are actually red herrings). Late that night following an establishing shot of the Bridge of Sighs **(182)**, Tessa Knight files her 'Stop Press' copy for the *Oxford Mail* – a piece it will be revealed she has put together after having stolen Morse's notebook when they met at the Lovelace College reception (or possibly afterwards in bed, as Thursday is later to surmise!). The following morning, Thursday buys a newspaper from a vendor in Holywell Street opposite New College, and is shocked at the headline story concerning the murders. It is only when he is dressing that Morse realises that his notebook is missing. Thursday and Morse drive down Merton Street **(216)** and visit the offices of the *Oxford Mail* – which seem to have been relocated from St. Helen's Passage **(224)** – where they take Dorothea Frazil and Tessa Knight to task under the watchful gaze of a portrait of Colin Dexter in the background. Afterwards Morse is reprimanded by Thursday as they walk down Logic Lane **(140)**. Bright is also displeased with Morse, and advises him to transfer away from Oxford to somewhere he is not known. He reminds Morse that he has made some pretty powerful enemies over the last three years, enemies who are determined to dog his career progress – the missing DS's examination paper being just one example.

Back on the case, Morse suggests enlisting the help of Jason to find the address of the unknown doctor with whom Miss Palfrey had had the affair in Binsey. Given that it is a small village, just asking any resident there would most likely have produced the information sought much quicker than the computer. As Jason works away during the night, Tessa Knight (for reasons never explained) visits the East Cowley Baths. Jason does his work admirably and comes up with three possible names and addresses, one of which (Leighton-Asprey) has a derelict cottage and boathouse in Binsey. Morse and Thursday investigate, and inside the abandoned property find a wall upon which is an array of plaster death masks, while in an over-sized fish tank they also find the body of Tessa Knight. Apart from masks for the four victims there are 'broken faces' masks of soldiers mutilated during World War I. There is also evidence of a boy and girl having lived at the property. A note, written in French, found hidden inside a cuddly toy talks about somebody watching the girl. Connections are finally starting to be made when Strange reveals that Edison Smalls had been in trouble with the police for having had a fight with a boy named Alexander, son of Dr. Leighton-Asprey, down at the youth club where they played chess together.

Morse is sent to look over Tessa Knight's flat which seems to be located in Holywell Street, at least that is where Morse is seen driving. It transpires that she was a fan of the books of Kent Finn. Upon questioning, Finn admits that he was having an affair with Tessa Knight. Dorothea Frazil is able to provide more connections as she covered the story when Leighton-Asprey's daughter, Penelope, drowned herself in the family boathouse. She too had stones in her pockets, mirroring the death of Dr. Nielsen. The father was actually a surgeon involved in face reconstruction for pilots wounded in World War II. Attention turns to the brother, Alexander, since at her inquest it was he who was blamed for driving his sister to suicide through his unnatural interest in her. There is no doubt that he is the person referred to in Penelope's note, the one Morse found in the cuddly toy. The final piece of the jigsaw puzzle is forthcoming from Strange who reports that one of Dr. Leighton-Asprey's patients was the father of one of those in the computer research group at Lovelace College. This person must be Alexander, who following the death of his sister was sent away and brought up under a different name.

136

Before an arrest can be made an alibi has to be broken. This involves Strange following, and losing, the suspect along Turl Street as they turn into Brasenose Lane **(209)**. Thursday and Morse return to Merton Street and the offices of the *Oxford Mail*, only to find that Dorothea Frazil has been kidnapped (though no explanation is given to why the busy office is devoid of any staff at that time of day). The suspect is later found swimming at the East Cowley Baths. Also found is Frazil's handbag next to a chess inscription (RXN CHECK MEAT) on the wall. It is only now that Morse realises that their suspect, Clifford Gibbs, is the not the murderer. The killer has been giving clues to their next victim all along e.g. the empty envelopes in the locker indicated the *Oxford Mail*. It is all a revenge plan against those Alexander did not like, or those he thought had slighted him in some way – such as Dorothea Frazil who wrote about him after the inquest into his sister's death.

There is a car chase, a crash, the kidnapped Dorothea Frazil escapes from the burning car unharmed, and the murderer is cornered in the boathouse by Morse. Here it becomes evident that the killer has had a breakdown, believing that they have seen Penelope recently, and have also received instructions to kill from Jason. Morse makes the arrest, but not before he falls into the river.

Morse's notebook, which was recovered by Thursday from the belongings of Tessa Knight, is returned to him, though Morse refuses to accept it back as it is evidence. The final (unnecessary scene) has an unknown person turning over a tarot card of 'The Hanged Man', which suggests ultimate surrender, sacrifice, or being suspended in time.

St. Pancras Baths

It was the Romans who introduced public baths to London, but this system of bathing – hot and cold baths, showers, sweating rooms, the application of ointment and oils – did not survive their departure. The reasons were a combination of the practical and spiritual: fear of catching the illness and religious disapproval of licentious mixed bathing. In 1357 the first major sanitary act was passed whereby 'all swine and dirt, dung, filth' was to be removed from the streets, but it wasn't until 1844 that a 'Committee for Promoting the Establishment of Baths and Wash-Houses for the Labouring Classes' was set up. By the following year the first such premises opened at Glasshouse Yard in dockland, and was an instant success attracting around 35,000 bathers in the first year of operation.

The St. Pancras Baths came into operation in 1903, and at the time was the largest municipal building in Kentish Town. It was designed by Thomas W. Aldwinckle, and originally had separate first and second class men's baths as well as a women's bath with a public hall. The main pool was 33 metres in length and covered by a glazed Gothic roof. In 2007 the baths closed when the boiler broke and bits of the roof started drooping into one of the three pools. It looked like the whole site would become housing and the baths lost forever, but although part of the building has been turned into flats, the pool has been saved and restored in a £25 million restoration project, and is now Grade II listed. It reopened in 2010.

[The Edwardian St. Pancras Baths]

KEMPTON STEAM MUSEUM

The engine house at Kempton Park Waterworks was begun in 1927 to serve the new post-World War I suburbs of North London with drinking water. The two 1,005 ton triple-expansion steam pumping engines were built by Worthington Simpson in Newark, near Nottingham, and installed between 1927 and 1928, before becoming operational in 1929 when Sir William Prescott, Chairman of the Metropolitan Water Board started them. Between them, the two triples pumped 38 million gallons of water 12 miles across London daily. They were augmented by a pair of steam turbines in 1933, and these worked in tandem with the triples until the engine house was closed by Thames Water in 1980.

[Top: Cowley pumping station where Edison Smalls works, and
Bottom: The unique triple-expansion steam engine]

The Kempton Great Engines Trust was formed 15 years later, and restoration work began on the now-derelict building and one of the two triples (No.6). After nearly a decade of work, the building reopened to the public as a museum and the restored triple was started in 2002 by HRH The Prince of Wales, making it the biggest working triple-expansion steam engine in the world.

Kempton's uniquely preserved building (a National Monument) and its interior, which is Grade II listed, has served as the ideal set for a long list of films and television productions. Notable among these are *The Golden Compass* (2007), *Poirot*, *Midsomer Murders*, and *Red Dwarf*. The triples have even been featured in documentaries about the *RMS Titanic* (where they have played the part of the engines on that ill-fated liner).

Kempton Steam Museum is open to the public on seven weekends a year, when the triple is operated at intervals throughout both days. Details about steaming weekends and weekday non-steaming viewing days can be found at www.kemptonsteam.org.

LOGIC LANE

[Looking north along Logic Lane toward the covered bridge]

The unusual name of this pedestrian path, which runs between High Street and Merton Street **(216)** and borders both University College and Merton College **(187)** to the west, is derived from a school of logicians that once stood at the north end. At that time is was spelt Logick Lane, but earlier in the 13th century it was known as Horseman/Horsemul(l) Lane due to a horse-mill being present in the thoroughfare. There was also a Horsemul Hall that stood at the end of Kibald Street.

The upper part of Logic Lane, beyond the angle of the 17th century house Kybald Twychen, retained the Horsemull name until around 1850. Later there was a dispute as to which college owned the lane until, in 1904, there was a court judgement in favour of University College. In the same year a covered bridge was built at the High Street end to link Radcliffe Quadrangle and the Durham Building of University College. In 1960 an archaeological dig to the east of Logic Lane revealed evidence of Bronze Age and Saxon remains.

ST. CATHERINE'S COLLEGE

[The clean modern architecture of Arne Jacobsen makes St. Catherine's College a popular place for students to live and study]

In 1868 the University of Oxford introduced the concept of 'unattached students', who were spared the considerable expense of membership of, and residence in, a college – a policy that was intended to attract students from poorer backgrounds.

141

The students had no fixed college, but were allowed to attend lectures at a number of locations e.g. Oriel College, The Queen's College, and University College allowed students to attend Pass lectures, while Balliol College went a step further and allowed them to attend Honours lectures. The initiative was a success, so in 1869 a social club called the Clarendon University Club was formed especially for such students. In 1874 a more ambitious venture, St. Catherine's Club, was started, but it went bankrupt by 1882. A problem with the 'unattached students' was that they produced poor academic results, with around 14% leaving Oxford without a degree. To improve matters, it was recognised that these students should have their own place of learning along with sporting and other facilities. The name St. Catherine's lived on as the St. Catherine's Society, which was to occupy what is now the Ruskin School of Art in High Street, where there was a library, two lecture theatres, and rooms for the use of tutors. In 1884 the term 'non-collegiate student' replaced that of 'unattached student'.

The site in High Street became inadequate, so in 1936 a new location (now the Faculty of Music) in St. Aldate's was found. The expansion continued such that in 1948 the St. Catherine's Society had 350 freshmen, making it the second largest institution within the University. It was clear that St. Catherine's needed to be a college in its own right, and this happened at a meeting of delegates on the 21st April 1956.

Merton College **(187)** was persuaded to sell (for £45,000) 6 acres of Holywell Great Meadow for the building of the new college which would have 'a lovely setting ... unexpectedly close to the historic centre of the University'. The undergraduate accommodation block cost £250,000 and was constructed such that the rooms 'were not to be of a standard noticeably higher than at other universities', with the consequence that the architect had to modify his design so that each room cost just £840. The whole project had a budget of £2 million, with much of the money and support coming from industry. Courtaulds, Arthur Guinness & Co., Shell Petroleum Company, Rolls-Royce, Esso Petroleum Company, the Ford Motor Company, and the Rockefeller Foundation were all donors. Controversially, the Danish architect Arne Jacobsen was chosen, but he produced a fine design that the *Daily Mail* said would make St. Catherine's 'the college to house the cold logic of nuclear youth'. It was constructed of exposed concrete beams filled with plate glass and sand-coloured bricks of a special 2 inch size. The strict geometry of the buildings is imaginatively softened throughout by the gardens which are unmatched in any other Oxford college.

The college admitted students in October 1962, though the official opening ceremony, presided over by the Chancellor, Harold Macmillan, was not to take place for another two years. By 1978 St. Catherine's had become the largest college within the University by student numbers. St. Catherine's College is especially strong in the sciences, though it does offer a full range of subjects with the exception of *Litarae Humaniores*.

HEALTH HYDRO

[The Health Hydro was designed and constructed by the Great Western Railway]

The Great Western Railway village was established in Swindon between 1841 and 1842, to provide 300 homes and associated facilities for a new community of workers, arriving from across the country, who would work in the Swindon railway works. The area also came to house an extensive and integrated design, engineering, construction and repair works for locomotives and other rolling stock and rails. The new village, laid out north of the existing town of Swindon, was intended to be largely self-contained, with its own new church, school, public houses, and even a cricket pitch.

The Great Western Railway Medical Fund Society, initially known as the Sick Club, was founded in 1847 with money raised by direct deductions from the wages of workers at the Swindon works. Daniel Gooch, the superintendent of the works, was prompted by the toll on the workforce of several accidents, together with epidemics of smallpox, typhoid, and cholera, to ask permission from the directors of the railway to set up a fund to improve the overall health of the workers, increasing reliability and encouraging skilled workers to stay with the

143

company. The fund initially provided for the services of a doctor, who could be consulted free of charge, by workers and their families (numbering 2,300 by 1850). As the works expanded, so did the provisions in public health and sanitation, with a swimming pool being constructed in 1868, and a block of washing baths at another location in 1869. This was extended to include Turkish baths in 1876.

In 1891 the first of the present buildings comprising the Health Hydro, were constructed with their entrances on Faringdon Road, using designs by Swindon architect J. J. Smith. It housed 2 swimming pools, medical consultation rooms, and a dispensary. The bricks used in the building were made at the railway brickworks, and the arching iron trusses for the roof were designed and cast at the railway works. The larger of the pools was initially for men, and the smaller, set behind the central main entrance, for women and children. A tunnel was constructed at basement level under the main entrance and continued northwards under the houses of the railway village directly to the carriage works, to allow the transport of coal and other supplies. A new building for extensive washing baths was added at the south-eastern corner of the block between 1898 and 1899, and in 1903, a large suite of dressing rooms for men and women were added at the south-western corner of the block, to provide better changing facilities. In 1905, a further major addition was made to the site: an extensive suite of Turkish baths, which included 3 hot rooms, a Russian (dry heat) bath and a plunge pool, with a shampooing (massage) room off the hot rooms.

During World War I, the buildings were used as a military hospital, with the swimming pools floored over to create a large hospital ward. In 1947, when the National Health Service was being planned, Aneurin Bevan visited and remarked, "There it was, a complete health service. All we had to do was to expand it to embrace the whole country!".

Between 1959 and 1963, the buildings underwent major refitting and some reordering, and there was a further refurbishment in the 1980s, so that today the buildings remain in use as a Health Hydro, with the pools and Turkish baths retaining their original uses, and the former consulting rooms and dispensary used for spa treatments. Good use of all the areas was made in *Game*.

CANTICLE
SERIES 4 EPISODE 2

PREMIER: 15th January 2017   **AUDIENCE:** 7.2 million

LENGTH: 89 minutes   **DIRECTOR:** Michael Lennox

GUEST STARS: Sagar Arya, Jonathan Barnwell, Paul Brown, Pearl Chanda, Dario Coates, Michael Fox, Kajsa Mohammar, Matthew Needham, Will Payne, David Sturzaker, Sylvestra Le Touzel.

SYNOPSIS

Canticle was not well received by audiences, and for good reason. Apart from the opening sequence, Oxford is missing from the story, which takes place primarily at Mapplewick Hall where the pop group, The Wildwood, hang out indulging in drugs, sex, and Indian mysticism. It is rather a slow episode as regards plot with some very one-dimensional characters, from the band members to Joy Pettybon (who is most certainly based on Mary Whitehouse, an activist who opposed the more permissive society). Nothing is added to our knowledge of the main cast either. The episode is set in the summer of 1967, when flower power was at its height during the 'Summer of Love', and when The Beatles released their album *Sgt. Peppers Lonely Hearts Club Band.*

The plot centres around the band, The Wildwood (Ken and Nick Wilding, Lee 'Stix' Noble, and Christopher Clark), who are filming a promotional sequence in Oxford and hoping to break into the American market. Away from that, there is a murder mystery for Morse to solve. The first victim is Barry Finch, a labourer, who is found dead in Oxford, but who it will soon transpire has a connection with Mapplewick Hall, and hence by association, with The Wildwood. DC Morse, though, is busy being a bodyguard to Mrs. Pettybon, who has received a death threat in the post. Unfortunately though, it is her keenest supporter, Reverend Mervyn Golightly, who dies after eating chocolates meant for Mrs. Pettybon. All is not quite as it first appears with the episode providing warnings about hypocrisy and jealousy, as well as the obvious message that drugs can permanently damage your health.

SCENE BY SCENE

The first 5 minutes of *Canticle* are the most memorable, as filming takes place on the lawn of the Front Quadrangle at New College **(190)**. It involves a choreographed sequence for a television show with girls dancing to The Wildwood's rather catchy song *Make Believe You Love Me Darling* (which is not too dissimilar from Rebecca Lynn's County and Western song of the same title from 1979). Also in the mix during the opening titles, are Joy Pettybon in her 'Keep Britain Decent' battle bus in Radcliffe Square **(222)**, Mapplewick Hall – actually West Wycombe Park **(151)** – where Finch is working, Morse receiving a jab in the bottom (though this seems to have no bearing – forgive the pun – on anything that follows), the landlord of The Crown public house discovering the body of Barry Finch while moving beer crates in the back yard, and finally Dudley Jessop (who ran the *Exiting Times* magazine) watching Pettybon's rally in Radcliffe Square.

Morse is called to the College following the finding of some drugs in the common room. Ralph Spender, The Wildwood's manager, is interviewed in the cloisters, but denies that his band are involved in any way with drugs. Meanwhile Mrs. Pettybon and the Reverend Golightly are with CS Bright and DI Thursday at Cowley Road police station showing them the hate mail that she has received threatening her life. Thursday assures her that their best man (Morse) will be assigned to protect her while she is in Oxford. Very soon it is time to attend The Crown where it is evident from marks on his body that Finch died elsewhere, was subsequently moved, and dumped at the public house after his death. Morse is introduced to Mrs. Pettybon (to whom he not surprisingly takes an immediate dislike) and her daughter, Bettina. Next it is over to Finch's home, and then on to Mapplewick Hall where he had been working. The interview with the band members yields very little, though Thursday and Morse do get to meet their remaining suspects – Pippa Leyton and Emma Carr (two groupies for the band), Anna-Britt Clark (wife of Christopher Clark), and Dr. Bakshi (who looks after the band's physical, mental and spiritual wellbeing).

At the mortuary Dr. DeBryn finds an anomaly. Although Barry Finch showed signs of strangulation it was not that, but a heart seizure that caused his death.

That evening, Morse accompanies Joy Pettybon to the Sierra Television Studios, supposedly near Birmingham, for her interview on *The Almanac Show*, unaware that The Wildwood are also appearing on the same programme. The location used for filming was actually Pinewood Studios **(148)** near London. The area where the band arrive and meet Morse, and where he subsequently talks with Bettina Pettybon, is the main corridor of the west wing administration building. Joy Pettybon is heckled by Dudley Jessop live on air, and because of this is subsequently beaten up by her supporters. Later that evening at Pettybon's hotel, Bettina wants Morse's company in her bedroom, while the Reverend Golightly helps himself to chocolates left by one of Joy Pettybon's admirers. Next morning the Reverend's dead body is found by a chambermaid.

Interviews are made. Joy Pettybon finds out about Morse being in Betinna's bedroom, and calls the Chief Constable to have him removed from the case. Ken and Nick Wilding talk at the appropriately named Music Temple at West Wycombe Park, and Dr. DeBryn reveals that the chocolates only contained a laxative not meant to kill. They only proved fatal in this case because the Reverend Golightly had weakened kidneys along with other health problems. It is WPC Trewlove who provides the clue about the marks found on Barry Finch's body – the impression of a wheel brace indicating that his body was transported in the boot of a car. Later a match to the wheel brace in Ralph Spender's car will be found, making him the chief suspect despite his alibi. Morse finds his own clue in the record markings on The Wildwood's latest single, *Jennifer Sometimes*. Bettina visit's Morse in his flat and confesses that she loves him. Morse returns to Mapplewick Hall and learns that *Jennifer Sometimes* was written with Emma Carr in mind. Fred Thursday does some basic detective work yielding Mrs. Pettybon's fingerprints on the adhesive side of the stamp used on the death threat letter, showing that she had sent it to herself.

That night the police are called to Mapplewick Hall because Nick Wilding has gone missing. A search is made, and he is found tripping on LSD at the Temple of Venus situated in the grounds. Although he will physically recover, his mind will never be the same again, and so this incident signals the end of the band. It is left up to Morse to find a vital clue, that a certain member of the band has been having sex with more than one girl at the same time, and rather carelessly has allowed the act to be photographed. DS Strange has also done some research and discovered that there is a skeleton in the cupboard of the Pettybon family, which will lead to Bettina leaving her mother for good. Finally, Trewlove provides a piece of information that breaks Ralph Spender's alibi for the night of Finch's death.

Simultaneously as Morse, at Mapplewick Hall again, discovers who the culprit is by chance, so does Thursday from his interview with Dudley Jessop who identifies the person who delivered the poisoned chocolates to the television studio. However, Morse is not quite quick enough in his deduction since he has unknowingly been drugged, and is about to be murdered. Luckily, Thursday and Strange arrive in the nick of time to save him, and to make an arrest. Morse will make a full recovery since he only received a concoction of various plant extracts, unlike Nick Wilding who was given a rather stronger dose of LSD.

As Morse convalesces at home, the newspaper headline announces the breakup of The Wildwood, but of more interest to the viewer is the side column, which tells of a local man having won a national crossword competition. Just above is a photograph of the man in question, who is, of course, Colin Dexter making his usual cameo appearance (and mirroring real life since Colin did win several such competitions during his lifetime). To end the episode, Morse receives a reverse charges telephone call at home, the person at the other end of the line never speaks, but the viewer is to assume that it is Joan Thursday. As with *Game* another tarot card is turned over by a mystery person – this time it is 'The Lovers' which denotes relationships and choices.

PINEWOOD STUDIOS

The old mansion at the centre of the Pinewood Studios complex was originally a private residence, called Heatherden House, before it was purchased by building tycoon Charles Boot and turned into an exclusive country club of some 156 acres. Boot subsequently changed the club's name to Pinewood, due to 'the number of trees that grew there'. However, his ultimate plan was to turn the estate into a film studio. In 1935 he entered into a partnership with J. Arthur Rank, a devout Methodist who wanted to make films with a religious or strong moral theme. Work soon commenced on the new studio, with the old mansion being kept for administrative purposes. Their dreams were finally realised on 30th September 1936 when Pinewood Studios Limited were officially opened by the Parliamentary Secretary to the Board of Trade. The same year Herbert Wilcox bought his way onto the board with a 50% stake, using the insurance money from his own studios, the British and Dominions at Elstree, which had been destroyed by fire.

[The Pinewood mansion]

By the outbreak of World War II, the studios had completed no fewer than 47 films before they closed due to financial difficulties in 1938. Productions were then transferred to Denham Studios, which were now owned by J. Arthur Rank. Once war was declared, the studios were requisitioned by the British Government and served variously as offices for Lloyds of London, as a base for the RAF and Crown Films Unit, and as an out-station for the Royal Mint (with comments being made that this was the first time that Pinewood Studios were in the money!). The studios were re-opened in 1946 and managed another 32 productions by the end of the decade including *Kind Hearts and Coronets* (1949), which although billed as an Ealing Comedy was shot here. However, the company was still not profitable, in part due to the advent of television, and in part due to an embargo on British films being shown in the States, in retaliation to the British government's 75% tax on box office earnings of American films being screened in the United Kingdom.

With the financial situation in mind, Pinewood Studios concentrated on filming comedy scripts that could be done on a low budget. They were successful too with films like *Genevieve* (1953), and *Doctor in the House* (1954) which spawned a whole series of Doctor films, as did the later Carry On titles. Just as things were looking up, the studios, with great publicity, announced that they were embarking on what became the most expensive non-event ever, *Cleopatra* (1963), starring Elizabeth Taylor, Richard Burton and Rex Harrison. Lavish sets were built, Elizabeth Taylor became seriously ill and needed a long period of convalescence. The English weather did not help either. In the end the film was made in Italy leaving a large hole in the company's finances once again.

Rescue was at hand though in the form of two film producers, one Canadian and the other American – Harry Saltzman and Albert R. Broccoli respectively – who having formed EON Productions, cast an unknown struggling actor called Sean Connery in role of James Bond in the first film of the series, *Doctor No* (1962). Other successes followed, with 160 films being made at Pinewood Studios in the 1960s, along with a few television productions. The 1970s saw an increase in television productions and a decrease of films to 125. In 1976 the world's largest soundstage, the 007 Stage, was built on the backlot. Although fewer films were being shot because of their scale, it only took a couple of blockbusters such as *Superman: The Movie* (1978) which occupied all twenty stages, to put Pinewood Studios in profit for a year.

In April 1985 the British government phased out the capital tax allowance scheme, which had encouraged British productions to be made in the United Kingdom. There was an immediate decline, with only 50 films being made at Pinewood Studios during the 1980s. In 1987 Pinewood Studios became a 'four-waller', meaning that it was no longer a fully- serviced studio, but that producers could hire freelance outside labour for their productions. Despite redundancies, it attracted many more productions in the 1990s, including work for television commercials, and overall increased profits to the extent that in 2000 the Rank Group plc sold Pinewood Studios for just over $99.2 million to a management buy-in team led by Michael Grade. Finally, in 2001 Pinewood and Shepperton Studios merged to form a studio with joint facilities to match any Hollywood enterprise, and today the place is busier than ever, and known not only for its facilities but for its technical expertise as well.

[The entrance to the Sierra Television Studios]

The gardens around Heatherden Hall are also another big attraction for film makers and have graced the screens in countless television series and films over the years. These formal gardens include a picturesque lake, fountain, and bridge, making it an irresistible attraction for film crews.

Pinewood Studios is now one of Europe's leading film, television, and media complexes. Recently plans have also been granted for the redevelopment of the existing studio site to improve the facilities. The vision is headlined as 'Project Pinewood, the first purpose-built living and working community for film, television, and the creative industries'.

Some of the country's most famous films have used the facilities here. These include, of course, most of the James Bond movies, *Slumdog Millionaire* (2008), *Mamma Mia* (2008), *The League of Extraordinary Gentlemen* (2003) and the aforementioned Carry On series, to name but a few. Television productions include *New Tricks, Jonathan Creek, Little Dorrit, The Avengers, UFO, Midsomer Murders* and the United Kingdom version of the quiz show, *The Weakest Link*, with host Anne Robinson.

Readers should remember that Pinewood Studios is not open to the public, and employs state-of-the-art security systems to keep film spotters away, so please under no circumstances visit expecting to gain entry.

WEST WYCOMBE PARK

[The Temple of Music with the main house in the background]

West Wycombe Park is a country mansion, built between 1740 and 1800, near the village of West Wycombe in Buckinghamshire and home to the Dashwoods. The house is a long rectangle with four facades that are columned and pedimented, and encapsulates the entire progression of British 18th century architecture from early idiosyncratic Palladian to the Neoclassical. The finest architects of the day submitted plans to transform the older family house into a then modern architectural extravaganza. Among them was Robert Adam, who submitted a plan for the west portico, but his idea was never adopted.

151

The two principal architects of the landscaped gardens were John Donowell and Nicholas Revett. They designed all of the ornamental buildings in the park. The landscape architect Thomas Cook began to execute the plans for the park, with a 9 acre man-made lake in the shape of a swan created from the nearby River Wye. The lake originally had a Spanish galleon for the amusement of Dashwood's guests, complete with a resident captain on board.

The Temple of Apollo was designed as a gateway, and later used for cock fighting; it also screened the view of the domestic service wing from the main house, while the Temple of Music is on an island in the lake, inspired by the Temple of Vesta in Rome. Opposite the temple is the garden's main cascade that has statues of two water nymphs. The present cascade has been remade, as the original was demolished in the 1830s. An octagonal tower known as the Temple of the Winds is based on the Tower of the Winds in Athens.

[The Temple of Venus where Nick Wilding is found]

Classical architecture continues along the path around the lake, with the Temple of Flora, a hidden summerhouse, and the Temple of Daphne, both reminiscent of a small temple on the Acropolis. Another hidden temple, the Round Temple, has a curved loggia, while the Temple of Diana has a small niche containing a statue of the goddess. Another goddess is celebrated in the Temple of Venus, and below this is an Exedra, a grotto (known as Venus's Parlour), and a statue of Mercury. This once held a copy of the Venus de' Medici; it was demolished in the 1820s but has recently been reconstructed and now holds a replica of the Venus de Milo. Today the house is open to the public during the summer, and owned by the National Trust, though it is also still home to Sir Edward Dashwood and his family.

Away from *Canticle* which made good use of the house, the lake, and the Temple of Venus this most picturesque of locations may also be spotted in *The Duchess* (2008), *What a Girl Wants* (2003), *The Importance of Being Earnest* (2002), the *Foyle's War* episode *Casualties of War, Cranford, An Ideal Husband* (1999), *Another Country* (1984), *Marple: A Pocket Full of Rye* (2008), *Dead Man's Folly* (1986), and *Lewis: Whom the Gods Would Destroy*.

LAZARETTO
SERIES 4 EPISODE 3

PREMIER: 22nd January 2017   **AUDIENCE:** 6.8 million

LENGTH: 89 minutes   **DIRECTOR:** Börkur Sigþórsson

GUEST STARS: Celine Buckens, John Hopkins, Amy Marston, Phoebe Nicholls, Sarah Winter, David Yelland.

SYNOPSIS

The central character in this episode is most certainly Cowley General Hospital where most of the action takes place. The plot and filming could be taken straight out of an Alfred Hitchcock film such as *Vertigo*, but, in fact, it is more akin to the 1978 Michael Douglas thriller *Coma*. In *Coma* the use of a certain operating theatre, designated for minor surgery, resulted in the brain death of the patients. Here it is bed No. 10 on Fosdick Ward that has proved unlucky for 3 patients over a 5 week period (with more deaths to follow presently).

The episode starts slow enough with the death of an elderly lady, Ethel Zacharides, who it will soon transpire has a connection to the hospital. Then there is Terry Bakewell, an informer under witness protection, who is there to undergo surgery, CS Bright who is admitted for an ulcer, and Burt Talbot a nosey patient and prophet of doom. This is the cast of characters of those who might die. As to suspects there is the rather cold Sister Clodagh McMahon, several other nurses (Jo-Beth Mills, Daisy Bennett, and Flora Byron), the eminent surgeon Sir Merlyn Chubb (who would not look out of place doubling for Sir Lancelot Spratt, after whom he is surely named, in the 1954 film *Doctor in the House*), and the younger Dr. Dean Powell (in the role of Simon Sparrow from the same film). There are a couple of side plots in which DC Morse tracks down Joan Thursday, and meets Monica Hicks (all too briefly), and Caroline Bryce-Morgan, the mother of his first true love, Susan Fallon (Wendy Spencer in the books). In the end it is a story of love, cover-ups, and revenge which Morse will unearth as he pieces all the information together, including one vital piece coming, unlikely as it may seem, from a parrot cage.

SCENE BY SCENE

Unusually the episode begins, not with snippets of different strands to the story to come, but with a single sequence to the strains of Mantovani and his Orchestra playing *Charmaine* as the viewer is introduced to the workings of Cowley General Hospital. It is night, and while Lester Fagan plays requests for patients on the hospital radio, Mr. Greeley's body (the latest patient to pass away in bed No. 10

155

on Fosdick Ward) is removed to the mortuary by porter Lyle Capper, while his personal effects are logged, and the bed made up by the nurses on duty (with a sweet pea being placed on the bed by some unknown person). The shots of the hospital exterior are actually Maidenhead Town Hall **(159)** which is quite appropriate given that this was the same building used for the hospital in the 1967 film *Carry on Doctor*.

The next morning sees Morse at home – following an establishing of Oxford, featuring the University Church of St. Mary the Virgin **(206)** – trying to trace the reverse charges telephone call that he received at the end of *Canticle*, before it is time to go and pick DI Thursday up at home **(245)**. Next up is the snooty Caroline Bryce-Morgan going to the hospital to visit her husband Edgar, who has had a stroke, and Sir Merlyn doing the rounds and being surprised at the death of Mr. Greeley. He orders a full post mortem examination.

Morse and Thursday arrive at the bungalow of Ethel Zacharides, who Dr. DeBryn says has been dead for around 3 days. There is nothing outwardly suspicious, but it seems that she was expecting a visitor around the time of her death. She also has a parrot that Morse will take care of at his flat. Meanwhile Terry Bakewell, who is about to inform on the Matthews gang (last heard of in *Coda*), is transferred to the hospital – Morse will be one of the officers assigned to protect him from any possible assassination attempt, and this will require him to be armed. To complete the picture, Bright collapses in his office from a peptic ulcer and is rushed to the hospital for immediate surgery. By coincidence Bright and Terry Bakewell will both be placed on Fosdick Ward, where there is a framed caricature of Colin Dexter hanging on the wall. It is while here on duty that Morse runs into the acidic Caroline Bryce-Morgan.

Another establishing shot of Oxford – the Radcliffe Camera on this occasion **(222)** – is followed by Morse interviewing Donna, the daughter of Ethel Zacharides, in the Fellows' Quadrangle of Merton College **(187)**. She tells Morse that her mother had been in dispute with the hospital over some missing personal items following her husband's death (and it will not be surprising to the viewer to learn that he died in bed No. 10 in Fosdick Ward), and further, that somebody from the hospital had written to her and was due to visit her at home on the day of her death.

That night in the hospital Morse challenges somebody acting suspiciously, and with good cause, since they turn out to be an assassin (Tam Fraser as it will later be revealed) sent to silence Terry Bakewell. A chase ensues in which shots are fired, but the culprit gets away.

156

The following day at the police station – which has moved from London **(246)** to the Sir William Dunn School of Pathology building in Oxford **(194)** – Thursday and DS Strange decide to find out the identity of the assassin by asking an informant named Gill. He is tracked down to St. Helen's Passage **(224)** and provides some useful background information.

Morse talks with ex-girlfriend Monica Hicks, who happens to be a nurse at the hospital, and she confirms Morse's suspicions, as told to him by Burt Talbot, that there is something wrong on Fosdick Ward as patient deaths are much higher than they should be, especially in bed No. 10. In addition, she imparts that it is common knowledge that there is a rivalry between the young and dashing Dr. Dean Powell, and Sir Merlyn Chubb who is suffering from shakes and past his best.

Next, it is the turn of Lester Fagan to be interviewed. His mother was a patient at the hospital, and he volunteers to run the book trolley and radio station by way of a 'thank you' for the care she received. Sister Clodagh MacMahon and Staff Nurse Jo-Beth Mills are both interviewed about Mr. Zacharides' missing possessions.

MacMahon is seen to keep a collection of pressed sweet peas locked in her desk. There is another secret in that Daisey Bennett is going out with Dr. Dean Powell, though she is warned against going out with staff doctors by Jo-Beth Mills.

In a touching aside, Thursday reveals his softer side as he admits that he does not know how to help when he finds his wife at home in a state of depression.

Meanwhile Morse has tracked down where the mysterious telephone call at the end of *Canticle* came from, and takes a day off to go and investigate. It does not take him long to find Joan Thursday, who is now the mistress of a married man and living in a flat in Leamington Spar. There is an awkward exchange of words between them, which leaves Morse in a dilemma about whether he should tell Fred Thursday of his visit.

On his return to Oxford, Morse drives up Holywell Street **(212)** and into the drive of Caroline Bryce-Morgan's home – which is actually Nether Winchendon House in Buckinghamshire **(160)**. Here he learns that Sir Merlyn is not about to retire anytime soon. Later Edgar Bryce-Morgan will die, and Morse will give his condolences to Caroline saying that Edgar had always been kind to him. Caroline's cutting reply will be that, "Edgar always had a weakness for failures."

The next morning Terry Bakewell is found dead in bed No. 10 along with a sweet pea in his hand. In the night he has been in some pain and had been prescribed some pills by Dr. Powell.

On her beat in Queen's Lane **(221)**, WPC Trewlove notices a parked black car with several parking tickets on the window and becomes suspicious – rightly so since in the boot is the body of Bakewell's would be assassin, Tam Fraser.

Some basic police work reveals that there have been 9 deaths in 6 months on Fosdick Ward, and all of them have been under the care of Dr. Powell. On duty for most of the deaths was Lyle Capper, while Burt Talbot was present on the ward for 4 of them. Lester Fagan also has a motive in that his former wife had been paralysed in a jewel robbery in which Terry Bakewell was a gang member. Dr. Powell has Bright moved to bed No. 10 so it is quite easy to guess whose life might be in danger next.

In the litter tray of the parrot cage, Morse finds the missing letter sent by the hospital to Mrs. Zacharides. It is from a Dr. Keenan, but when asked Sir Merlyn confirms that there has never been a doctor of that name at Cowley General.

Dr. DeBryn provides a clue, Terry Bakewell has a syringe mark on his body even though he was only given oral medication. He also has high levels of insulin in his body. Could it be that somebody is murdering the patients via a hypodermic injection of insulin, which causes the release of adrenalin, which in turn causes an electrical disturbance in the heart and ultimately death? To test this hypothesis, a former dead occupant of bed No. 10, Arthur Carpenter, is dug up and upon examination he too has an unexplained needle mark.

Another clue is discovered, when it is revealed that while Dr. Powell was at Longhampton, his previous hospital, one of his patients, a child named Molly Keenan, died. Her parents held Dr. Powell responsible. She died in Longhampton's bed No. 10. Dr. Powell was cleared of any negligence largely upon the testimony of Clodagh MacMahon (who was then just a nurse). What is more, Molly Keenan died of an insulin overdose, with the blame being placed on the student nurse who had prepared the injection. That nurse had later committed suicide. It looks even worse for Dr. Powell when the missing items from Mr. Zacharides are found in his office and home.

All is not as it seems, for Morse will soon discover from a photograph (just as in *Canticle*) that Dr. Powell is being set up by a sibling of Molly Keenan, who now works at the hospital. It is a case of revenge for a sister's death by bringing disgrace upon the doctor who was absent from the ward (and with Clodagh MacMahon with whom he was having an affair) when most needed. More pressingly, that person is now about to kill Bright with an insulin overdose. Clodagh MacMahon also realises who is responsible and follows them. A fight ensues. Thursday and Morse arrive just in time to make an arrest and save Bright. The two heroes have a drink together. Morse attends the funeral of Edgar Bryce-

Morgan, and finally another tarot card is turned over. This time the card of 'Death' is placed on top of 'The Tower' indicating that following danger, crisis, and destruction there will be an end, a profound change, or failure, but not necessarily physical death.

MAIDENHEAD TOWN HALL

[The entrance to Maidenhead Town Hall could be mistaken for a hospital]

Maidenhead comes under the auspices of Windsor, so the original Town Hall that was built in 1686 by Sir Thomas Fitz on the site of the old Market House is in Windsor. Although Maidenhead has a long history of settlement, since the Anglo-Saxon and Roman periods, there is no evidence of this in architectural remains today. The historic heart of the town has been given over to redevelopment, primarily office space, high technology company headquarters, and flats, making it a rather nondescript place. The only features of note are the clock tower (built for Queen Victoria's diamond jubilee), Maidenhead Bridge, All Saints' Church, and Boulter's Lock.

The current Town Hall in St. Ives Road was designed by Guy North and built between 1960 and 1962. It recently underwent a major renovation which included replacing all the existing windows with new aluminium frames to the same original design. Since 1972 it has served the 23 wards, who elect 57 councillors, that currently make up the Royal Borough of Windsor and Maidenhead, and from 1998 it has been a unitary authority assuming the powers and functions of Berkshire County Council. Politically, it is seen as being one of the safest

Conservative seats in the country, with 41 out of the 57 councillors representing that party, 1 representing the Liberal Democrats and the remaining councillors being independent members as of January 2019.

NETHER WINCHENDON HOUSE

[The crenellations of Nether Winchendon House]

This Grade I listed house was built on the site of an Augustinian priory that was a daughter house of Notley Abbey in Long Crendon. Jasper Tudor, Duke of Bedford, bought, and largely remodelled, the priory in the 16th century. In 1771 the estate passed to Sir Francis Bernard and it has been part of that family ever since. What remains today is an enchanting medieval and Tudor manor house set in 7 acres of gardens, and surrounded by 600 acres of parkland. The house is crenelated and partially encased in stucco from its medieval originals, but with curling Tudor chimneys.

The house has appeared in series such as *Agatha Christie's Marple*, *Chef!*, *Lovejoy*, *Kavanagh Q.C.*, and *Midsomer Murders*.

160

HARVEST
SERIES 4 EPISODE 4

PREMIER: 29th January 2017   **AUDIENCE:** 6.8 million

LENGTH: 89 minutes   **DIRECTOR:** Jim Loach

GUEST STARS: Natalie Burt, Chris Coghill, Emily Forbes, Grahame Fox, Sheila Hancock, Sam Hoare, Joanna Horton, Adam Levy, Simon Meacock, Michael Pennington, Matthew Walker, Alex Wyndham.

SYNOPSIS

For many of the *Endeavour* episodes, there is a clear inspiration from a film, and here the influence is very much from the 1973 cult classic *The Wicker Man*, but with a little of *The China Syndrome* (from 1979) thrown in for good measure.

Throughout the episode there are symbols of paganism set against a backdrop of the village harvest and the Autumnal equinox. In addition, there is a reveal, in that the person who has been turning over tarot cards at the end of each episode in this series is none other than Sheila Hancock (thus ensuring that there are two members of the Thaw family in this adventure). She portrays a witch-like character by the name of Dowsable Chattox, who has a son, Seth, who works on the farm of Zebulon Sadler. All this flummery has little to do with the actual story, however, which centres around a body being found on an archaeological dig at Bramford Mere in the close vicinity of the local nuclear power plant (where the viewer just knows that something is going to go wrong sooner or later). Immediately DI Thursday links the find to the disappearance of botanist Dr. Matthew Laxman, who went missing there exactly five years earlier. There is a setback when Dr. DeBryn proclaims that the bones are closer to being 2,000 years old, and belonging to a man who died in what may have been a ritual sacrifice.

That would be the end of the story if it were not for DC Morse who, rather fortuitously, spies a pair of glasses at the dig that do belong to the missing academic. Soon a link is found between the power station and Dr. Laxman. He was against nuclear power, and furthermore had a Geiger counter with him at the time of his death, adding suspicion that his interest in Bramford Mere was not purely botanical. The residents of the village of Bramford will be of little help since they deny any knowledge of Dr. Laxman. Among them are the chief suspects for this episode, but also one who will come forward with some useful information. This will lead ultimately to a climax at the power station, and an explosive ending which will earn both Thursday and Morse medals for bravery.

SCENE BY SCENE

The episode starts with a flashback to the events of September 1962 and Dr. Laxman driving to Bramford. He puts his Geiger counter on the back seat of his car as he offers a lift to Nigel Warren, another opponent of nuclear power. Shortly afterwards he is run off the road by a truck coming from the Bramford A nuclear power station. Fast forwarding to the present day the viewer sees Nigel Warren preaching his doctrine in Catte Street (211) opposite the Bridge of Sighs (182). Attention soon turns to the archaeological dig at Bramford Mere, the house in the woods – which was actually specially built for the series in Black Park (240) – where Dowsable Chattox is doing her thing with tarot cards, and to Thursday at his house (245) and Morse in his flat.

The news comes in that a body has been found at Bramford Mere and Thursday immediately assumes that it is that of the missing botanist Dr. Laxman. The dig itself is at Port Meadow (173) where Dr. DeBryn disappoints Thursday by saying that the body is not that of the missing academic. Morse finds the pair of glasses, and when Dr. Laxman's wife, Alison, is interviewed at the Oxford Botanic Garden (171), she confirms that her husband did have a similar pair, but that his colleague, Professor Donald Bagley of Wolsey College, who spent much more time with her husband than she did, may be of greater help in this respect. The fictional Wolsey College is actually Magdalen College (184) where good use is made of the chapel and Cloister Quadrangle. Nigel Warren, who is still preaching in the same spot in Catte Street as in the opening titles, is also interviewed. Afterwards Thursday and Morse walk through Bodleian Quadrangle (197) in the direction of Radcliffe Square (222).

Morse drives out to Bramford, which is actually the village of Hambleden (231) last seen in *Home*. The difference this time is that a nuclear power station has been superimposed into the background. In fact, the village has unspoilt countryside in all directions, and the power station in question is that of the disused Fawley power station (166) in Hampshire. It is in the village that Morse first comes across the tight-lipped locals who still engage in their pagan rituals, with a group of Morris Men practicing their figures in front of the church. The action takes place at the Hambleden Village Stores & Post Office, the Stag & Huntsman Garage, and Wheelers Butchery as Morse tries to find anybody who will talk to him about Dr. Laxman. Finally, he comes across an American, Mrs. Ros Levin whose husband, Dr. John Levin, works at the power station – she is willing to talk, but is of little help since she has not been in the area that long. She suggests a visit to Dowsable Chattox who lives in a house in the woods. The visit is fruitless, so Morse next visits the church (used so effectively in *Home*) and is soon joined by Thursday. In the graveyard they meet Zebulon Sadler who, as well as being a farmer, is the Sexton of the church, and Dr. Tristan Berger (who appears to be the only normal resident of the village).

Morse thinks it strange that nobody ever interviewed the workers at the power station. He goes there the following day, but is refused entry without an appointment. That night it is off down the pub – The Royal Standard of England **(229)** – for a quiz night. This is followed by a fish & chips take away from a shop in Ship Street **(174)** in the company of DS Strange. As they walk and talk Strange mentions a police job in London that might suit Morse. They part with Strange walking along Turl Street **(225)**. There is an unhappy end to the evening as on arrival at Wellington Square **(226)** Morse finds that his flat has been broken into with much damage having being done, and several items having been stolen.

Next day it is back to Bramford as Dr. Berger's sister, Selina, has telephoned the police station and has some relevant information to impart. She says that when she went on a bus 5 years ago on her way to the cinema in Oxford, that she noted a black car at the side of the road. Suspiciously though, she doesn't seem to remember which film she saw.

Back in Oxford on a bench in Radcliffe Square Morse talks with Dorothea Frazil of the *Oxford Mail*, who reveals that (a) the second phase of the power station (Bramford B) is about to open that weekend and (b) that there is local opposition to because land is going to be flooded to make a reservoir for Bramford B. She will also be of practical help since she has an invite to view the facility, and will take Morse along with her in the guise of photographer 'Snappy' Jenkins. They meet Elliott Blake, the director of operations, who gives them a tour of the site. He reveals that Professor Bagley, who has been so instrumental in the development of nuclear power, has been turned against it since his wife died from leukaemia following exposure to radiation during nuclear testing. Morse talks with Dr. Levin who slips up in revealing that although he has not lived in England for long, he had visit Professor Bagley several times prior to his arrival, and was in the area when Dr. Laxman went missing. On their way back from Bramford B, Morse decides to walk some of the way. By chance he rests in a field beside a scarecrow, which he soon realises is wearing Dr. Laxman's clothes. Part of the clue is that the scarecrow is wearing a radiation dose detector similar to that given to Morse at the power station (which is strange given that there is no evidence that Dr. Laxman ever went inside the power station). What is more, there is an intact tarot card in his pocket which leads Morse back to Dowsable Chattox. It transpires that Chattox did a reading for Dr. Laxman, and now Morse will have one done as well, which results in him finding out that Zebulon Sadler owns the field containing the scarecrow.

In a barn (just outside Hambleden village) while searching for Sadler, Morse finds Dr. Laxman's car in a barn under a tarpaulin. It seems clear that the farmer had found the vehicle at the roadside and towed it back to the barn with the intention of selling it later, but that he had nothing to do with Dr. Laxman's death. In the glove compartment is a map, and evidence of what appears to be an appointment at Dr. Berger's house. This is suspicious, since Morse knows that Dr. Berger was away that particular weekend. Selina Berger, upon further questioning, changes her earlier statement and now says that she and Dr. Laxman met and went to the cinema together on the night in question, and it wasn't until the following morning that she noted his car at the roadside.

In an aside, Thursday examines some of the items recovered from Morse's burgled flat, and among them is Joan Thursday's address in Leamington Spa. An establishing shot of Lincoln College library **(169)** indicates nightfall. The following day Thursday travels to see his daughter and takes an instant dislike to Ray Morton, the married man with whom she is currently living. Later Thursday will threaten him, and beat him up. His visit does have one positive effect though, it will prompt Joan Thursday to contact her mother by telephone.

Next is another establishing shot of Oxford involving The Radcliffe Camera **(222)**, Brasenose College **(177)** , and Exeter College **(179)**. Professor Bagley who reads in the newspaper of Bramford B becoming operational at the weekend, goes to see Alison Laxman. He asks her if he can leave some things with her for safekeeping as he is going away for a little while. The location of Wolsey College has now moved from Magdalen College, since this scene was filmed by the memorial plaque at Exeter College.

After his various interviews, Morse decides to go for a drink in Bramford's local public house, The Hanged Man. The actual name is the Stag and Huntsman at Hambleden. He is probably contemplating his future, for a little later he informs CS Bright of his intention to transfer to London, where he has been offered the job which Strange mentioned to him earlier in the episode. It comes with increased salary and rank. Meanwhile Thursday goes to see Professor Bagley to ask why Dr. Laxman would have need of a Geiger counter in his work. In Professor Bagley's office at the College, Colin Dexter makes his appearance in the form of a bronze bust situated next to the bookshelves.

That night, when Morse returns home, Joan Thursday is waiting for him outside his flat in Wellington Square. She has a black eye, and has been chucked out of her home by Ray Morton. Morse offers to marry her, but is rejected. In the end she takes some money he gives her, and returns to Morton, though Morse is at a loss to understand why.

At Cowley Road police station **(194)**, it has been discovered that the radiation dose metre on Dr. Laxman's suit jacket had been exposed to a high level of radiation, even though he never went inside the power plant. Hence there must have been some sort of accident whereby the local area had been exposed to radiation. Upon being interviewed, Zebulon Sadler says that he got the jacket from Seth Chattox who had found it in the water at Bramford Mere. A visit with a Geiger counter soon points to where Dr. Laxman's body has been buried all this time.

Coincidently, the Bramford locals are out in force to celebrate the Autumnal Equinox in exactly the same location where Dr. Laxman's body is being recovered. However, the investigation is interrupted when the siren at the power station goes off – it is too early in the day to be a drill. Thursday and Morse race to Bramford B only to find that Nigel Warren and Professor Bagley have gained access to the control room where they are holding Elliott Blake and Jon Levin at gunpoint. They are attempting to cause radioactive cooling water to be purged from the reactor and enter the ground water. This is exactly what happened at Bramford A in an accident six years earlier. This time Professor Bagley hopes that there will be no cover up, and that the subsequent bad publicity will lead to the plant being closed down. He is convinced (wrongly) that Dr. Laxman was murdered by somebody at the power station. Thursday diffuses the situation and disarms Professor Bagley, but Warren has a grenade. It will explode but quick thinking by Morse will ensure that the damage is minimal.

But if it wasn't anybody from the power station that was responsible for Dr. Laxman's death, just who was the murderer? Thursday and Morse realise that it is a case of unrequited love and jealousy from somebody who did not wish to see Selina Berger going out with Dr. Laxman. But, before that person can be taken into custody, they are shot dead by another central character from the episode.

Just as it looks like everything has been resolved satisfactorily, there is a final reveal when Morse is called to Cowley General Hospital where Joan Thursday has been admitted. Luckily, she has not been assigned bed No. 10 on Fosdick Ward (as in *Lazaretto*), but has suffered a 'bad fall' and has tragically lost the baby she was carrying. It is now clear why, earlier in the episode, she felt the need to return to Morton rather than stay with Morse.

The 4th series ends with Thursday and Morse both being rewarded. A happy Thursday, along with his wife, attends Buckingham Palace **(167)** to receive the George Medal. Morse is also to receive the George Medal, but has in the interim also been promoted to DS (perhaps a wise move by Bright behind the scenes to ensure that his best detective remains in Oxford). Morse does not appear overjoyed by either his promotion or his medal.

FAWLEY POWER STATION

**[The imposing Fawley power station whose chimney
is one of the tallest landmarks in Hampshire]**

The immediate error in using Fawley power station in *Harvest* is that it is not a nuclear power station, but an oil-fired affair located on the western side of Southampton Water, between the villages of Fawley and Calshot. Although this method of energy production is more expensive than coal or natural gas, it made economic sense given that the plant was adjacent to the Fawley oil refinery. Indeed, it had a direct pipeline to the power station, but was always regarded as a reserve source of energy, and hence was only fully operational at times of peak demand. There was also a dock built so that oil could be delivered by ship, though this remained virtually unused.

The architect was Colin Morse, with Mitchell Construction being the builder appointed by the Central Electricity Generating Board. It was commissioned in 1971 as a 2,000 megawatt power station comprising four units of 500 megawatts which supplied steam to a turbine, that powered the generator. At the time the cooling pumps were the largest in the country at a flow rate of 210,000 gallons per minute.

In the 1980s there was talk of a second coal-fired power station at the site but nothing came of the proposal. Two of the units were mothballed in 1995, and in 2013 the remaining two units were shut down (in part due to the European Union's

166

Large Combustion Plant Directive aimed at limiting flue gas emissions). One of the many drawbacks of the power station was that when it was operating the screens on the cooling water lines were found to kill as many as 50,000 fish a week (though it only affected certain species such as bass). In 2017 it was announced that the site would be turned into a development for 1,500 homes.

[The futuristic control room]

The most striking feature of the station, apart from the 198 metre tall chimney, was the futuristic circular 'flying saucer' control centre which has featured in film and television several times e.g. in *Rollerball* (1975) it became the world control centre. Other appearances are in *Mission: Impossible – Rogue Nation* (2015), *Red Dwarf* and even the Star Wars film *Solo: A Star Wars Story* (2018).

BUCKINGHAM PALACE

Buckingham House (as it was originally called) was said to be the most ostentatious private house in London. It was built between 1702 and 1705 for the Duke of Buckingham, whose third wife was an illegitimate daughter of King James II, and who intended it to overshadow King William III's residence, St. James's Palace. This may be why, in 1761, King George III purchased the house from the Duke's descendant Sir Charles Sheffield, as a private retreat for Queen Charlotte in place of Somerset House.

[Buckingham Palace where Thursday receives his Queen's Police Medal]

King George IV wanted to demolish Buckingham House and replace it with a palace costing, in 1819, an estimated £500,000, but parliament was only willing to provide £150,000 in funding. The King was stubborn, however, and had John Nash draw up plans, while at the same time he managed to secure a sum that 'might not be less than £200,000' for 'repair and improvement' from parliament. The compromise was that Nash, as architect, was to retain the outer shell of the earlier house. Even so, the costs rose to over £330,000 with the work far from complete. The design was for a three-sided court open at the east, in front of which was to stand the Marble Arch. The two towers at each end were to be square, and there was a central dome in the shape of an inverted egg-cup. In 1828 the Duke of Wellington became Prime Minister. By now Nash wanted to pull down the two wings, which did not meet with the King's approval, but this needed more money to continue, and Wellington was not willing to give it. The work, once begun though, could not very well be abandoned, and so yet more funding was forthcoming. The final cost was in the region of £700,000, excluding the cost of the Marble Arch.

King George IV did not live to see the palace finished. His successor, King William IV, never wanted to live there, and his successor, Queen Victoria, was scarcely in residence during the early years of her reign. It was, in fact, a badly designed building. The drains were faulty; there were no sinks for the chambermaids on the bedroom floors; few of the lavatories were ventilated; the

168

bells would not ring; some of the doors would not close; and many of the thousand windows would not open. Nash was dismissed in 1830, and replaced by Edward Blore, who removed the dome in favour of an attic, and enclosed the courtyard by adding the east front (what most people regard as the main entrance, where the Queen makes public appearances from the balcony). The Marble Arch was also removed from the site where the Queen Victoria Memorial currently stands.

Buckingham Palace comprises some 600 rooms, only around a dozen being the private domain of the Royal Family. The State Rooms, which include the Throne Room, Ballroom, Dining Room, Music Room, Drawing Rooms, and connecting galleries, are open to the public during the summer months. The garden of some 45 acres, was landscaped by W. T. Aiton and contains expansive lawns, a lake, and a wide variety of trees and flowers (including a mulberry tree originally planted by King James I).

LINCOLN COLLEGE LIBRARY

The College of the Blessed Mary and All Saints, Lincoln in the University of Oxford (to give the College its full title) was founded on 13th October 1427 by Richard Fleming, the then Bishop of Lincoln, and is one of the older colleges in the city. He intended it to be 'a little college' with the aim of training the clergy 'in true theology' so that they could 'defend the mysteries of Scripture against those ignorant laymen who profaned with swinish snouts its most holy pearls'.

To achieve this, he obtained a charter for a college from King Henry VI, which combined the parishes of All Saints, St. Michael's at the North Gate, and St. Mildred's (which was demolished) within the college under a rector, and thus provided a revenue, albeit small.

For much of its history the College was impoverished, but one highlight was the library (now with 60,000 volumes housed in the old church of All Saints after the building was remodelled as a library by Robert Potter in 1971-1975). Between 1465 and 1474 Robert Fleming (Dean of Lincoln) gave a rich collection of manuscripts to the College, that were added to the already useful collection of scholastic books.

Today the upper reading room, or Cohen Room, has an elaborate plastered ceiling, and the Senior Library (downstairs) holds some of the College's older books. These include pamphlets from the English Civil War period, Wesleyana, and plays dating from the late 17th and early 18th centuries, as well as a small collection of manuscripts. The science library is also to be found downstairs.

The College expanded slowly due to its lack of land from which revenue could be taken. There were benefactors, however, such as the Bishop of Rotherham, who brought into the College's possession the Bicester Inn (now the Mitre Hotel), and Bishop William Smyth of Lincoln who gave the College the manor of Bushbury in Wolverhampton. In 1608-1609, through the beneficence of Sir Thomas Rotheram the west range of the chapel quadrangle was built, which was followed in 1629-1631 by the east range and the chapel itself. In 1640 a new cellar was excavated under the hall, and a ball court and bowling green created. Just as the College fortunes seemed to be secure, the Civil War broke out with the consequence that the College silver went to swell the royal mint, and when the Parliamentarians won, the loyalist Fellows were all expelled and replaced by nominees chosen by the parliamentary regime (5 of them were later deprived of their position after the Restoration in 1660). The College again thrived although was inconspicuous among its other richer and more distinguished neighbours.

In 1726, John Wesley was elected a Fellow (a position which he held until his marriage in 1751 when he was obliged to resign). His presence brought the College to prominence, since members of his Holy Club met in his rooms and the College was regarded as the cradle of Methodism. His portrait still hangs in the Hall, and his bust overlooks the front quadrangle. Following this fame, came obscurity in the form of Edward Tatham, who became rector in 1792. He was a brusque Yorkshireman who became unpopular with his own Fellows as well as heads of other Oxford institutions (e.g. he opposed the conferral of an honorary degree on Edmund Burke) to the point where the College suffered a severe decline in numbers and prestige.

Even today, despite many additions over the years, Lincoln still remains in many respects a classic example of a small 15th century college, and it is seen as a conservative institution which failed to admit female students until 1979.

Lincoln also has a long-standing rivalry with its neighbour, Brasenose College **(177)**, which was also founded by a Bishop of Lincoln, in that the two Colleges share a tradition revived annually on Ascension Day. Legend has it that, at one time, a mob chased students through the town and the Lincoln porter only allowed his own students to pass, refusing entry to a Brasenose member who was subsequently killed by the mob. An alternative (although less colourful story) is that the student actually died as a result of a duel with a Lincoln student. As a penance, on Ascension Day, members of Brasenose College are invited through the one door connecting the two Colleges for free beer (said to be flavoured with ivy so as to discourage excessive consumption).

Famous alumni include Dr. Seuss, John le Carré and John Radcliffe (who later fell out with the College).

OXFORD BOTANIC GARDEN

[The Oxford Botanic Garden with Magdalen Tower in the background]

In 1621 the Oxford Physic Garden was established by Henry Danvers (Earl of Danby). It is, surely the oldest such garden after those of Pisa and Leyden. The objective was to use the garden for 'the advancement of the faculty of medicine' but in fact it was used for botany, medicine, and practical gardening from the start. In 1840 it was renamed the Botanic Garden, and today it boasts an alpine garden, a fernery, a grass garden, herbaceous borders, a water garden, and a collection of historical roses. In the greenhouses are tropical plants (including bananas and rice), collections of ferns, succulents, orchids, insect-eating plants and water lilies. Notable firsts for the garden were the production of its own weed, the Oxford ragwort (*Senecio squalidus*), and the London plane tree (a hybrid of an oriental and American species raised in 1665).

[The Inigo Jones gate at the botanic gardens]

Danby had originally leased 5 acres of land from Magdalen College **(184)** for his garden, which had formerly been a Jewish burial ground. The ground had to be raised above the River Cherwell flood plain, which took 4,000 loads of 'mucke and dunge'. The gateway was built by Inigo Jones's master mason, Nicholas Stone, in 1632. An innkeeper, Jacob Bobart, who was also a competent gardener, became the first Keeper in 1642. The job had been offered to John Tradescant, most associated with the Ashmolean Museum, who due to failing health was unable to accept the post. Bobart was a good choice, and he produced the first catalogue of plants in 1648, by which time there were 1,600 specimens. The formal design of the garden was by Robert Morison, first Professor of Botany in Oxford, who had been superintendent of the Duke of Orlean's famous garden at Blois.

Bobart's son succeeded his father as Keeper, and after Morison's death became Professor of Botany. It was Professor Daubeny, appointed in 1834, who changed the name of the garden, and was the first to use it for experimental research. He also gave a party there for the victorious Darwinians after the famous debate between Huxley and Wilberforce, over which he had presided at the Oxford British Association meeting in 1860. A garden outside the entrance, designed by

172

Sylvia Crowe, now commemorates Oxford's wartime contribution to the science of antibiotics through the development of penicillin.

PORT MEADOW

[Some of the residents of Port Meadow]

The flat expanse known as Port Meadow (originally Portmaneit), has been common land since at least since 1086 when it was recorded in the Domesday Book as a place where 'all the burgesses of Oxford have a pasture outside the city wall in common, which pays 6s. 8d.'. Freemen of Oxford still have the right to graze horses and cattle on the land, and to make this easier in 1841 a bridge (Sheriff's Bridge) was built linking Walton Well Road **(131)** to the meadow. Pasturing is controlled by annual drives across the land by the Sheriff of Oxford. All animals present are impounded with Freemen and commoners with grazing rights being able to retrieve their animals for a nominal fee, while all others are fined. Sheep are not allowed on the meadow. Up until the 19th century horse racing also took place here on a pear-shaped course at the Wolvercote end. Although marshy in places, it was described as being 'more suited for a race-course than the one at Epsom' by Zacharias Conrad von Uffenbach when he visited in 1710.

Port Meadow was up to 500 acres in size, but by 1720 had been reduced to 439 acres, and more recently in 1970 to just 342 acres. There is a Bronze Age burial mound known as Round Hill on the east side of the meadow, and during World

173

War I an airfield was built on the north side. Since the ground has never been ploughed floating sweet-grass, water mint, and Oxford ragwort all thrive here, making Port Meadow a Site of Special Scientific Interest.

SHIP STREET

[Ship Street where Morse and Strange go for their supper]

This road, which runs from St. Michael at the North gate in Cornmarket to Turl Street **(225)**, has had many names in its time. In 1385 it was known as Somenors Lane after a man who rented the Blue Anchor inn here. In the 16th century it became Lawrence Lane after Lawrence Hall which stood on the east side of the churchyard, but by 1679 it was known as both St. Michael's Lane (after the church) and Jesus Lane (after the college in Turl Street). Before 1623 the road wound on through Catte Street **(211)**, ending at the City wall close to the East Gate.

At that time William of Wykeham bought the eastern part of the road, while Exeter College **(179)** owned most of the remainder. The name Ship Lane was not ascribed to the street until the 1760s, and may have been a mistake given that there was a sheep market nearby. It may well have originally been Sheep Lane. Nevertheless, by 1850 it was certainly Ship Street. Nearly all the houses in the street are Grade II listed, and survive unspoilt by modern development, making the street ideal for filming purposes. The City wall runs at the back of the houses on the north side of the street, and there is a bastion 26 feet high behind Nos. 1-3. St. Anne's College started life in Ship Street and its magazine is still called *The Ship*.

PART II
THE USUAL SUSPECTS*

*Locations used more than once in the series.

[*Endeavour* filming in Catte Street, Oxford]

OXFORD COLLEGES

BRASENOSE COLLEGE

SEEN IN: *Neverland, Arcadia, Harvest.*

[Brasenose College from Radcliffe Square]

The College takes its name from the bronze sanctuary knocker, first recorded in a document of 1279, which used to be attached to the main gate of the Brasenose Hall. The importance of the knocker was that colleges, like churches, were regarded as sanctuaries and so fugitives were safe from the authorities once they had clutched the knocker. It was removed to Stamford in the 1330s, since Oxford was considered at that time to be too turbulent a place for it to be secure. In 1890 it was brought back to Oxford and has hung ever since in the hall, above high table. Over the centuries many halls have occupied the site which today is Brasenose College. These included Burwaldescote (1247-1469), Amsterdam, St. Thomas's Hall (formerly Staple Hall), Sheld Hall, Ivy Hall, Little University Hall, Salysbury Hall, and Little Edmund Hall.

Brasenose College was founded in 1509 by William Smyth, Bishop of Lincoln, and Richard Sutton, a successful lawyer. Since at this time the original knocker was at Stamford, a new brazen nose was produced which contains the caricature of a human face. This knocker is currently located at the apex of the main gate,

177

while stained-glass representations may be found in the northern oriel window in the hall, alongside portraits of the two founders. The college coat of arms consists of devices of the founders and the diocese of Lincoln, and is one of only three known examples of tierced arms in England, the others belonging to Lincoln College and Corpus Christi College.

The College prospered due to the generosity of the early benefactors, though there was discontent among the Junior Fellows, who considered their income too low in comparison to the Senior Fellows and the Principal. It was not without financial scandal, to the extent that in 1643 some Fellows petitioned King Charles I to institute a Visitation. Most of these abuses flourished under the autocratic rule of Principal Radcliffe (1614-1648). However, despite these setbacks the college expanded to 21 Fellows from the original dozen. Probably the most famous Principal of the 16th century was Alexander Nowell, who is also credited with the invention of bottled beer.

[Left: The brazen nose knocker above the entrance, and Right: The sundial, dating from 1719, on the north side of the Old Quadrangle are the two most famous icons at Brasenose College]

After the Civil War in 1647 the College was in debt again and experienced a Parliamentary Visitation. Principal Radcliffe was ousted and Daniel Greenwood put in his place. He was largely responsible for turning the College finances around and ensuring the stability of Brasenose for the next century, during which time the place became firmly Jacobite. Whereas the 18th century saw Brasenose as a place of intellectual distinction, the 19th century saw it acquire a new reputation for sporting achievements, particularly in rowing and cricket.

Among the notables of Brasenose College are Sir Charles Holmes (director of the National Gallery from 1916-1928), John Buchan, Field-Marshall Earl Haig, Lord Scarman, Robert Runcie (former Archbishop of Canterbury), and John Mortimer. Today the College has 40 Fellows, 23 lecturers, 92 graduates and 329 undergraduates. Since 1974 it has been co-residential. In architecture the building is a curious amalgam of Gothic and Baroque.

As far as filming is concerned, Brasenose College can usually be recognised since producers often go for shots which incorporate the sundial – which adds a burst of gold against blue which emphasises the sunlit nature of the College's precincts – and with the Radcliffe Camera **(222)** looming large in the background.

EXETER COLLEGE

SEEN IN: *Fugue, Home, Nocturne, Ride, Arcadia, Coda, Harvest.*

[The chapel is heavily inspired by Sainte-Chapelle in Paris]

179

Walter de Stapledon (Bishop of Exeter and Treasurer to Edward II) was the founder of the Exeter College in 1314, though at that time it was known as Stapledon Hall. It was mainly a place for the education of prospective parish clergy and as such was one of the poorest of Oxford establishments and often in debt. In fact, the only income was from tithes of the Cornish church of Gwinear, and those from Long Wittenham in Berkshire, along with some Oxford property that in total amounted to not much more than £50 per annum in 1355. Originally there were only 13 Fellows, including the Rector and Chaplain, and the statutes stated that all of these, with the exception of the Chaplain, were to come from the diocese of Exeter and to study philosophy. There was no provision for the study of theology and the maximum term of stay was 13 years (comparatively short for those times). In 1405 the name was changed to Exeter College and by now more buildings had been added – St. Stephen's Hall, a chapel, a library, and what was known as Palmer's tower.

Fortunes were to change when William Petre, a former undergraduate of the College, became both powerful and wealthy, and on his retirement in 1566 devoted some time to reorganising the place. He endowed 7 new Fellowships that were now widened to include people from Devon, Somerset, Dorset, Oxfordshire and Essex. He gave four Oxford rectories (Kidlington, Merton, South Newington, and Yarnton) which provided financial stability, and made the Fellows' appointments for life. By the early 17th century the College had become a fashionable place for lawyers and politicians as well as the clergy, but all was to change again during the Civil War when King Charles I took much of the valuable silver for his own use.

It was not until the Victorian era that the College once again prospered, with Fellowships not being restricted by geography, and much building work taking place, with Sir George Gilbert Scott, who was also the architect behind the Martyrs' Memorial, being responsible for the present chapel, library, Rector's lodgings, Broad Street **(210)** gateway, and tower, and the range running west from the tower. The style was most certainly Gothic.

Among the famous who studied here are William Morris, Charles Lyell, R. D. Blackmore, J. R. R. Tolkien, Richard Burton, Alan Bennett, Sir Roger Bannister, and even Ralph Sherwin who was executed for his faith in 1581 and was later canonised by Pope Paul VI in 1970 and thus becomes the only Fellow of the college to become a saint.

Exeter College has been a favourite with both the *Inspector Morse* and *Lewis* production teams, having been used several times (most famously as the location where Morse has his final heart attack causing him to collapse on the lawn of Front Quadrangle). The College is also the setting for the fictional Jordan College in Philip Pullman's trilogy *His Dark Materials*, and it also appeared in the film adaptation of *The Golden Compass* (2007).

[The ramparts, where Joan Thursday takes her lunch in *Home*, overlook Radcliffe Square and the Radcliffe Camera]

HERTFORD COLLEGE (INCLUDING THE 'BRIDGE OF SIGHS')

SEEN IN: *First Bus to Woodstock, Girl, Trove, Arcadia, Game, Harvest.*

[The spiral staircase in the north-west corner of Old Quadrangle]

Hart Hall and Magdalen Hall are the true origins of Hertford College. The former site was bought by Elias de Hertford in 1283, but by 1490 was in the possession of Exeter College **(179)**. In 1572, there was much building work done to both Hart Hall, and the adjacent Blackhall (both halls being leased by Philip Randell, ex-Principal of Exeter College), which became linked with a passage and gateway forming the main entrance to both. John Donne, the poet, was a member of Hart Hall at this time.

182

The next major programme of building took place under the auspices of Principal Thornton, who was responsible for the original monumental gateway in Catte Street **(211)** which contained the library above. His successor, Dr. Newton aimed to have Hart Hall become a college in its own right within the University. Though this idea was not without opposition for many years, and consequently it did not receive its charter until November 1740. Dr. Newton wished the new Hertford College to be exclusively for the education of clergymen, and then only for scholars from middle-class families. As a concession he accepted gentlemen-commoners provided they agreed to pay double the fees. The college fortunes were erratic, in 1805 there were no students and only 2 Fellows. Without a qualified Principal the statutes of 1747 stated that the college must be wound up. Consequently, the buildings became part of Magdalen Hall, which had been founded in the late 15th century by William of Waynflete. The fact that it was an independent hall did not stop Magdalen College **(184)** making two unsuccessful attempts to gain control of it during the 17th century. In 1813, Dr. Macbride was appointed Principal to supervise the integration of Hertford College into Magdalen Hall. He was most successful, and even managed to defray all expenses in this connection, including the repair of Hertford College buildings and the construction of new ones, to Exeter College.

[Hertford Bridge, quite a tricky place to drive a bus under]

The fortunes of the hall improved, and in 1868 the new Principal, Dr. Michell, resolved to reinstate Hertford College. Again, there was opposition, but he had financial backing of Thomas Charles Baring who donated £30,000 for the endowment of 5 Fellowships. Later Baring was also to endow 30 undergraduate scholarships. Since then the college's academic performance has strikingly improved, and today it has around 600 undergraduates, and sits in the middle of the Norrington Table rankings of academic excellence.

Hertford Bridge, or the Bridge of Sighs as it is known to almost all, derives its name from the misconception that it resembles the bridge of the same name in Venice. In fact, its construction is more akin to the nearby, and much larger, Rialto Bridge. Hertford Bridge, was built by Sir Thomas Jackson in 1913-14, to simply link the two parts of Hertford College. There is an old (untrue) story that because of the bridge Hertford College students became the heaviest in Oxford, and consequently the authorities had to close it in an attempt to give the students more exercise. It is, however, a distinctive city landmark at the bottom end of Broad Street **(210)**, over New College Lane **(217)**, which today is a dead end, although in 1965 it seems that this was a major thoroughfare since the coach carrying a young Morse passes under the bridge at the beginning of *First Bus to Woodstock*.

MAGDALEN COLLEGE (INCLUDING MAGDALEN BRIDGE)

SEEN IN: *Trove, Game, Harvest.*

One of the most frequent images of Oxford used by artists, is Magdalen College as seen from Magdalen Bridge. The latter spans the River Cherwell and may be the original 'ox ford'. A bridge has been here since 1004. During the Middle Ages bridge-hermits were employed to help travellers with any difficulties. It is thought that first bridge was of wood and was replaced only in the 16th century by a stone structure of around 500 feet long with arches every 25 feet.

It is believed that William Waynflete, the founder of Magdalen College, may have paid for bridge repairs in the 15th century, and certainly by 1723 there are records to show that the University of Oxford was responsible for this task.

[Magdalen Bridge (date unknown)]

However, this was not enough, as the bridge was later condemned as being dangerous and was consequently rebuilt between 1772 and 1778 to the design of

184

John Gwynn. It was a toll bridge, complete with a tollhouse and gates across the road. The balustrade was designed by John Townesend. Apart from being widened in 1835, and again in 1882, the bridge remains much the same today.

[Cloister with Great Tower behind]

Magdalen College owes its founding to the aforementioned William Waynflete. The Hospital of St. John the Baptist, whose function it was to tend the sick and

185

assist needy travellers, was to become the home of Magdalen College. By 1458, while Waynflete was Chancellor of England, the number of brethren at the hospital had fallen to just five, which made it easy for him to suppress the hospital and transfer its buildings over to a new college for the study of theology and philosophy. However, although remodelling did not start until 1474, the main buildings were completed by 1481 thanks to the generosity of Waynflete himself and several endowments (including that of Ralph de Cromwell) which made it the wealthiest college in Oxford. The College was successful, and by 1565 had 132 'gentlemen-commoners' along with their servants.

During the Civil War the College was most certainly royalist, and even lent King Charles I the sum of £1,000. After the battle of Edgehill (which the royalists lost), Oxford became a garrison town, with Magdalen tower being used as an observation point and stocked with missiles to defend the London road. When the roundheads won the war, the chapel was stripped and most of the remaining College Plate and ornaments were sold off or destroyed.

[The New Building, River Cherwell and Addison Walk]

It was not until 1877 that sciences were allowed to be taught and 'ordinary-commoners admitted'. Only after World War I was an emphasis placed on academic achievement over social or sporting attainment. In 2010, the College topped the Norrington Table of academic excellence with the highest score achieved by any institution to date.

Within the College grounds is Addison's Walk, named after Joseph Addison (1672-1719) who was a fellow of Magdalen. It extends around a small island in the River Cherwell, and was a favourite walk of C. S. Lewis. The College is also fortunate enough to have a large meadow, The Grove, which occupies most of the ground north-west of the New Building and the Grove Quadrangle up to Holywell Ford. In the 16th century it consisted of gardens, orchards, and bowling greens, but today it is a large open space occupied by fallow deer.

From the top of Magdalen Great Tower each May Day choristers sing an invocation to summer and 'according to an ancient custom, salute flora at 4 o'clock in the morning with vocal music of several parts'. This custom probably originated in the 16th century, but by the 18th century listeners to the choir were in danger of being bombarded with rotten eggs and flour by undergraduates in the tower. Today the tradition continues, only at a slightly more civilised 6 o'clock, and includes Morris Dancers, punting, and champagne breakfasts.

MERTON COLLEGE

SEEN IN: *First Bus to Woodstock, Trove, Lazaretto.*

[The magnificent ironwork of St. Alban's Quadrangle]

Walter de Merton was an only son with no fewer than 7 sisters and 13 first cousins, and it was the size of his family that led him to establish an educational institution. He was a rich man, and at his death in 1277 he had 15 manors and pieces of land to his name. His first endowment was to be administered by Merton Priory, and entirely devoted to the support of male members of his family. By 1264 he had plans for an institution in Oxford to support 20 Fellows. Hence Merton College lays claim to being the oldest Oxford college, although at this time it had no buildings, only a statute.

Merton himself had been Chancellor to both King Henry III and King Edward I, and during his service had drawn up the aforementioned statutes for an independent academic community that most importantly would be self-governing, with all endowments going straight to the Warden and Fellows (with the only right of intervention being by the Visitor or Archbishop of Canterbury). By 1274 when he retired from royal service, there was an academic community consolidated at the present site of the college with a rapid programme of building taking place.

The initial acquisition included the parish church of St. John (which was superseded by the chapel when the former fell into 'a ruinous state') and three houses to the east of the church which now comprise the north range of the Front Quadrangle. De Merton also obtained permission from the King to extend south from these properties to the old City wall forming an approximately square site. The College continued to acquire other properties as they became available on both sides of Merton Street **(216)**.

The strength of Merton College lay in the teaching of medicine and theology as well as the arts, with what became known as the Merton School making considerable contributions to the study of mechanics, geometry, and physics throughout the Middle Ages.

Merton, unlike some other colleges picked its Fellows wisely since they had to be elected as vacancies became available and as resources allowed. Also, all Fellows had to already hold a degree and were expected to complete a probationary period of a year before being fully admitted to the College. Merton, therefore, became one of the most prestigious and wealthy of the Oxford colleges. For example, in 1599 the College was able to speculate and purchase the manor of Gamlingay St. George in Cambridgeshire for £1,830, and from this and other rents was able to build a large new quadrangle. Indeed, perhaps because of the somewhat better academic standards expected here, Merton men tended to gain positions of power and wealth and seldom forgot their old college in their turn.

188

[The Great Tower at Merton College was completed in 1450]

In 1548 the independent St. Alban Hall, owned by the convent of Littlemore, was purchased and incorporated into the College, although it continued as a separate institution until 1881 when it was finally annexed. During the Civil War the College was royalist to the extent that it provided both silver plate for the cause and accommodation for the Queen. However, the Warden was suspected of supporting the parliamentarians, and for this reason the College is often cited as being the only one in Oxford to side with parliament, with the actual College being moved to London at this time and the Oxford buildings being commandeered by the royalists.

189

The site of Merton College is rather hemmed in, with Merton Street and the old City wall providing barriers to the front and rear of the College, and Corpus Christi College and the old Littlemore Priory on the remaining two sides. Consequently, Merton was never able to develop its site further, but instead has remained a place of exceptional learning, wealth, and beauty. Since 2004 it has appeared at the top of the Norrington Table of academic excellence for Oxford 7 times. Famous alumni include Sir Basil Blackwell, Sir Thomas Bodley, Randolph Churchill, T. S. Eliot, William Harvey, and J. R. R. Tolkien.

Other premises owned by Merton College include the Old Walden's Lodgings **(83)** and the Old Faculty of Philosophy Building **(130)**, both of which have featured in *Endeavour*.

NEW COLLEGE

SEEN IN: *Sway, Canticle.*

Until 1400 this college was known as St. Mary College of Winchester in Oxford, its name was changed to distinguish it from the other St. Mary's College that later became Oriel College. Originally it was one of the 6 theology colleges, and was by far the largest, attended principally by those entering the clergy, with only scholars from Winchester being eligible to become Fellows. New College was the first to be based around a quadrangle that contained all the major buildings. The construction was overseen by the College founder, William of Wykeham, the Bishop of Winchester, who also was also responsible for the building of the royal lodgings at Windsor Castle. He was a shrewd businessman as well, for the site of the College was chosen because it could be bought cheaply since it was to be built on the site of a number of small plots that had been particularly affected by plague, and described at the time as 'full of filth, dirt, and stinking carcasses'. The foundation stone was laid on 5th March 1380, with the buildings being erected in increments between then and 1403, when the bell-tower was completed.

One of the most interesting buildings is the chapel, which is T-shaped, with an antechapel at right-angles to the nave. This allowed for worship in the nave simultaneously with private Masses conducted in the antechapel, where disputations and elections were also held. The chapel was built in the Perpendicular style, though decoration was restrained. The original roof was probably a tiebeam construction, but today a taller hammerbeam roof designed by Sir George Gilbert Scott survives, along with 62 of the original misericords in the Fellows' stalls, many of which show rich images of Oxford life, from a doctor lecturing, to scholars fighting with daggers. The rest of the wooden features and the figures on the reredos belong firmly in the Victorian era.

[The main entrance and Porters' Lodge from Holywell Quadrangle]

The Protestant Reformation was felt in the College when in 1528 the then Warden, Dr. London, deprived John Quinbey of his Fellowship because of his heresy. He was subsequently imprisoned in the bell-tower where he starved to death. While obeying the commands of King Henry VIII, which included destruction of many of the College's precious manuscripts, the College remained a centre for the

191

Catholic faith. This was to continue until Queen Elizabeth I purged many of the Catholic Fellows. In addition, the chapel altar was removed, much of the Medieval glass destroyed, and the reredos plastered over. As a result, the College was no longer seen as being at the forefront of religious leadership in Oxford.

However, New College continued to grow in size and even the Civil War did little to change the place, despite the cloisters acting as the main arsenal for the King's army, following the defeat at Edgehill in 1642. Cromwell did have 50 of the Fellows ejected, to be replaced by 55 new Fellows along with a new Warden, George Marshall, a Cambridge man. This was short-lived, for during the Restoration the College was again to thrive with the expulsion and appointment of yet more Fellows. Indeed, New College became the richest in revenues save for the colleges of Christ Church **(62)** and Magdalen **(184)**, although academically, with Fellowships being bought and sold, standards were to fall, as the College became more of a club where Fellows were 'much given to drinking and gaming and vain brutish pleasure' and where 'they degenerate in learning'.

There was at this time much building and redesigning taking place and nowhere more than in the chapel. Between 1736 and 1740 William Price of Hatton Garden restored the windows on the south side of the nave, while in 1765 William Peckitt of York repaired the north side and west window (the removed glass was sold to York Minster where it remains to this day). The Fellows disliked the new west window so much that in 1777 they had the glass moved to a window in the north-east of the nave, and commissioned Joshua Reynolds to design another west window, depicting the Nativity. Further, between 1789 and 1794 James Wyatt made a plaster vault in the roof and replaced the reredos with plaster imitations of the originals (though these were in turn replaced during the Victorian era by ones in stone, whose niches were filled with sculptures by J. L. Pearson).

With refurbished buildings came more rigorous academic standards, and from 1810, a consequent rise in undergraduate numbers, though for many years the college preserved its right of exempting its members from the University examinations. It was not until 1857 that various reforms (along with others over the next 30 years) were agreed upon, which brought the college into line with others. Today the New College is particularly strong in the sciences.

St. John's College

SEEN IN: *First Bus to Woodstock, Rocket, Arcadia.*

St. John's College was originally a monastic college called St. Bernard's and dates from 1437. In design the buildings, especially the Front Quadrangle, were based on those of New College **(190)**, though not as lavish due to lack of funding at the time. The tower was constructed in the 1470s, while the chapel was not consecrated until 1530. The east range was never completed.

[Front Quadrangle]

In 1539 St. Bernard's College was dissolved, although it remained an academic hall, and was given to Christ Church College **(62)**. Nine years later it was bought by Sir Thomas White, a Merchant Taylor and Alderman (and later Lord Mayor) of the City of London. It was he who founded St. John's College on the 29th May 1555, naming it after the patron saint of tailors. To help fund the College, he also made over 7 manors and enough money to purchase 2 further ones at Walton Oseney and Walton Godstow in North Oxford. Much of St. Giles' adjacent to the College was, and still is, owned by the St. John's College. In 1583 Bagley Wood was added, but despite all this (mainly undeveloped) land, the College remained poor and consequently little expansion took place, save for the Old Library which was constructed in 1596.

Canterbury Quadrangle in the Tudor Gothic style of the Old Library was also added. It had arcaded loggias, pedimented frontpieces, and Mannerist detailing, making it the first classical quadrangle in Oxford. It cost £3,000, and when opened in 1636, King Charles I and Henrietta Maria came to the College and were entertained by a play and dinner in the Laudian Library (for which the cost was

193

nearly as much as that for the construction of the building). Today, those parcels of land, which have now been developed, make St. John's one of the wealthiest colleges in Oxford.

[Canterbury Quadrangle]

Like many institutions, St. John's went through a period of hardship during the Civil War, but its fortunes changed during the Restoration at which time close relations with the government were resumed. It was traditionally a place of High Tory politics, at least until 1728 when a Whig President, William Holmes, was elected. To partially redress the balance, it should also be pointed out that Labour Prime Minister, Tony Blair, was an undergraduate here in the 1970s.

The remainder of the 18th century was a quiet time, and also one of stability, for the College. It returned to its earlier political views in the 19th century, and in 1834 entertained the Duke of Wellington upon his installation as Chancellor of the University. St. John's resisted all attempts to become a 'modern' institution with the last Fellow holding under the founder's statutes surviving until 1930. Up until then there had only been 4 heads in the previous 136 years. Today, the College is as 'modern' as any in Oxford, and can boast over 300 undergraduates, 100 graduates and 50 Fellows. Among the best-known alumni are Robert Graves, Philip Larkin, Kingsley Amis, and A. E. Housman.

SIR WILLIAM DUNN SCHOOL OF PATHOLOGY

SEEN IN: *Lazaretto, Harvest.*

Pathology was first taught at Oxford as part of general medical instruction, but by the mid-19th century had become a subject in its own right, along with anatomy

194

and physiology. When Sir Henry Acland became Reader of Anatomy in 1845, pathology was taught at Christ Church College **(62)** in the Anatomy School, but with the opening of the University Museum **(71)** in 1860, the collection of pathological specimens was transferred from Christ Church to Acland's new laboratory within the medical department of the Museum. Simultaneously, George Rolleston was appointed Linacre Professor of Anatomy and Physiology, and included pathological instruction in his lectures.

[The functional Sir William Dunn School of Pathology Building]

In 1899, with the University purchasing a large collection of pathological specimens from Holland the time was right for expansion. Fortuitously, an anonymous benefactor offered the University £5,000 for this purpose, and it was matched by another £5,000 from the University itself, so that in 1901 a new department could be opened. However, there was only an annual grant of £150 towards staff, and certainly no money for a Chair, which had to wait until 1907 when Danish experimental pathologist Georges Dreyer was appointed.

In 1922 the trustees of the late Sir William Dunn (a London banker, merchant and philanthropist who died in 1912), who had already made a grant to the University of Cambridge for a department and Chair in Biochemistry, were approached. There was opposition from anti-vivisectionists and those not wanting the 3 acres of the University Parks earmarked for a building being lost. However, on the 21st

195

November 1922 the sum of £100,000 was gifted to the University and in May the following year the foundation stone of the Sir William Dunn School of Pathology was laid. The architect was E. P. Warren, who worked closely with Professor Dreyer. Together they produced a design that has continued to be perfectly functional toady, albeit with one extension since its opening in 1927. Today the department performs research in cellular and molecular biology of pathogens, the immune response, cancer, and cardiovascular disease, as well as teaching undergraduate and graduate courses in the medical sciences.

. —. —.. . . — .... — ——— ... — .—.

Oxford Places

Bodleian Library

Seen in: *Fugue, Arcadia, Coda, Game, Lazaretto.*

[The statue of William Herbert, 3rd Earl of Pembroke and
Chancellor of the University of Oxford, outside the main
entrance to the Bodleian Library]

Opened in 1602 the Bodleian Library is one of the oldest libraries in Europe,
though not the first academic library in Oxford. That was situated in a room above
the congregation house at the University Church of St. Mary the Virgin **(206)**, and
contained books donated between 1317 and 1327 by Thomas Cobham, Bishop of
Worcester. The books were dispersed after his death to pay for his debts and

197

funeral expenses, but later redeemed and deposited in Oriel College. Around 1337 the Commissary of the University declared the library the property of the University of Oxford and had the books moved back to St. Mary's.

[Duke Humfrey's Library (date unknown)]

Other books followed from the library of Humfrey, Duke of Gloucester and younger brother of King Henry V. With this addition the room was not large enough, so the collection was scheduled to be moved to the Divinity School, then under construction. This was not to be completed, however, until 1489, more than 40 years after Humfrey's death in 1447. It was called the Duke Humfrey's Library and has an elaborate ceiling with arms of the University in the panels and the arms of Thomas Bodley at the intersections.

By the middle of the 16th century the University was in financial crisis, and according to Sir Thomas Bodley the Library 'in every part' lay 'in ruined and waste'. Much of the collection had also been dispersed, and it was Bodley who offered to bring the Library back to 'its proper use, and to make it fitte, and handsome with seates, and shelves and Deskes'. The building was refitted and restocked with books at the expense of Bodley, and other benefactors, and reopened on 8th November 1602.

In 1610 Bodley came to an agreement with the Stationers' Company, which undertook to send a copy of every book registered at Stationers' Hall to the Library. As might be imagined, the number of books in the Library increased dramatically, though Bodley did not accept everything sent to him since he considered many volumes to be 'idle bookes, & riffe raffes' which ought never to 'com into the Librarie'. Due to his own biases there was a poor representation of English literature and a complete absence of early editions of Jacobean dramatists for many years.

Soon extensions to the Library building were needed. The first was constructed over the Divinity School, between 1610 and 1612, and became known as the Arts End. The ceiling was painted with numerous coats of arms and the folios were chained to the lower shelves. Next the two-storey quadrangle, used for lectures, was rebuilt and a third storey for storage was added in 1624. This is the Schools Quadrangle. The old building was extended in the same style as the Arts End and became known as the Selden End, after John Selden, who gave eight thousand volumes to the Library along with a collection of oriental manuscripts. On the second floor is a frieze of some 200 famous men painted around 1620. Books continued to flood in from numerous benefactors including Alexander Pope, Benjamin Franklin, and Samuel Johnson, to the extent that by 1861 the library once more needed to expand – which it did by taking over the Radcliffe Camera **(222)**.

Space again needed to be found and in 1939, thanks mainly to a large donation by the Rockefeller Foundation, the New Bodleian Library building was completed. It should also be mentioned that Kenneth Grahame made the Bodleian Library his heir, and bequeathed the income resulting from the copyright of *The Wind in the Willows* in addition to the original holograph manuscript. Today the library has absorbed those of the Radcliffe Science Library, the Indian Institute, Rhodes House, the Law Library and the John Johnson Collection. It has around 11 million books on over 100 miles of shelving and is, as ever, in need of further room to expand.

BROAD WALK, MERTON FIELD & CHRIST CHURCH MEADOW

SEEN IN: *First Bus to Woodstock, Trove, Arcadia, Game.*

**[Broad Walk with Christ Church Meadow to the left
and Merton Field to the right]**

Just to the south of Christ Church College **(62)**, is Christ Church Meadow which runs behind the Faculty of Music and St. Aldate's police station. It is still grazed upon by cattle and in 1346 was said to be 46 acres in size. In fact, part of the land was a gift by Lady Montacute to maintain her chantry in the Lady Chapel in the original priory. The tourist should beware since there are restrictions to entry, outlined on the notice board in Rose Lane:

> The Meadow Keepers and Constables are hereby instructed to prevent the entrance into the Meadow of all beggars, all persons in ragged or very dirty clothes, persons of improper character or who are not decent in appearance and behaviour; and to prevent indecent, rude or disorderly conduct of every description.

Merton Field is a fenced off grass playing field north of the main part of Christ Church Meadow and south of Merton College **(187)**. Along the northern perimeter is Dead Man's Walk which follows the line of the old city wall, and Grove Walk **(111)** which leads to Merton Street **(216)**. Near to the eastern end of Dead Man's Walk is a plaque marking the first hot air balloon ascent in Britain, made by James Sadler in 1783.

200

[Top: Cricket being played on Merton Field, and Bottom: A break
between scenes with Broad Walk in the background]

Broad Walk is a wide avenue which runs between Christ Church Meadow on one side and Merton Field on the other. It was lined on both sides by elm trees, planted by John Fell in 1668, but they had to be cut down in 1976 due to Dutch elm disease. They were replaced by alternating oriental plane trees and hybrid plane. Appropriately enough the first hybrid plane was cultivated in the adjacent Oxford Botanic Garden **(171)** in 1665. Despite an attempt to make Broad Walk into a road, Merton Mall, it remains a pedestrian zone.

LAMB AND FLAG

**SEEN IN:** *First Bus to Woodstock, Arcadia.*

Originally owned by Godstow Abbey it was purchased by St. John's College **(192)**, along with the rest of St. Giles', around 1695 when it was just known as The Lamb (the current name referring to the symbol for St. John the Baptist). Much of the original building remains with clinker rooms and uneven floors adding to the atmosphere to the place. The main bar is adorned by heraldic crests of every college in Oxford.

[The Lamb and Flag in St. Giles', with Lamb and Flag Passage to the right of the building]

In *Endeavour* it is implied that this is the public house where Thursday has his lunchtime sandwiches, although invariably the interior is that of The Royal Standard of England **(229)** near Beaconsfield.

202

REWLEY HOUSE (DEPARTMENT OF EXTERNAL STUDIES)

SEEN IN: *Girl, Rocket.*

[Student accommodation, and a residence for Morse]

Rewley House occupies Nos. 3-7 Wellington Square **(226)** and belongs to the Department of External Studies. It is named after Rewley Abbey, founded in 1280 by Edmund, second Earl of Cornwall, and served as the residence for Cistercian monks studying at the University. It was abandoned at the time of the Dissolution of the Monasteries. The present structure dates from 1873 when Rewley House was erected as a girls' school. The school moved out in 1903, and the building became a furniture warehouse until 1926 when it was acquired by the University. It was refurbished by Thomas Rayson and opened in 1907 as the Centre for Extra-Mural Students. Another refurbishment took place in 1982 thanks to a grant of $3

203

million from the Kellogg Foundation, and it now contains a library, lecture theatre, dining and common rooms, teaching rooms, offices, and improved student accommodation.

It was as early as 1850 that the idea of taking the University to the masses was put forward by the Rev. William Sewell, who 3 years earlier had founded Radley College, Abingdon. He had to wait until 1878 though, for adult extension work to start. It was a success since by 1890 there were over 20,000 students taking such classes. Alongside classes, summer schools were introduced in 1888. In 1924 the extension lectures were to combine with classes given by the Workers' Educational Association to form the Delegacy for Extra-Mural Studies. International links were formed soon after World War II for which accommodation was required. Initially, in 1965, the Kellogg Foundation provided funding for residential accommodation for 67 persons. In time the Delegacy came under the General Board of Faculties as a University department based at Rewley House. Today around 4,000 non-residential, and 2,500 residential students, take upwards of 200 courses annually. In addition, about 3,500 students are accommodated at 14 summer schools housed in various colleges during the University holidays.

SHELDONIAN THEATRE

SEEN IN: *Fugue, Ride, Arcadia, Prey, Game.*

It was Gilbert Sheldon, Chancellor of the University, who commissioned and in doing so gave his name to this theatre. It was meant to be a building in which University business could be enacted, including ceremonies which had previously taken place in the University Church of St. Mary the Virgin **(206)**. Sheldon gave about £14,500 for the construction. The building was designed by a young architect friend of his by the name Christopher Wren, at that time the Savilian Professor of Astronomy. It is, in part, inspired by the open-air Theatre of Marcellus in Rome, and being classical in nature was said at the time to be revolutionary since it was like no other Oxford building. Completed in 1669, it was constructed from high quality stone in the lower half, but cheaper Headington stone elsewhere as money ran out. This part of the building did not last well and needed extensive renovation between 1959 and 1960.

The roof is of special interest since it allowed a span of 70 feet by 80 feet without supporting crossbeams. This was suggested to Wren by the mathematician John Wallis, who had been appointed Professor of Geometry in 1649. Originally the roof had dormer windows, but in 1838 these were replaced by the octagonal cupola designed by Edward Blore. The theatre holds two thousand seated people in tiers, and has an allegorical ceiling painting by Robert Streeter, sergeant painter to King Charles I, representing *Truth*, surrounded by *Justice, Law, Music,*

Geometry, Drama, Architecture, and *Astronomy*, triumphing over *Envy, Hatred,* and *Malice.* The woodwork includes a fine Chancellor's throne and two orators' pulpits, and there is also an organ dating from 1877.

[Students in academic attire exiting the Sheldonian Theatre under the watchful eye of a bowler-hatted University official, and two Emperors]

There is a large room over the ceiling that was the original headquarters of the Oxford University Press before it moved to the adjacent Clarendon Building. Books printed during this time have the inscription *E Teatro Sheldoniano.* Today the theatre is used for *Encaenia* (a meeting of Convocation presided over by the Chancellor on the Wednesday in the 9th week of the Trinity Term), degree ceremonies, voting by Convocation, and occasional concerts.

Christopher Wren commissioned William Byrd, an Oxford stonecutter and mason, to carve 14 stone heads for the front of the building. The heads were erected on stone columns in 1669, though it is not known whom the heads represent. They are known by many names including the Emperors' Heads, the Faceless Caesars, the Philosophers, and the Twelve Apostles, and may represent emperors, gods, or wise men. They were carved in good Headington stone and lasted two hundred years before they needed replacing. In fact, due to the construction of the Clarendon Building, there was only room for 13 of them to be replaced. However, these replacements were carved from poor quality Headington stone, which by the middle of the 20th century needed replacing again. So worn were they that John Betjeman compared them with 'illustrations in a medical textbook on skin diseases'. In 1970 they were taken down, and new heads, weighing about a ton each, and carved in Clipsham stone by Michael Black, were erected over the next 2 years. They were based, as far as possible, on the originals, although only 11 of them could be traced (mainly to private gardens around Oxford). Each has a beard, which has led Michael Black to state that they represent a history of beards.

UNIVERSITY CHURCH OF ST. MARY THE VIRGIN

SEEN IN: *Game, Lazaretto.*

The University Church of St. Mary the Virgin can justifiably be said to be at the heart of the City and University. For a start, it is located at the very centre of the old walled City, and in Medieval times when the City had no University buildings of its own, the scholars lived among their teachers in houses and adopted St. Mary's church as its centre. Indeed, as well as being a parish church, by the early 13th century the building was also the seat of University government and academic disputation, and the place where the degrees were awarded.

A century later, as the various colleges were being founded, more room was needed, so the Old Congregation House at the north-east side of the church, abutting the tower, was built with the help of money endowed by Bishop Cobham specifically to house his books. Hence the upper room now became the University library, with the books chained in place, along with the University chest (literally since this is where the University's money was kept in a chest), while the lower room (now the café) was the University's parliament. This practice remained in place until the middle of the 17th century, although today this is still the church where the University worships, with the formal University sermon being preached here in front of the Vice-Chancellor and Proctors on two Sundays each term.

The Church also has a connection with the 3 Oxford martyrs (Latimer, Ridley and Cranmer) who were first tried in the chancel in April 1554, with Ridley and

Latimer being tried here a second time in 1555 before being burnt at the stake on the 16th October the same year for their rejection of the doctrine of transubstantiation. Another famous figure associated with the Church is John Wesley, the founder of Methodism, who during his days as a Fellow of Lincoln College gave some of his most notable and stirring sermons here, including one in 1744 in which he denounced the 'laxity and sloth' of the senior members of the University. Not an entire surprise then, that following this sermon he was never asked to preach here again! He was in no way regretful of his actions, writing 'I have preached, I suppose, the last time in St. Mary's. Be it so. I am now clear of the blood of these men. I have fully delivered my soul'.

[The building that is the very heart of Oxford]

207

In 1828 St. Mary's welcomed a new vicar, John Newman, who was a Fellow at Oriel College and thought by many to be the most intelligent man in Oxford, as a consequence undergraduates flocked to his sermons. Matthew Arnold, an undergraduate at that time, wrote, 'Who could resist the charm of that spiritual apparition, gliding in the dim afternoon light through the aisles of St. Mary's, rising into the pulpit, and then, in the most entrancing of voices breaking the silence with words and thoughts which were a religious movement, subtle, sweet, mournful?' It was, however, the Assize Sermon on the 14th July 1833, preached by John Keble, which is considered to have launched the famous Oxford Movement in which Newman's leadership was so central. By 1843, Newman had become disillusioned with Anglicanism and resigned from St. Mary's. He was soon to be accepted into the Roman Catholic faith, and in 1879 became one of its cardinals.

Today visitors can walk around the Adam de Brome Chapel (which is furnished as a courtroom reflecting its earlier use), and the chancel where the aforementioned Oxford martyrs were tried, take refreshment in the coffee shop located in the vaults, or, for the more energetic, climb the tower for panoramic views of the city.

OXFORD STREETS

BRASENOSE LANE

SEEN IN: *Girl, Trove, Nocturne, Sway, Neverland, Arcadia, Game.*

[Disappointingly there are no parked cars for bodies to fall on]

Brasenose Lane is always easy to spot on film, since it has a gutter, or kennel, running down the centre of the street, just as it did in Medieval times when it was called Vicus St. Mildridae after St. Mildred's Church which once stood on the site where Lincoln College is today. It wasn't until the 17th century that it became Brasenose Lane after Brasenose College **(177)**, though in 1750 it is shown on

maps as being Exeter Lane after Exeter College **(179)**. The lane is not open to cars, though it is often used by scooters and motorcycles.

[Rain temporarily stops *Endeavour* filming in Brasenose Lane]

BROAD STREET

SEEN IN: *Girl, Trove.*

[Period coaches parked in Broad Street during filming of *Girl*]

The derivation of the street name is quite logical, though it was originally known as Horsemonger Street in the 13th century on account of it being a place where horses were sold. It was in this street, at a point marked by a white cross in the road surface (and also by a plaque on the wall of Balliol College), that the Oxford martyrs, Bishops Latimer and Ridley and Archbishop Cranmer, were burnt at the stake. Up until 1928 the centre of the street was used as a cab-stand, but since then it has been given over to car parking. Oxfam opened its first shop at No. 17 in 1948, and it remained the charity's headquarters until 1954. Blackwell's Bookshop has several premises in the street, including Nos. 48-51 and 53 in between which may be found the White Horse public house **(28)**.

Apart from the aforementioned Balliol College, Exeter College **(179)**, and Trinity College **(37)** may also be found here, along with the Museum of the History of Science **(33)**, the Sheldonian Theatre **(204)**, the Clarendon Building, and the latest extension of the Bodleian library **(197)** on the corner opposite the King's Arms public house **(51)**.

CATTE STREET

SEEN IN: *Girl, Fugue, Home, Sway, Arcadia, Prey, Harvest.*

[Actors are directed to their starting positions during the filming of *Girl* in Catte Street – Sean Evans is already onboard the double-decker bus]

This street runs from High Street to Broad Street **(210)** via the east side of Radcliffe Square **(222)**. All Souls College **(82)**, Hertford College **(182)**, and the

History Faculty Building are on the east side, while on the west side are the University Church of St. Mary the Virgin **(206)**, the Radcliffe Camera **(222)**, and part of the Bodleian Library **(197)**. So many iconic buildings, and the fact that it is a no through road, makes Catte Street ideal for filming purposes. The road has been here since around 1210 when it was known as Kattestreete, though over the years it has also been called Cate Street, Kate Street, and Cat Street. It was even referred to as the 'street of mouse-catchers'. In the 14th century it housed shops and small tenements on both sides. The street name is the diminutive of Catherine, and hence in the 19th century it was known as St. Catherine's Street. It was only in 1930 that the City Council decided to revert to Cat Street, but with the older spelling of Catte. Up until 1973 when it was pedestrianised it was a heavily congested road since it was the main route between east and west Oxford.

[Left: The telephone box from which Denis Bradley makes a call in *Girl*, and Right: The Norris residence in *Home*, which is actually part of Hertford College]

HOLYWELL STREET

SEEN IN: *Girl, Home, Neverland, Ride, Arcadia, Coda, Game, Lazaretto.*

Once part of Holywell Manor (and owned by Merton College since the 13th century) this street, which runs between Broad Street **(210)** and Longwall Street, contains many 17th and 18th century houses. No. 17, which was used in filming *Girl*, was at one time the King's Head public house with the timber frame dating from the 16th century. The author, J. R. R. Tolkien lived at No. 99 between 1950 and 1953.

**[Looking up Holywell Street from New College, with the
Alternative Tuck Shop, where Thursday is a regular
patron, on the very right of the picture]**

The two most notable buildings in the road are the Holywell Music Room (an historic chamber music venue built in 1742) and New College's Holywell Building **(190)** designed by Sir George Gilbert Scott and Basil Champneys, and built between 1872 and 1896. Running behind is the best-preserved section of the original City wall. Another favourite *Endeavour* location is the Alternative Tuck Shop on the corner with Mansfield Road from which Thursday can be seen periodically purchasing his tobacco. Since 1975 there has been a gate across the eastern end, making Holywell Street closed to through-traffic, and consequently ideal for filming.

KING EDWARD STREET

SEEN IN: *First Bus to Woodstock, Sway.*

Unusually for Oxford, this street has had the same name since it first came into existence in 1872. It is one of only two major streets, the other being New Road, that was made within the City walls since the Middle Ages. It was cut by Oriel College through its own property, and necessitated the demolition of Nos. 109 and

110 High Street (to make the road wide enough) for which the College had to pay £600. The rebuilt No. 109 High Street, now a corner property, is the premises of University outfitters Shepherd and Woodward. The houses in the street were in the main designed by Frederick Codd who was a supporter of Gothic Revival architecture. In 1881 Cecil Rhodes kept an academic residence at No. 6 King Edward Street.

[**The entrance to the residences of Miles Percival and Luisa Armstrong in *First Bus to Woodstock* and *Sway* respectively**]

MARKET STREET

SEEN IN: *Girl, Ride, Coda.*

Between 1330 and 1340 it was known as Le Cheyne Lane for it had a chain, probably supported on posts, at the west end. The road lead from Lorineria, that part of Cornmarket devoted to harness fittings made of metal, to Turl Street **(225)** close to Jesus College. Indeed, it was later known as Jesus College Lane, but also Bedford Lane and Adynton's Lane after two families who had property here. It was only with the building of the covered market between 1772 and 1774 that people started to refer to it as Market Street, or Market Lane, though right up until

214

1837 it still appears on some maps as Jesus Lane. There was also the Church of St. Mildred that stood on the site of Lincoln College (at the junction with Turl Street at its east end), so it is probable that at some point it was also known locally as Mildred Lane. As far as filming is concerned it has been used in *Endeavour* as the place where buses and coaches seem to have their city terminus.

[In *Endeavour* **Market Street seems to be the departure point and terminus for all Oxford buses and coaches**]

215

MERTON STREET

SEEN IN: *Fugue, Trove, Nocturne, Arcadia, Coda, Game.*

[Looking north along Merton Street]

Being the only significant remaining cobbled road (with the exception of Radcliffe Square which is not open to traffic) in Oxford, Merton Street is invariably used in filming whenever possible. It runs from Oriel Square **(19)** to High Street passing Merton College **(187)**, Corpus Christi College, Christ Church College **(62)**, the back of University College, Grove Walk **(111)**, Logic Lane **(140)**, Old Warden's Lodgings **(83)**, and the (old) Faculty of Philosophy Building **(130)**.

216

In the 13th century this L-shaped street was called Vicus Sancti Johannis (and later between 1661 and 1666 as St. John Baptist's Street) after the church, now Merton College's chapel. By 1751 the whole street had become King Street, and the street retained this name until the late 19th century. Merton Street only referred to the entire length of the road in the 20th century (though the eastern section of the road was known as Merton Street in around 1838). In the mid-18th century there was a public house on the west side of the lane, and for this reason the eastern portion of the road adjoining High Street was known as Coach and Horses Lane. Famous residents have included Siegfried Sassoon (No. 14), Michael Brock, and J. R. R. Tolkien who took rooms here in the 1970s shortly before his death in 1973.

NEW COLLEGE LANE

SEEN IN: *First Bus to Woodstock, Trove, Arcadia.*

[The Old Lodge entrance to New College in New College Lane]

217

Named after New College **(190)**, the lane runs from Catte Street **(211)**, under the Bridge of Sighs **(182)** until, after two right-angled bends, it joins Queen's Lane **(221)** by the lodgings of the Provost of The Queen's College. It also leads to the Old Lodge entrance of New College. It has been called New College Lane from at least 1648, but was originally a longer thoroughfare since it continued on from Catte Street to High Street.

St. Helen's Passage **(224)** leads off from the lane close to the Bridge of Sighs, and is next to the house once occupied by Edmond Halley (discoverer of Hailey's Comet). There is also a small gate, known as 'the non licet gate', which the Lord Mayor and members of the Oxford City Council use on their traditional periodic inspection of the City walls located within the bounds of New College. The College is obliged to open the gate whenever a representative of the City knocks on it, after which the robed civic party, enters and climbs the walls to inspect them.

PARK TOWN

SEEN IN: *First Bus to Woodstock, Fugue, Trove, Sway, Neverland, Ride.*

[The curved roofs in Park Town are unique for Oxford]

Park Town is one of the most well-known streets in central North Oxford, and was also one of the earliest planned suburban developments in the area. The Park Town Estate Company was formed in September 1857, through the efforts of Samuel Lipscomb Seckham. The elegant houses and gardens that resulted were originally surrounded by ornamental iron railings. Unfortunately, many of these were removed during World War I to help war effort in manufacturing guns and ships. Park Town includes two crescents of townhouses, surrounding communal gardens, together with a number of larger villas.

[Morse is billeted here in *First Bus to Woodstock*]

Miss Sarah Angelina Acland, daughter of Sir Henry Wentworth Acland, lived at No. 10 for a time. Her interest in colour photography at the turn of the century produced a number of interesting early examples, which are held at the Museum of the History of Science **(33)** in central Oxford. It seems to be a favourite residence for Morse too, for it is here in Park Town that he first has accommodation in *First Bus to Woodstock*, and also the place to which he returns to share a flat in the main crescent with Monica Hicks for several episodes, just a few doors down from where Dr. Daniel Cronyn lived in *Fugue*.

It is a very much sought-after area with most of the properties being Grade II listed and extending over 4 floors with high ceilings. They were built in the Regency style, and although many have been converted into flats, single occupancy residences can be found on the market for around £2 million.

219

[Morse and Monica Hick's inhabited the end of terrace residence]

PUSEY STREET

SEEN IN: *First Bus to Woodstock, Home.*

Edward Bouverie Pusey was the grandson of the 1st Viscount Folkestone, and the son of Philip Bouverie, who changed his name to Pusey on inheriting the family's estate in the Berkshire village of the same name. He attended Eton College in 1812, and 7 years later went on to study Classics at Christ Church College **(62)**. After this he became a Fellow at Oriel College, where he developed a close friendship with John Keble and John Henry Newman, both of whom were also Fellows of the College. He went on to study German and theological literature, as well as oriental languages, and was subsequently ordained into the Anglican Church. Later he was appointed Regius Professor of Hebrew and spent time cataloguing the Arabic manuscripts in the Bodleian Library **(197)**.

He opposed liberalism in the Church, and by the 1830s was a leader in the Oxford Movement. It was said that he exercised a profound influence in Oxford due to his preaching in Oxford's two main churches, Christ Church Cathedral and at the University Church of St. Mary the Virgin **(206)**. He was not without controversy since after one sermon he was suspended from preaching by the University for 2 years.

[The entrance to the Moonlight Rooms]

It seems appropriate then, that such a man be commemorated with a street name, and in 1925 the Oxford City Council decided to rename Alfred Street, St. Giles' as Pusey Street. No. 5 is a Grade II listed building while on the other side of the street is Regent's Park College, the entrance of which became that of the Moonlight Rooms in *Home*.

QUEEN'S LANE

SEEN IN: *Fugue, Trove, Arcadia, Lazaretto.*

Prior to Queen's Lane there was a thoroughfare here called Torald Street. Its line was slightly different and went straight through from High Street to Holywell Street **(212)**. On a 1762 map of Oxford the part of the street that passes St. Edmund Hall **(26)** was known as St. Edmund Hall Lane, a name that continued to be in common use until at least 1821. Queen's Lane also passes the church of St. Peter-in-the-East **(36)**. Today, the street, which runs from New College Lane **(217)** to High Street, is narrow and in the main flanked by high stone walls. It also affords excellent views of some good examples of gargoyles on the college buildings beyond the walls.

[In *Lazaretto* the body of the would be assassin, Tam Fraser, was found in a car parked in this section of Queen's Lane]

RADCLIFFE SQUARE & RADCLIFFE CAMERA

SEEN IN: *Girl, Home, Sway, Neverland, Ride, Arcadia, Coda, Game, Canticle, Lazaretto, Harvest.*

When he died in 1714, John Radcliffe, the physician, academic, and politician, left £40,000 for the building of a library in Oxford. It took over 20 years for this plan to come to fruition however. The rotunda form for the structure was originally proposed by Nicholas Hawksmoor, but the final design was based on plans created by James Gibbs. The building was begun in 1737, and was completed in 1748, and was opened in 1749 by Dr. William King, the Vice-Chancellor and Principal of St. Mary Hall. It is believed to be the first round library in the country, and was originally intended to be a science library, though today the books found there are mainly devoted to the arts.

[The Radcliffe Camera dominates Radcliffe Square]

The plasterwork in the splendid domed upper room is by Joseph Artari, Charles Stanley, and Thomas Roberts. The square is the 'heart of Oxford' and according to Sir Nikolaus Pevsner 'is unique in the world'. He later added, 'or, if that seems a hazardous statement, it is certainly unparalleled at Cambridge'. It was at one time condemned due to the large size of its pebbles, which were ruinous to shoes. The defeat of Napoleon was celebrated here in 1814 by a dinner given to four thousand poor people.

The whole area is a favourite filming location, for nothing says Oxford more than a shot of this Square and its surroundings. On the north side is the Bodleian Library **(197)**, running through the Square from north to south on the east side is Catte Street **(211)** which passes All Souls College **(82)**, while the south side of the Square is taken up entirely with the University Church of St. Mary the Virgin **(206)**, and on the west side can be found the entrance to Brasenose College **(177)**, one end of Brasenose Lane **(209)** as well as Lincoln College and Exeter College **(179)** both of which back onto the Square.

St. Helen's Passage

SEEN IN: *First Bus to Woodstock, Lazaretto.*

[Stairway to the *Oxford Mail*]

St. Helen's Passage is a narrow alleyway off New College Lane **(217)**, which leads to the Turf Tavern and Bath Place. It winds to avoid buildings in New College Lane and also Holywell Quadrangle of Hertford College **(182)**. This pedestrian passage had formerly been known as Hell Passage, though it is not certain if this because of the disreputable gaming house that was once here, or the fact that it is very dark due to the high City wall which runs along one side of the aforementioned Turf Tavern. In 1963 future Australian Prime Minister, Bob Hawke, set a Guinness World Record by drinking a yard glass of ale in just 11 seconds. President Bill Clinton famously did 'not inhale' here during an evening session while he was an Oxford Rhodes Scholar.

St. John Street

SEEN IN: *First Bus to Woodstock, Girl.*

The first St. John Street is now Merton Street **(216)**. The new one runs from Wellington Square **(226)** to Beaumont Street. It was begun in 1825 as part of a speculative development by St. John's College **(192)**, and completed around 10 years later. It comprises unified terraces, in a simple Georgian style, of 3-storey houses with cellars. Each is constructed of brick, but with Bath stone fronts, moulded cornices and parapets. Today they are all Grade II listed properties.

[Left: Wendy Spencer's home, and Right: Looking from Pusey Street to the junction with St. John Street used in the final scene of *First Bus to Woodstock*]

William Turner, the Oxford painter (not to be confused with the more famous J. M. W. Turner), was a long-time resident at No. 16. Other notable residents have included P. D. James and J. R. R. Tolkien. It was at No. 12 that Mensa International was founded in 1946 by Lancelot Ware and Roland Berrill. On the corner of St. John Street and Wellington Square is Rewley House **(202)**, and at the other end of the street is the Sackler Library. In *First Bus to Woodstock* it is at the junction of St. John Street and Pusey Street **(220)** that fake traffic lights were set up so that while stationary Thursday can ask Morse where he sees himself in 10 years time – the answer being given visually as Morse looks into the rear view mirror of the Jaguar and sees the eyes of John Thaw. It is also at this junction that Wendy Spencer, Morse's first great love, lived at No. 22.

TURL STREET

SEEN IN: *Rocket, Trove, Neverland, Coda, Game, Harvest.*

This is an ancient street running between Broad Street **(210)** and High Street. It gets its name from a revolving (twirling) gate which was in a postern in the City wall at the Broad Street end, but was demolished in 1722. Almost the whole of the east side of the street is taken up by Exeter College **(179)** and Lincoln College, while the west side has a row of mainly late 18th century stucco and timber-framed houses, along with Jesus College. At No. 15 is the Oxfam bookshop which has featured as a number of establishments in the *Endeavour* series.

[The Oxfam bookshop and Norah's Antiques in Turl Street –
both have appeared as different establishments in *Endeavour*]

WELLINGTON SQUARE

SEEN IN: *Arcadia, Prey, Harvest.*

[Morse's basement flat on the
east side of Wellington Square]

The Square was formerly the site of a workhouse built in 1772 to accommodate 200 paupers. In the 1790s a nursery, and a ward for the elderly and infirmed people were added. It was not a desirable area given that nearby was Rats and Mice Hill, so named after a hillock of rubbish inhabited by said rodents. The workhouse moved to Cowley Road in 1860, and between 1869 and 1876 the Square was developed by the University, resulting in the dwellings that can be seen today. It is named after the Duke of Wellington, who apart from all his other achievements, had also been the Chancellor of the University (1834-1852).

226

The houses on the north side of the street were pulled down in 1969 to make way for the University Offices (i.e. the central administration building which among other things deals with undergraduate admissions). On the corner with St. John Street **(224)** is Rewley House **(202)**.

BUCKINGHAMSHIRE

FORTY GREEN - THE ROYAL STANDARD OF ENGLAND

SEEN IN: *First Bus to Woodstock, Trove, Nocturne, Sway, Neverland, Arcadia, Prey, Harvest.*

[The Royal Standard of England where you can get 'drunk for a penny']

Forty Green, near Beaconsfield, is reputedly the home of one of England's oldest public houses. Once known by the local West Saxons as *Se Scip,* meaning 'the ship', The Royal Standard of England public house lies tucked away in a tiny

229

country lane. Legend has it that young Prince Charles hid away in the pub's priest hole whilst on his way to escaping to France in 1651, after the battle of Worcester.

After King Charles II's restoration to the throne, the new king honoured the landlord for his support by agreeing to change the name from The Ship to The Royal Standard of England. An alternative account says that the public house got its name because the King often met his mistresses in one of the bedrooms.

[The bench where Thursday takes his sandwich lunch with Morse]

In the early days, the alehouse was used as a meeting place for local villagers. The Saxons even brewed ale on the site. Because it is so old, it is inevitable that there are ghost stories associated with the location. The most famous dating from the Civil War, tells of a group of parliamentarian soldiers who staked a group of cavalier's heads on pikes outside the door. Included among these was that of a 12 year-old drummer boy, who is said to haunt the building today. Another tells of an unfortunate traveller who was crushed to death by a speeding stagecoach, and is said to haunt the bar.

At the beginning of the 18th century, the upstairs rooms were used for gambling, whoring, and drinking large quantities of alcohol, to the extent that the sign over the doorway still depicts the famous legend: 'Drunk for a penny, Dead drunk for two pennies, Clean straw for nothing'.

This atmospheric public house has attracted various filming and television productions including *Hot Fuzz* (2007), *The Boys are Back in Town* (2008), *The Theory of Everything* (2014), and several *Midsomer Murders* episodes.

[The stained-glass panel often appears in shot]

HAMBLEDEN - ST. MARY THE VIRGIN CHURCH & VILLAGE

SEEN IN: *Girl, Home, Harvest.*

The well-preserved village of Hambleden, about 3 miles from Henley-on-Thames, is actually at the heart of the Hambleden Estate, which comprises some 1,600 acres of mature beech woods, pastures, and chalk valleys in the Chilterns. The name Hambleden originates from the Anglo-Saxon for 'crooked or irregularly-shaped hill', and is listed in the Domesday book as Hanbledene, though it was also known as Hamelan dene at least until 1015.

The manor house, opposite the church, the home of Maria Carmela Viscountess Hambleden, was built in 1603 in the Jacobean style for Emanuel, the 11th Baron Scrope (who later became the Earl of Sunderland). King Charles I stayed in the house overnight in 1646, while fleeing from Oxford. Lord Cardigan, famous for leading the ill-fated Charge of the Light Brigade, was born here in 1797 (and until recently his sea chest could be seen in the church – unfortunately it was stolen). In 1932 the manor was bought by the Right Honourable W. H. Smith, a descendant of the founder of the newspaper shop chain of the same name. It remained in the Smith family until 2008, when the western part of the estate was sold to the Swiss financier Urs Schwarzenbach.

Cottages of brick and flint, with dormer windows and topped with red tiles make up the majority of the properties in the village. There is also a water pump, a post office, a village store, a church, and a chestnut tree in the middle of the village. Visitors are often surprised to discover that this place is not in deepest rural England, but only 40 miles from the centre of London.

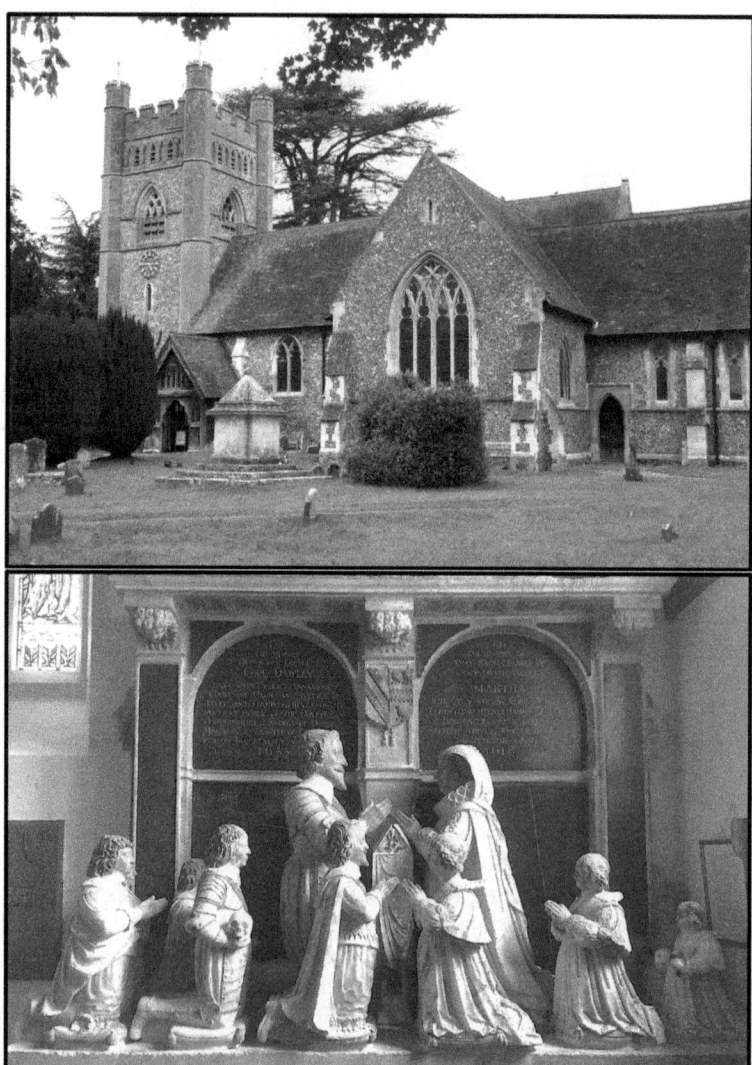

[Top: The church which plays a central role in *Girl*, and
Bottom: The Cope D'Oyley memorial]

232

The large church of St. Mary the Virgin dates from the 12th century, and in keeping with other buildings in the village is constructed from local flint and chalk with stone dressings under an old tiled roof. The tower boasts 8 bells, the oldest of which dates back to the 15th century, and is one of the few pre-Reformation bells still in use. Inside there is an impressive 17th century memorial to Cope D'Oyley, his wife, and his ten children.

[Previous Page, Top: In *Home*, Morse returns to the family house,
supposedly in Lincolnshire, but actually just outside the village,
Previous Page, Bottom: In *Harvest*, Morse makes (unsuccessful)
enquiries about Dr. Laxman along this row of cottages,
This Page: and also asks about the disappearance at the butchers,
Following Page, Top: the local garage and finally,
Following Page Bottom: at the Post Office and general stores]

234

[Top: Dr. Berger's house from *Harvest*, and
[Bottom: the Levin home from the same episode]

236

[The Stag and Huntsman became the Hanged Man in *Harvest*]

The village and its surroundings can be seen in a range of film productions including *Chitty Chitty Bang Bang* (1968), *Dance with a Stranger* (1985), *101 Dalmatians* (1996), *The Avengers* (1998), *Sleepy Hollow* (1999), *Band of Brothers* (2001), *Nanny McPhee and the Big Bang* (2010), and *Into the Woods* (2014). On the small screen it has made appearances in *As Time Goes By*, *Shelley*, *Cranford*, *Poirot*, *Marple*, *Rosemary & Thyme*, *Down to Earth*, and *The New Avengers*, as well as several episodes of *Midsomer Murders*.

QUAINTON - BUCKINGHAMSHIRE RAILWAY CENTRE

SEEN IN: *Fugue, Neverland.*

With around 1,300 inhabitants, Quainton village lies in the Vale of Aylesbury, about 5 miles from Aylesbury's busy town centre. The name is Old English meaning 'Queen's Estate' (*cwen tun*), which probably refers to Edith, the wife of

King Edward the Confessor. This is feasible since Edward had a palace at nearby Brill. Originally the village was called Quainton Malet, which referred to the Malet family who owned the local manor from 1066 to 1348. The family had associations with the Order of the Hospitallers, who are credited with both the rebuilding of the Church of St. Mary & the Holy Cross around 1340, and the erection of the preaching cross on the village green. The shaft and base of the cross still remain. Many of the half-timbered and thatched cottages, which the village is renowned for, can be found around the green. An imposing windmill towers over the heart of the village. This huge structure, 65 feet high to the top of the brickwork and a further 8 feet to the top of the dome, was built between 1830 and 1832, but sadly stood derelict for most of the 20th century. It is the tallest mill in Buckinghamshire and is a Grade I listed building.

**[It was along this stretch of track that the body
of Eric Patterson is found in *Neverland*]**

Close to Quainton is the Buckinghamshire Railway Centre, a working steam museum, which provides a step back in time to its visitors (www.bucksrailcentre.org). The London Railway Preservation Society was formed in 1962. However, they did not have suitable space to display their exhibits. In 1971 they were absorbed by the Quainton Railway Society who had taken possession of the old Metropolitan Line railway station of Quainton Road. Apart from the station, there were extensive sidings to which was added a former building from Wembley Park that became the maintenance shed. A bonus was the fact that the mainline from Aylesbury passes through the site, so it is possible to run special trains to and from Aylesbury, and further afield.

[The body of Evelyn Balfour, along with a written clue, is found in a freight van in the sidings behind the steam locomotive in *Fugue*]

What started as a modest collection housed on a 25 acre site, has grown into around 170 items of locomotives and rolling stock in buildings dating from 1874 to the 1960s (and includes World War II warehouses of the Ministry of Food Buffer Depot). The museum actually has two stations, since in 1999 the old Rewley Road station (the Oxford terminus of the Oxford to Cambridge line) was re-erected and is used as part of the visitor centre and main offices.

Films such as *Otley* (1969), *11 Harrowhouse* (1974), *The Masks of Death* (1984), *The Woman in Black* (1989), and *The Crucifer of Blood* (1991) have all been filmed here, and it has made television appearances in *Doctor Who: The Black Orchid*, and *Midsomer Murders*.

WEXHAM - BLACK PARK

SEEN IN: *Ride, Prey, Harvest.*

[The magnificent lake at Black Park which Morse lives beside in *Ride*]

Black Park is a country park in Wexham, between Slough and Iver Heath, which rather conveniently backs onto Pinewood Studios **(148)**, and has a private gate to allow unhindered access for film crews. Managed by Buckinghamshire County Council, it covers over 500 acres of woodland, heathland, grassland, and a large lake (covering 14 acres), with some areas being designated as Sites of Special Scientific Interest. The park is actually part of the historic Langley Estate. First mentioned in 1202, it has belonged variously to Henry VIII, Princess Elizabeth and the 3rd and 4th Dukes of Marlborough. The lake contains carp, bream, pike, perch, and roach, while on the surface visitors can see swans, grebes, coots, and moorhens. There are around 13 miles of footpaths, cycle paths, and majestic pine tree-lined avenues (which lend their name to the adjacent film studios) all of which are accessible to the public every day of the year between 8 o'clock and dusk.

It should come as no surprise, then, that the park continues to be used by many film and television companies. In the past the woods and lake featured prominently in the Hammer Horror films from the late 1950s to the 1970s. In these films the location was often used to represent Transylvania. The park has also been used 4 times in the James Bond films. It first became Switzerland for part of the famous Aston Martin DB5 car chase scene in *Goldfinger* (1964) as James Bond tries unsuccessfully to evade Oddjob. It appeared again in *Octopussy* (1983) as India, with James Bond emerging from the lake in a crocodile camouflage. In *The World is Not Enough* (1999) Black Park's versatility was again illustrated when it doubled for Azerbaijan, where tree felling from a

240

specially equipped helicopter was very much in evidence, and most recently it was a substitute for Uganda and the meeting between Le Chiffre and Obanno (the leader of a guerrilla group) in *Casino Royale* (2006). Five Carry On films, several Harry Potter productions, Monty Python's *And Now For Something Completely Different* (1971), *Atonement* (2007), *A Challenge for Robin Hood* (1967), *Wombling Free* (1977), *Batman* (1989), *Scrooge* (1970), *Stardust* (2007), *Treasure Island* (1950), *Willow* (1988), *The Wolfman* (2010), *The Charge of the Light Brigade* (1968), *Eden Lake* (2008), *Fahrenheit 451* (1966), *Johnny English* (2003) where the park café was used, *Superman II* (1980), *Supergirl* (1984), *Agent Cody Banks* (2003), *Sleepy Hollow* (1999), and *Alice in Wonderland* (2010) are among many other productions that have all been filmed here.

On the small screen the location was used in *Regan* (the pilot of *The Sweeney*), *The Sweeney* (3 episodes), *The Professionals* (2 episodes) *Blake's 7* (where it appears as various different planets in 3 episodes), *UFO* (5 episodes), *Film Fever*, *Doctor Who* (2 episodes), *Midsomer Murders*, *New Tricks*, and *Waking the Dead* (in which a car was driven into the lake and later recovered).

In fact, during an average year there are around 200 days that the park is rented out for filming, bringing much needed income to the authorities, who charge anywhere between £2,500 and £4,000 a day. However, a filming day also includes the time to set up a production as well as clearing the site after filming. For example, the Harry Potter crew actually inhabited the park for the best part of 3 months, although the scenes shot lasted on screen for less than 2 minutes and were filmed over just 5 days.

If you proceed from the café and information centre along the east side of the lake, you would find the place where scenes from *The Lost Prince* (2003), *Wolfman* (2010), *First Knight* (1995), *Robin Hood* (2010), *Son of Rambow* (2007), and the Lumberjack's song from *And Now For Something Completely Different* (1971) were all filmed. It should be noted that the lake is equally at home substituting for a river, and has been the River Thames more than once in its film career.

Continuing on from the top of the lake, you will soon come to a clearing where parts of *Henry VIII* (2003) with Ray Winstone, the guerrilla camp scene in *Casino Royale* (2006), *The Mummy Returns* (2001), *Midsomer Murders* where a body is found on Whiteoaks golf course in the 2009 episode entitled *The Dogleg Murders*, and most importantly the first two Harry Potter films were all shot. In *Harry Potter and the Philosopher's Stone* and *Harry Potter and the Chamber of Secrets* this became the Forbidden Forest, and on the far side of the open space is where Rubeus Hagrid's hut could be found. It was a small wooden cabin situated on the edge of the Forbidden Forest and to the north-east of Hogwarts Castle. Not much further along the main path the walker will come to a junction at which you should turn right and follow the line of trees to a crossroads. Here you would appear to be in the middle of a forest, with a wide track in every direction cutting through dense pine woods. This is where the helicopter tree-felling scene in *The World is Not Enough* (1999) and many of the Hammer Horror and Carry On films were shot. It is where nearly 3 months of preparation were involved for the shooting of *Harry Potter and the Order of the Phoenix*, and also the location where the body of Jeannie Hearne is discovered in *Ride*.

[Close to here is where the body of Jeannie Hearne was dumped]

From here you need to turn right (i.e. south) and follow the main path back towards the lake. You will pass the spot where Morse resides in his lakeside shack. In fact, you are now walking parallel to the path you took from the visitor's centre, and will soon come across a clearing of great film significance. Not only was this the site for part of the alpine car chase in *Goldfinger* (1964) and the location of Fort Knox in the same film, but it is also where one might find giant spiders, hippogriffs, unicorns, dragons in cages, and the odd basilisk. Close to the bench in memory of Mervyn Jenkins is where scenes in *Harry Potter and the Philosopher's Stone*, *Harry Potter and the Chamber of Secrets*, *Harry Potter and the Prisoner of Azkaban*, and *Harry Potter and the Goblet of Fire* were all filmed.

Finally, on the left, and fairly close to the park café, is where the residence for Dowsable Chattox was built for *Harvest*.

GREATER LONDON

BARNET - COURTHOUSE ROAD

SEEN IN: *Fugue, Home, Trove, Nocturne, Neverland, Ride, Arcadia, Prey, Coda, Game, Lazaretto, Harvest.*

[A typical 1930s house in Courthouse Road, and the one used for Interiors of the Thursday home]

The area of Finchley dates from the 13th century with the land belonging to the Bishop of London. In medieval times the Great North Road ran through here and was notorious for highwaymen right up until the 19th century. The Northern Line

245

railway station in West Finchley was opened in 1933 to serve the new housing developing in the area. This included Courthouse Road, where Mamta Hardy was approached by a location manager who was impressed with the original windows of her home. This, along with other 1930s features, made her house perfect for that for the interior of the Thursday residence. Even so the lounge and hallway had to be refurbished with new carpets, wallpapers, and light fittings all in the manner of 1960s designs, including a television, a radio, a lamp, a clock, wooden furniture, and a tea set. Even the door handles were changed and radiators covered up, such is the attention to detail of the *Endeavour* crew. Apart from the fictional Thursday family the most notable resident of Courthouse Road was Harry Beck, who created the design for the present London Underground map, who lived at No. 60.

ENFIELD - PRYTANEUM COURT

SEEN IN: *Home, Trove, Nocturne, Sway, Neverland, Ride, Arcadia, Prey, Lazaretto.*

The Enfield area was historically part of the parish of Edmonton. In 1850 the residents formed a local board of health to govern the area, and in 1879 the ratepayers of Southgate petitioned for a separate Southgate Local Board, which was established two years later. It became an urban district under the Local Government Act of 1894, and by 1900 was large enough to have 12 councillors. As the district grew it became a municipal borough with a mayor, 7 aldermen, and 21 councillors. In 1965, the borough was abolished and the district merged with Edmonton to form the modern Borough of Enfield, which was administered from Southgate Town Hall.

The name of the building derives from ancient Greece, where each state, city, or village possessed its own central hearth and sacred fire, representing the unity and vitality of the community. The fire was kept alight continuously, and tended by the king or members of his family. The building in which this fire was kept was the Prytaneum, and the chieftain (the king or prytanis) lived here too. In fact, the fire was the holy fire of Hestia, the goddess of the hearth, and symbol of the life of the city.

The Prytaneum was regarded as the religious and political centre of the community and was thus the nucleus of all government, and the official home of the whole people. When members of the state went forth to found a new colony, they took with them a brand from the Prytaneum altar to kindle the new fire in the colony.

There was also a court of justice called the Prytaneum which tried murderers that could not be found, and inanimate objects which had caused death.

[Cowley Road police station in Enfield]

The site of the Prytaneum in Athens is not known for certain, but that in Enfield, Prytaneum Court and former Southgate Town Hall, is located at Green Lanes in Palmers Green. It was in 2013 that the building was sold with planning permission to convert it into around 30-40 (1-, 2- and 3-bedroom) flats. The exterior appeared in 9 *Endeavour* episodes as Cowley Road police station.

247

OXFORDSHIRE

BINSEY - RIVER THAMES

SEEN IN: *First Bus to Woodstock, Game.*

[**The River Thames at Binsey, close to the spot where Morse first encounters Dr. DeBryn in** *First Bus to Woodstock*]

The village of Binsey, around 1.5 miles north-west of Oxford, is on the opposite side of the river from Port Meadow **(173)**. The most famous structure here is the Church of St. Margaret, a 12th century Grade I listed affair, adjacent to which is St. Margaret's Well, a Grade II listed building, which was the inspiration for the Treacle Well in *Alice's Adventures in Wonderland*. The well is dedicated to St. Frideswide, the patron saint of Oxford, who it is said that she fled to Binsey in a bid to escape marriage to the king of Mercia. In the event, she need not have worried since the king was struck blind at the gates to Oxford. St. Frideswide prayed for him, and received her miracle in the form of a healing spring that was brought forth and whose waters cured the king. The spring was walled and became a site of pilgrimage. Treacle in medieval times referred to any medicine composed of many ingredients that was used as an antidote treatment for poisons and other ailments.

The village was owned by St. Frideswide's Priory until the Dissolution of the Monasteries when it was incorporated into the assets of Christ Church College **(62)**, who today own all but one building. There is a total of 9 listed structures in the village, including the popular Perch Inn, and it is just along the River Thames a short distance from here, that the initial meeting between Morse and Dr. DeBryn took place over the dead body of Miles Percival in *First Bus to Woodstock*. It is a popular spot for corpses, since Binsey is also the location in *Prey* where Dr. DeBryn examines Dr. Richard Nielsen who has been found dead in the river with stones in his pockets.

SHIRBURN - ALL SAINTS CHURCH

SEEN IN: *Home, Ride, Arcadia.*

[All Saints Church nestles beside Shirburn Castle]

Shirburn village is located to the south of Oxford and around 6 miles from Thame. It was a spring line settlement at the foot of the Chiltern escarpment and the manor of Shirburn is mentioned in the Domesday Book of 1086. In 1872 the Watlington and Princes Risborough Railway was built through the parish with the terminus just half a mile away in Watlington. The line was closed to passengers in 1957, and to freight in 1961.

The castle was built in 1377 and became a centre of Recusancy throughout the 16th and 17th centuries. It was originally the seat of the Earls of Macclesfield. George Parker, 2nd Earl of Macclesfield, was a keen scientist and astronomer and built an observatory and chemical laboratory here. In its time it was said to be 'equipped with the finest existing instruments' with astronomer Thomas Hornsby using it to observe the transit of Venus from here in 1761. The castle is not open to the public and is, in fact, subject to a long running and acrimonious dispute between the Parker family and Beechwood Estates, an argument which in 2004 resulted in Richard Parker, 9th Earl of Macclesfield, being evicted from the family seat.

All Saints Church on the estate is classed as a historic redundant church and is open by appointment with Beechwood Estates. It dates from the late 11th or early 12th century, with additions and alterations being made in the 13th, 14th and 18th centuries. In the 19th century the north transept was added. In *Ride* this is where Joss Bixby is laid to rest at the end of the episode, and where Thursday tells Morse that he is a good detective, but a poor policeman, just before the end credits roll. Earlier in *Home* the same churchyard was the resting place for Constance Morse (assumed to be in Lincolnshire), while close to here is the entrance to the caves where Verity Richardson is being kept hostage in *Arcadia*.

The castle was built in 1377 and became a centre of Recusancy throughout the 16th and 17th centuries. It was originally the seat of the Earls of Macclesfield. George Parker, 2nd Earl of Macclesfield, was a keen scientist and astronomer and built an observatory and chemical laboratory here. In its time it was said to be 'equipped with the finest existing instruments' with astronomer Thomas Hornsby using it to observe the transit of Venus from here in 1761. The castle is not open to the public and is, in fact, subject to a long running and acrimonious dispute between the Parker family and Beechwood Estates, an argument which in 2004 resulted in Richard Parker, 9th Earl of Macclesfield, being evicted from the family seat.

All Saints Church on the estate is classed as a historic redundant church and is open by appointment with Beechwood Estates. It dates from the late 11th or early 12th century, with additions and alterations being made in the 13th, 14th and 18th centuries. In the 19th century the north transept was added. In *Ride* this is where Joss Bixby is laid to rest at the end of the episode, and where Thursday tells Morse that he is a good detective, but a poor policeman, just before the end credits roll. Earlier in *Home* the same churchyard was the resting place for Constance Morse (assumed to be in Lincolnshire), while close to here is the entrance to the caves where Verity Richardson is being kept hostage in *Arcadia*.

ENDEAVOUR ON LOCATION MAPS

The following maps are merely intended to show the relative positions of the various locations covered in the text and are not meant to be to scale. The associated tables give both the type of place according to the defined symbols in the table below, along with the page number in brackets for that location and the postcode. In so doing it is hoped that the maps will help the reader when planning their own visits to these places of interest.

Building (Small or General)	Building (Large or Important)	Church (Religious Establishment)
Museum (Tourist Attraction)	Park (Garden or Open Space)	Place of Learning (College or Library)
Public House	Street	O Other Point of Interest

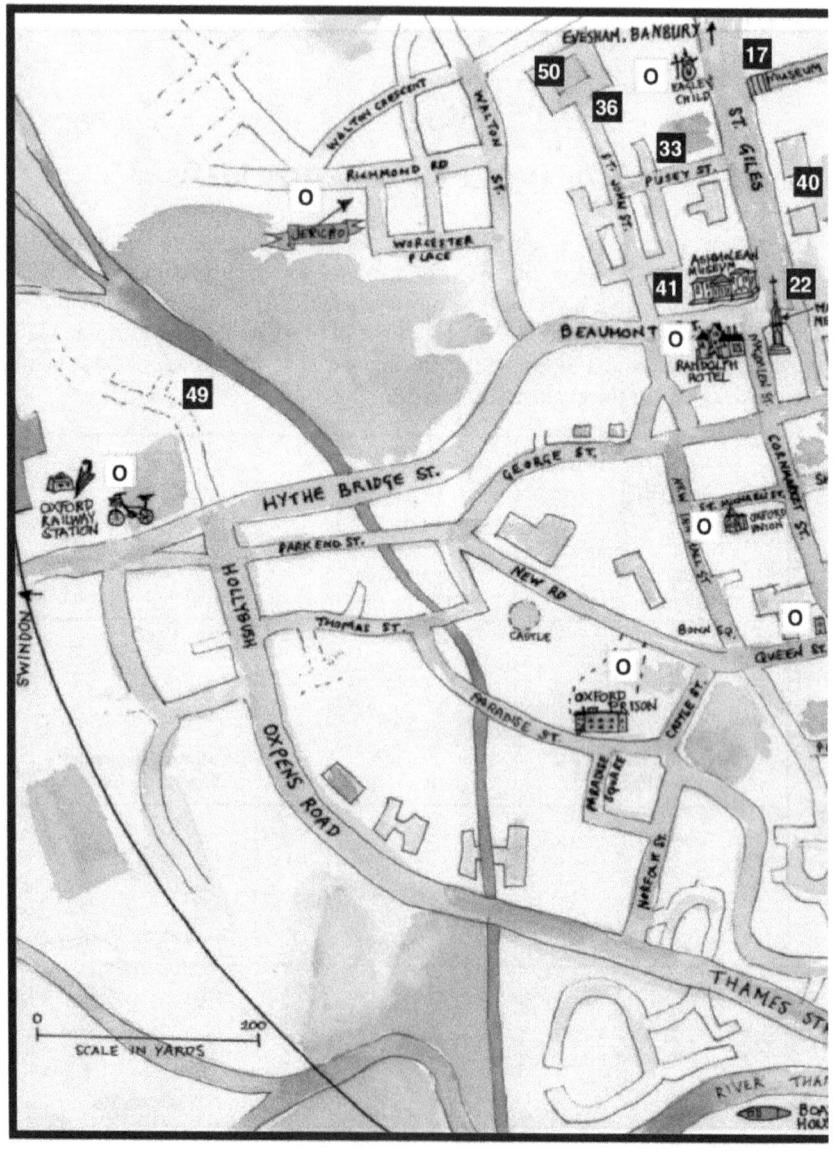

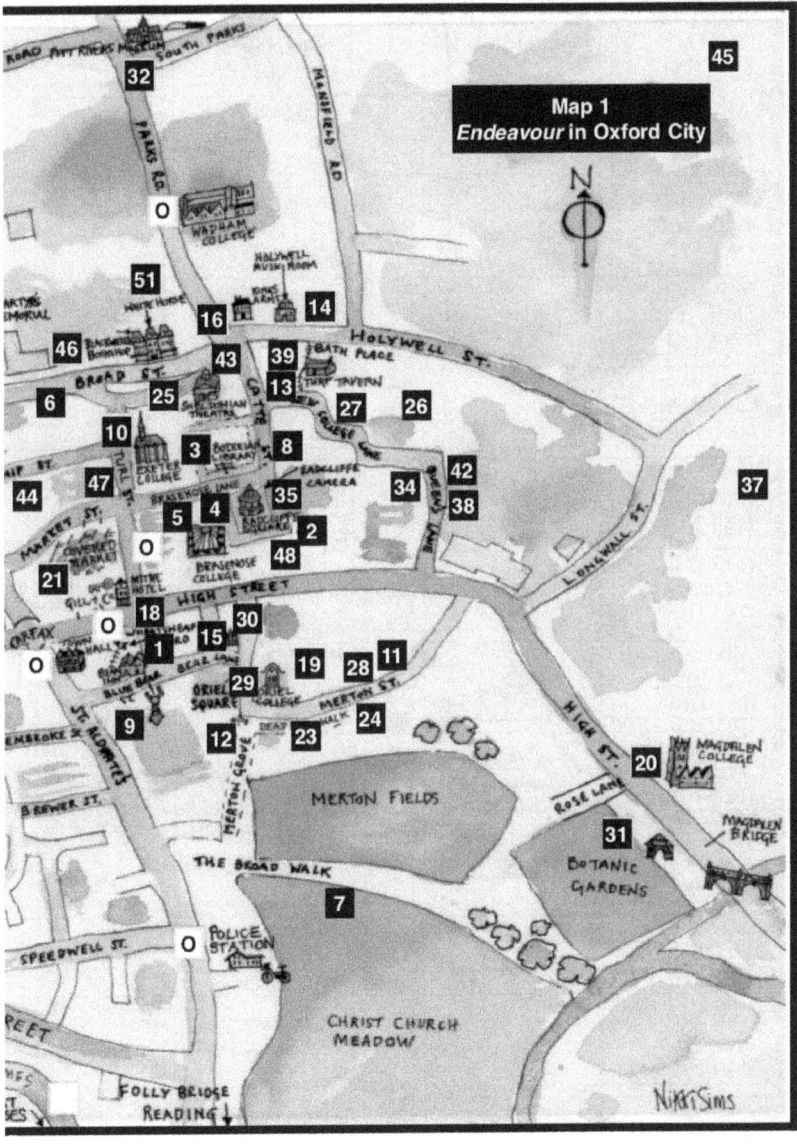

Key to Map 1 – *Endeavour* in Oxford

1	Alfred Lane (61) OX1 4EH		14	Holywell Street (212) OX1 3SB	
2	All Souls College (82) OX1 4AL		15	King Edward Street (213) OX1 4HS	
3	Bodleian Library (197) OX1 3BG		16	King's Arms (51) OX1 3SP	
4	Brasenose College (177) OX1 4AJ		17	Lamb and Flag (202) OX1 3JS	
5	Brasenose Lane (209) OX1 3DQ		18	Lincoln Col. Library (169) OX1 3DR	
6	Broad Street (210) OX1 3AS		19	Logic Lane (140) OX1 4EX	
7	Broad Walk[1] (200) OX1 1RA		20	Magdalen College[3] (184) OX1 4AU	
8	Catte Street (211) OX1 3BW		21	Market Street (214) OX1 3EF	
9	Christ Church College (62) OX1 1DP		22	Martyrs' Memorial (34) OX1 3AE	
10	Exeter College (179) OX1 3DP		23	Merton College (187) OX1 4JD	
11	Faculty of Phil. (130) OX1 4JD		24	Merton Street (216) OX1 4JD	
12	Grove Walk (111) OX1 4JE		25	Museum His. of Sci. (33) OX1 3AZ	
13	Hertford College[2] (182) OX1 3BW		26	New College (190) OX1 3BN	

27	New College Lane (217) OX1 3BL		40	St. John's College (192) OX1 3JP	
28	Old Walden's Lodgings (83) OX1 4JD		41	St. John Street (224) OX1 2LH	
29	Oriel Square (19) OX1 4EW		42	St. Peter's-in-the-East (6) OX1 4AR	
30	Oriel Street (62) OX1 4EW		43	Sheldonian Theatre (204) OX1 3AZ	
31	O. Botanic Garden (171) OX1 4AZ		44	Ship Street (174) OX1 3DA	
32	O. U. Museum Nat. Hist. (71) OX1 3PW		45	Sir W. Dunn Sch. of P. (194) OX1 3RE	
33	Pusey Street (220) OX1 2LA		46	Trinity College (37) OX1 3BH	
34	Queen's Lane (24) OX1 4AR		47	Turl Street (225) OX1 3DR	
35	Radcliffe Sq. & Camera (222) OX1 4AJ		48	U. C. of St. Mary (206) OX1 4BJ	
36	Rewley House (203) OX1 2JA		49	Upper Fisher Row (111) OX1 2EZ	
37	St. Catherine's College (141) OX1 3UJ		50	Wellington Square (226) OX1 2JH	
38	St. Edmund Hall (26) OX1 4AR		51	White Horse (28) OX1 3BB	
39	St. Helen's Passage (224) OX1 1TR				

[1] Including Merton Field & Christ Church Meadow

[2] Including the Bridge of Sighs

[3] Including Magdalen Bridge

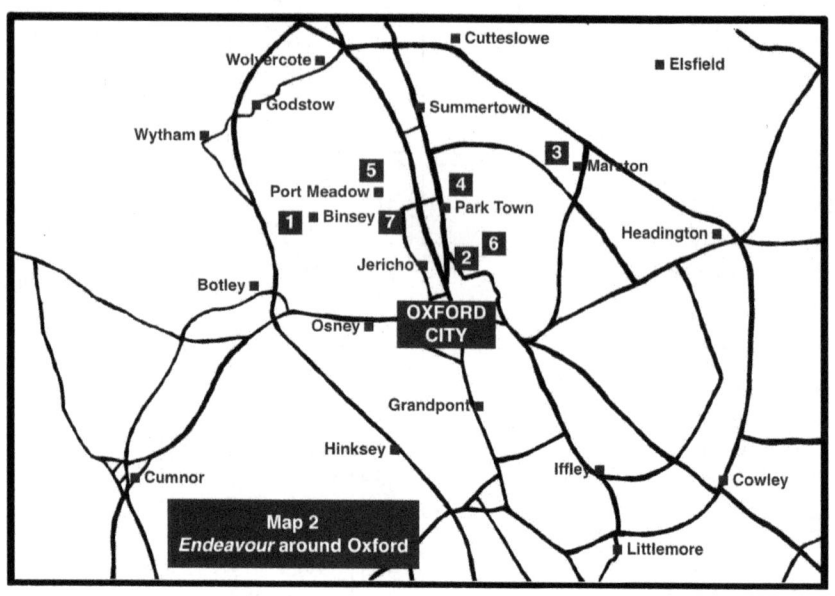

Map 2
Endeavour around Oxford

Key to Map 2 – *Endeavour* around Oxford

1	**Binsey** **(249)** **OX2 0NG**		5	**Port Meadow** **(173)** **OX2 8PU**	
2	**Keble College** **(49)** **OX1 3PG**		6	**University** **Parks (121)** **OX1 3RF**	
3	**Old Marston** **(18)** **OX3 0PZ**		7	**Walton Well** **Road (131)** **OX2 6ED**	
4	**Park Town** **(218)** **OX2 6SJ**				

258

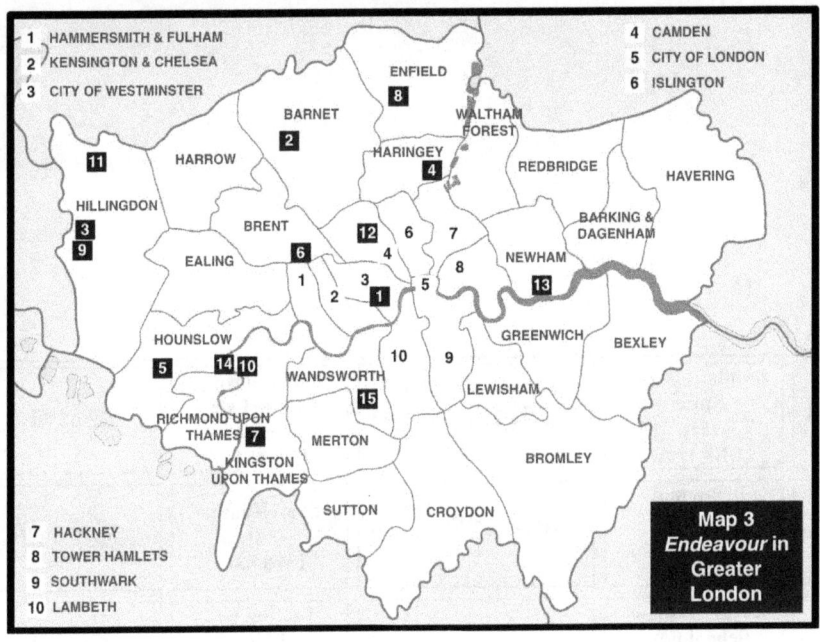

Key to Map 3 – *Endeavour* in Greater London

1	Buckingham Palace (167) SW1A 1AA		5	Kempton Steam Museum (138) TW13 6XH	
2	Courthouse Road (245) N12 7PJ		6	Kensal Green Cemetery (129) W10 4RA	
3	Glebe Avenue (25) UB10 8PA		7	Kingston upon Thames Cty. Hall (91) KT1 2DW	
4	Hornsey Wood Reservoir (59) N14 4AX		8	Prytaneum Court (246) N13 4DQ	

9	Randalls Dept. Store (81) UB8 1LA			13	Silvertown Tate & Lyle Factory (42) E16 2EW	
10	Richmond Theatre (16) TW9 1QJ			14	Syon House (14) TW8 8JF	
11	Royal Masonic School For Girls (17) WD3 4HF			15	Tooting Bec Lido (60) SW16 1RU	
12	St. Pancras Baths (137) NW5 3LE					

260

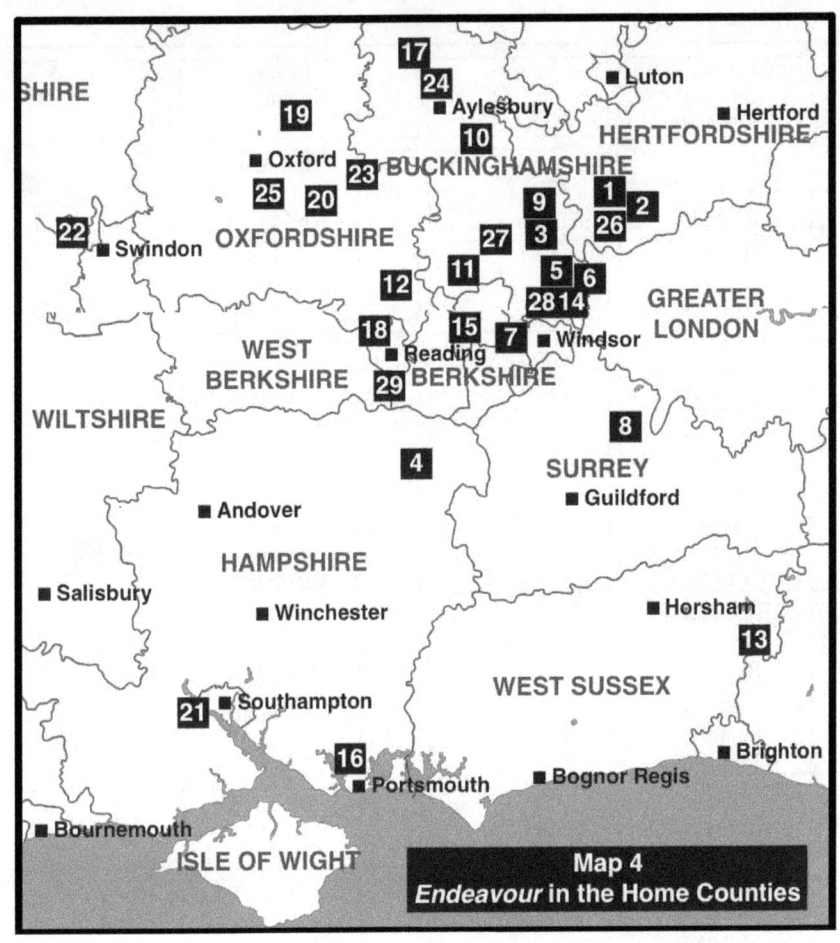

Key to Map 4 – *Endeavour* in the Home Counties

1	Abbots Langley (90) WD4 8RW		3	Beaconsfield (13) HP9 2LA	
2	Aldenham (25) WD25 9DB		4	Camberley (102) GU17 9JT	

261

5	Chalfont St. Giles (107) HP8 4QQ		18	Reading (80) RG1 3AS	
6	Chalfont St. Peter (108) HP8 4AB		19	Rousham (123) OX25 4QX	
7	Dorney (199) S14 6QP		20	Shirburn (250) OX49 5DL	
8	Esher (43) KT10 9JL		21	Southampton (166) SO45 1BD	
9	Forty Green (229) HP9 1XT		22	Swindon (143) SN1 5JA	
10	Halton (96) HP22 5NN		23	Thame (160) HP18 0DY	
11	Hambleden (231) RG9 6RP		24	Waddesdon (99) HP18 0JH	
12	Henley on Thames (92) RG9 2BS		25	Wallingford (112) OX10 6AN	
13	Horsted Keynes (52) RH17 7BB		26	Watford (110) WD17 2UB	
14	Iver Heath (148) SL0 0NH		27	W. Wycombe (109 & 151) HP14 3AE	
15	Maidenhead (159) SL6 1RF		28	Wexham (240) S13 6DS	
16	Portsmouth (89) PO3 6AS		29	Winnersh (70) RG43 5BG	
17	Quainton (237) HP22 4BY				

PLACES INDEX

263

Church (Religious Establishment)

Museum (Other Tourist Attraction/Open to the Public)

Park (Garden or Open Space)

Place of Learning (College or Library)

Public House

Street

Episode Index

267

ACKNOWLEDGMENTS

All the photographs in this publication are by the authors unless otherwise stated. The line illustrations on pages 62, 64, 184 and 198 are taken from *Old England: a pictorial Museum of Royal, Ecclesiastical, Municipal, Baronial, and popular Antiquities* edited by Charles Knight and printed in the middle of the 19th century by *James Sangster & Co.*, Paternoster Row, London. The line illustration on page 34 is taken from *A Hand-Book for Visitors to Oxford*, 1847. Photographs on page 14 (Brigadier & Mrs. J. F. Moffatt), page 15 (Ed Sexton), page 25 (Robert Eva), page 43 (Wybe/CC BY-SA), page 59 (Matt Emmett), page 80, page 81, page 90 (Basher Eyre), page 102 (Martinvl), page 109 (Art Deco Society), page 110, page 120 (Michael Garlick), page 143, page 166 (Geni), and page 167 (Jim Champion) are from public domain sources. The authors would also like to thank Michael Blackburn for permission to use his photograph on page 52, and the Kempton Steam Museum for their help with information and the supply of photographs on page 139.

Two online resources that give reviews of *Endeavour* along with other useful information are: *denofgeek.com* and Chris Sullivan's in depth *morselewisendeavour.com* site which is to be highly recommended.

FURTHER READING

Hibbert, Christopher (Editor) & Hibbert, Edward (Associate Editor), *The Encyclopaedia of Oxford*, Macmillan London Limited, (1988), ISBN: 978 0333486 14 6, 562 pages. Essential reading for anybody interested in the history of Oxford.

Weinreb, Ben (Editor) & Hibbert, Christopher (Editor), *The London Encyclopaedia*, 1120 pages, MacMillan Reference, (2010), ISBN: 978-1405049252. Quite simply the definitive and most comprehensive book on London ever published.

Lightning Source UK Ltd.
Milton Keynes UK
UKHW020742150922
408910UK00009B/883